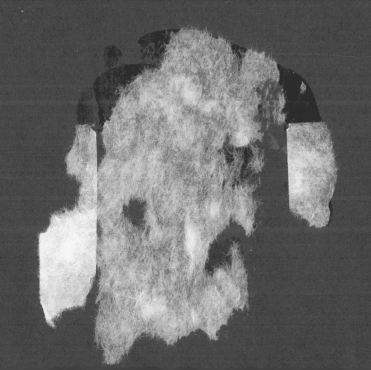

The Battle for Morningside Heights

By the same author

The Passionate People

The World of John Lardner (Edited)

The Battle for Morningside Heights
Why Students Rebel

BY **ROGER KAHN**

Foreword by Senator Eugene McCarthy

William Morrow and Company, Inc.

1970 NEW YORK

378.198
K12b
74969
august, 1971

First Printing

For Alice

CONTENTS

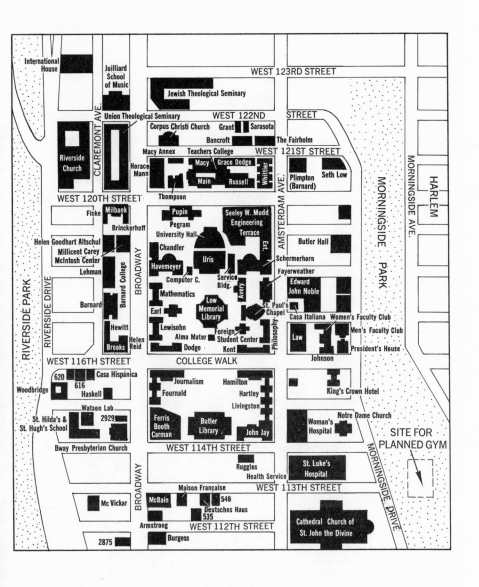

INTRODUCTION

By SENATOR EUGENE J. McCARTHY

UNTIL VERY recent times it was possible for the university to fulfill with reasonable effectiveness the function of the medieval *studium*. It could stand apart from the centers of power in society, seeking truth, defining and clarifying principles, and passing a kind of reserved judgment upon the procedures of its own age. The intellectual community had the protection of both time and distance.

This is not the case today. The university is involved in contemporary problems and in contemporary history. Consequently, the university must be prepared to defend its integrity and its specific function in society on a day by day basis.

The threats to this integrity arise primarily from two basic changes which have taken place in the relationship of society to the university and of the university to society.

The first is the change in the method of supporting the university and its work. The earlier commitment was a general one to the institution itself, leaving it for the most part free to use the money according to its own determinations. Although this kind of support continues, there has been a growing tendency toward specialized support both from government and from private sources. The consequent competition for funds, for research projects, for prestige and the kind of competition which seeks identification with public objectives can, unless guarded against, unbalance the university program and destroy its position of detachment and independence and weaken its role as an independent center.

The second change is a more subtle one and, therefore, more difficult to guard against. This is the change by which the university has become more immediately and directly involved in contemporary society and in its problems. It is expected not only to provide government and society with information and data of immediate applicability but also to pass judgment—scientific, historical, psychological, moral and social—affecting current decisions.

Revolt on the campus reflects the changing role and function of the university. Today there are at least three demands bearing upon university life which are fundamental to this revolt.

The first is that of the war in Vietnam itself, which demands a practical judgment within the movement of history and also a moral judgment with regard to individual commitment. These judgments are demanded of students because they are students and because they are citizens, but more immediately because it is the young people of this country who are called upon to do the actual fighting and to commit their time and lives.

The second is that of racial discrimination and injustice. The response on campuses again has two aspects: a detached one which is required of students as they try to pass an academic and a historical judgment on the racial problems of the United States; and a personal and moral one, involving discrimination on campus—if such discrimination does exist—and beyond that a judgment as to one's own personal responsibility for discrimination or exploitation.

And the third is concern over process or participation, over freedom and dependence, over the institutionalization of life and freedom within a social structure.

Of most serious concern to students is the militarization of American life as well as the militarization of academic life.

Universities are in trouble which is to a large extent of their own making, either because of what they have done or permitted to happen, or because of what they have not done or what they have not prevented from happening.

This book by Roger Kahn is the story of student protest on the Columbia University campus. It is a thorough report of the personalities and the issues, the confusion and the complexities and the contradictions on that campus. Whereas it cannot be claimed that this book is a guide to understanding the troubles on every campus, as the trouble varies from campus to campus and in some respects reflects differences in personalities and differences in the immediate provocations, it is, in my opinion, the most important book which has been written on the issue of student unrest. Anyone who reads it will have not only knowledge of what happened at Columbia University but a better understanding of what students are thinking and of what they are most concerned about—of their aspirations, their fears, their hopes, their desperate uncertainties—and of what they would like from the university and from American society.

The spring shenanigans were unfortunate, truly unfortunate.
                    —*Dr. Grayson Kirk*

The concentration camps finished Christianity. Now we have to turn to Marx and Lenin.
                    —*Antony Papert, Columbia student leader.*

If this isn't 1917, then it's 1905.
                    —*Anonymous Columbia student leftist.*

It's *our* university; it's *our* university.
                    —*Students, in chant, at helmeted members of the Tactical Patrol Force.*

It's not their university, and it isn't a social welfare agency, either.
                    —*Dr. David Truman, former vice-president.*

Roar like a lion, Columbia. We have our finger up your ass.
                    —*Pamphlet written by black militants.*

AUTHOR TO READER

THIS is the story of a rebellion on a single American campus. What makes the rebellion memorable, apart from courage, brutality, slogans, jokes, impotence, sex, injuries and ambitions, is that it fired the national student uprising.

Before the battle for Morningside Heights, we had protest and we had Berkeley. The California radicals of the Free Speech Movement had a vision. "In a healthy university," Mario Savio wrote in the spring of 1965, "an undergraduate student would have time to do nothing, to read, to waste time dreaming in the eucalyptus grove." But Savio's movement withered. The Berkeley uprising lit the autumn of '64. The FSM was dead within a year.

After that the symptoms of unrest became erratic; protests developed at Howard University, Colgate, Michigan, Bowie State, and Trinity College. But each seemed to be isolated. No one bothered to count the numbers of the left.

Recently, according to *The New York Times*, there were 635,000 radical students and fellow travelers studying on campuses. That the anti-left *Times* would report the tabulation is significant and the numbers, even if understated, speak for themselves. During the Columbia anniversary spring of 1969, one researcher counted student disruptions at eighty-three separate campuses from San Francisco State to City College of New York. On a single day in April, 1969, student demonstrators were occupying buildings on seventeen American campuses.

17

The dissident campus was done. We now faced the campus martial: the campus of riot, chemical Mace and tears.

The change angered and frightened conservatives. Two congressional committees, each dominated by a conservative politician, investigated the developing student movement. When the president of Notre Dame announced that he would allow protesters on his clerical preserve ten minutes of meditation before he summoned police, he was hailed by *The Reader's Digest.* The President of the United States was reported to be preparing a similarly severe speech until the White House liberal urged him not to be "simplistic."

But the liberals were equally, if less raucously, discomfited. It is one thing to fight for the right of a campus socialist club to exist or the right of a Negro to attend law school. It is considerably more difficult to reach a satisfactory position on that mix of cursing blacks and hirsute whites who insist on taunting policemen and possibly kidnapping deans. The beginning of understanding, it seems to me, proceeds from Columbia.

In that wet and chilly spring of 1968, several thousand men and women, boys and girls, policemen and journalists, blacks and whites, played out a bloody and leaderless drama on the Morningside Heights campus. The high ground towers above the Hudson River and Harlem like a barony. Before this drama ran its frightful course, Columbia's splendid isolation was defiled. The radical storm, the present, had engulfed her.

Radical is the essential word. The Columbia events and their aftermaths sweep beyond the Morningside campus; they sweep beyond campuses everywhere into the bland suburban avenues and the mean city streets that are the antithetic markings of American life. The first and transcendent conclusion that Columbia drives home is inescapable. Radicalism, with its confrontations, violence, tears and roars of pain, is the most potent means of forcing action in the United States today.

Most of the demands framed by the Columbia leftists have been realized. Construction of a subtly racist ten-story gymnasium between Columbia and Harlem has terminated. It will not be resumed. Columbia's direct affiliation with the Institute for Defense Analyses, a peacetime war-planning board, has been severed. Criminal charges against most of the 524 registered Columbia students who were arrested have been dropped. The university's structure and its disciplinary processes are being reconsidered. Most remarkable of all, both the president and the first vice-president of Columbia are put to rout. Grayson Kirk, the former president, has retired to full-time canvassing. David Truman, the former vice-president and provost, has resigned; he is now the president of Mount Holyoke, a well-endowed college for women set in the tranquillity of South Hadley, Massachusetts.

These changes were wrought not by reason (although some of them are innately reasonable) or by debate or evolution. They were forced by confrontation. Within certain limits, it is valid to suggest, as some of the radicals do, "The student left has brought Columbia to its knees." But one must not forget the limits. Columbia is still essentially what it was before the violent spring of 1968. It is an elitist institution, controlled by businessmen-trustees and supported by the federal government. The changes forced by the radicals have not been radical changes. The hide bears different mottles. The beast itself is the same. The question that the serious radicals have begun asking is, *What really did we win?* Then if they follow a particular subbranch of Marxism they say, *What could we win? How could we change capitalist imperialist Columbia as long as the society that supports her remains a fortress of imperialist capitalism?*

As a neutralist, without prior bias, I spent half a year wandering Columbia, wearing not only many hats, but many costumes. When I talked with deans I favored dark suits and blue button-down shirts, an outfit also suitable for discussions with conservative students. With radicals, I preferred open-collar sports shirts; a visible fringe of chest hair seemed to contribute to trust. I enjoyed and respected individual deans and teachers, including Harry Coleman and Carl Hovde. Dean Coleman, who actually was kidnapped by radicals, explains that at the club, his wife calls her golf ball "Mark Rudd." That way, she is certain to give it a sharp whack. It was pleasant swapping stories with Dean Hovde, and I understand why the radicals can have no dialogue with him. He stands for order, moderate change and the pure aesthetic. Revolutionaries oppose and suspect him the way they oppose Social Democrats, the way they argue that A. E. Housman's work is irrelevant. I enjoyed many of the radicals, too, without accepting the wisdom of their philosophies. They are young, unfinished people, very brave and very open. Few have read every page of Marcuse's seminal *One Dimensional Man.* Fewer still have read every page of *Das Kapital.* But the bright ones are working toward something, and when they have done their homework and added years, it is these people, rather than twenty-two-year-olds who voted for Nixon, who will embody hope—America's and the world's.

Even knowing its multitudinous and continuing sins, it is difficult not to be touched by the Columbia circumstance. This is after all a university, a special place, and as best they know how, the finest Columbia people are working toward constructive change. But there is pathetically little understanding, among faculty and administration, of the way things really are; most changes they discuss are trivial. While New York City descends toward chaos, Columbia academicians rhapsodize about a faculty senate, which has finally been created, five decades too late. They live in a commodious womb, the leading academicians, with their ample salaries, their lifetime security, their esoteric specialities. They talk about slums as though slums were another country; they deplore and they regret and they consider. But there is no inclination among the academic princes to do what academicians will have to do if the universities are to help save the urbs. They do not go out and mix, blond wasps beside blacks and browns, and meet the angry poor and share their beer, and get slowly into nostril, mouth and lung the terrible stench of poverty. The uncommitted intellect is a Columbia misfortune.

My sympathies stop abruptly at the point where Columbia contributes freely and blindly to the Defense-State complex.

At least twelve trustees and high executives maintain primary connections with Defense-State; an indeterminate but a substantial number of professors scramble for this establishment's grants. The Columbia faculty hires out to help fashion weapons and tactics while relinquishing the right to say whether these—the fruits of their intellectual pains—are put to just use. I am not cheered by the reality that this is analogous to an America that in the 1968 presidential elections contrived to deny itself a major party candidate who was opposed to the Vietnam War.

To many of the young people on campus and to many of the police who battled them in the buildings, Columbia represents society. What was wrong with Columbia (or what was wrong with the young people), they believed paralleled what was wrong with America. In fighting then, they fought for a better America. This devotional belief fanned passions on both sides.

Actually, Columbia does not represent the United States at all. It was, and is, too intellectual, too white, too Jewish, too self-righteously liberal and above all too wealthy to represent anything more than the upper reaches of America. Columbia is only the America of *Commentary*, Suzy Knickerbocker and Stephen Birmingham.

But the Columbia affair was not mere campus business. A university went out of control. As it did we suddenly saw, within and beyond the university, disparate elements of embattled America. New Lefters pushed the crisis. Angry blacks stood beside them, and turned away. The Defense-State combine protected its flanks. The police stormed the campus, overran it. The working press observed and made judgments on what to report and on what was just. And when all this was done, it seems to me, we had as balanced a picture as any specific event can provide of America at war with herself.

Roger Kahn
New York City
1969

1 AFTER THE FALL

THE worst had happened, there was no denying that. Here on a campus, disaster came as handmaiden to that spring of 1968. With it went force, blood, oaths, shrieks and everywhere a wash of tears.

James Shenton wept. He is a history professor; still the police beat him as he stood close to the library named for the father of Seth Low. Rabbi Bruce Goldman cried. He was a campus chaplain; still he was clubbed by police officers who would not let him near young people who might (or might not) want his guidance. A dignified young woman cried when a policeman bent her legs the wrong way, toward the nape of her neck, as she slumped immobile, her black tights snagged on the wires of a fence. Even David Truman had been seen weeping. Truman was the vice-president of Columbia, and an assured man, who ordinarily commands his emotions. Finally Richard Greeman wept. He was a young assistant professor of French, a bearded and committed leftist. He found himself standing near the campus, with his wife, watching dawn light the wreckage. Dick Greeman looked at his wife, with whom he'd walked the campus five hundred times, and she looked back at him. Then without words they embraced, weeping.

Now in the autumn of 1968 emotions were coming under check. There was a different sense, a different pace, different dramatis personnae. Except for a few plainclothesmen—it was impossible to mistake these gruff aggressive men for graduate students—the police were gone. The faculty had returned to research laboratories. Most of the students were back in class. Under Acting President Andrew Cordier, a professional diplomat, the university was working to assume a tranquil image. That was the first thing. Erase the memory of April blood.

"But, wait," one radical student said in September. "We're learning how to make Molotov cocktails. Next time the cops try to take over the campus, we're gonna burn 'em."

The cold reality of autumn at Columbia was pushing matches, marches that led nowhere, press releases for *The New York Times* and unreported speeches in which the word *motherfucker* was chanted, the *kyrie* of the season. It was a dangerous situation, far from tranquil. Perhaps rioting would really come again. Then Columbia could become fixed in the public mind as a boiling radical center and wealthy conservatives might place donations elsewhere.

Against this threat to the vital stream of endowment, the diplomatic forces of Columbia marshaled an ultimate effort. They would demonstrate the return of normality. The accepted norms of campus allow limited turmoil, and what Columbia wanted to get across was that a search for justice had been excited by the events of spring. "We move forward," one professor announced, "not always easily."

On Thursday, September 26, 1968, John Hastings telephoned to tell me about "a big story upcoming on the twenty-eighth." Hastings is a cheerful, square-jawed man, a sports fan and former newspaperman, who is Columbia's assistant vice-president for public information. He had worked under two directors of public relations during twenty-one years at Columbia, but there was no director for public relations in the fall of 1968. The position was vacant, turned down by at least two men since Wesley First departed following the Strickman cigarette filter fiasco. "The Cox Commission report," Hastings said on the telephone, "is going to be released. Fred Friendly's office is handling it."

I telephoned the office of Fred W. Friendly, former president of CBS News, now Edward R. Murrow Professor in the Graduate School of Journalism. Friendly is famous at CBS for courageous news coverage and for his summation of interstaff relations: "I don't get ulcers. I give them." A secretary answered my call.

"I understand you people are handling publicity on the Cox report."

"What do you mean *publicity*?" The secretary's voice was belligerently British. "And it's not the Cox report. It's the fact hyphen finding commission report."

"To whom am I speaking?" I said.

Her name was Miss Reading. After I identified myself, Miss Reading conceded that the report would be released a day later and that

I was welcome to witness the release if I acceded to various conditions. I could see a copy of the report at ten the next morning in the World Room of the Journalism Building. To do that, however, I would have to sign a statement promising not to leave the World Room until being dismissed and that, even after leaving, I would not publish the report before the following morning.

"I don't intend to publish for months," I said.

"You'll still have to sign," Miss Reading told me.

The day of the release—Saturday—was significant. Since courts, legislatures, schools and most businesses are closed, Saturday is a light day for news. A light news day plus careful solicitation of journalists gave the Cox report a reasonable chance of seizing the lead position in what Columbia authorities consider the most important media of all: *The Sunday New York Times.* There could be no better display for Columbia as a justice-seeker.

On Saturday morning, at about eleven o'clock, a pleasant-faced black in the nondescript uniform of a Columbia campus policeman stood before the Journalism Building holding a billy.

"World Room?" I said.

"Third floor."

"I hear the radical kids are planning to bust up the press conference."

"We're ready."

He winked, one man of substance and authority to another.

The World Room in the Columbia School of Journalism takes its name from the most lamented inscription in the long necrology of American newspapers. The old *New York World* perished in the Depression and is remembered for its best deeds rather than its worst. Its best deeds were considerable, and the *World* is regarded as a kind of Camelot among newspapers.

At the rear of the room, a Statue of Liberty raises her torch in a massive stained-glass panel. The panel is green and blue and red. It smacks of a Maxfield Parrish mural, but it is not intended to be camp. Underneath one reads, "In Memoriam: Herbert Bayard Swope." He was the most famous of the old *World*'s editors.

Fred W. Friendly, whom I recognized from photographs, was standing close to the entranceway. Someone offered me a pen and presented two documents—the promises to embargo the story—and after I signed, I was given a copy of the Cox Commission Report. It was a paperback book, bound in gray and blue and black and white, and available to the public for $1.95. With the book came a press release:

MAKING OF CRISIS AT COLUMBIA MAY BE FASTEST BOOK PRODUCTION JOB
ON RECORD.
RANDOM HOUSE HAD FINISHED BOOKS READY ONE WEEK AFTER DELIV-
ERY OF MANUSCRIPT.

Five paragraphs followed, explaining how Steven A. Baron, the
Random House production manager, Miss Jane Seitz, an editorial
assistant, the printing firm of Brown Brothers and the Colonial Press
of Clinton, Mass., combined to produce the book *Crisis at Columbia*
in a week.

I was musing about all that speed when Fred W. Friendly said hello.
He is a tall man, with a large fleshy face and an air of one accustomed
to command. "Good you could come," he said, warmly. "There's
coffee or tea, whatever you'd like for breakfast over there."

"I'm doing a book about Columbia," I said.

"Read this," Friendly said, holding up the blue, white, gray and
black paperback. "Your work has been done for you." I took Professor
Friendly's advice, found a seat and began to read.

The Cox report takes its name from Archibald Cox, an experienced
arbitrator and a professor of law at Harvard. Early in May, 1968, Cox
responded to an appeal from the Executive Committee of Columbia
Faculties—the leadership of professors with tenure—and assumed
chairmanship of a commission to "investigate and report on the disturbances on campus during the week of April 23-30, 1968." The Columbia administration "cooperated fully." The trustees, from whom
all power flows, supported the investigation. But neither the radical
Students for a Democratic Society nor the militant Students Afro-
American Society cooperated. Thus the Cox committee could swear
in only representatives from the conservative and moderate sides.

The investigators worked gratis and with enormous diligence.
Twenty-one days of hearings. Seventy witnesses. A hearing transcript
of 3,790 pages. Still, as I opened the blue, gray, black and white book
in the World Room I wondered if the report would have been as it is
had Cox been able to break through suspicions of the radical young.

I made good time across Archibald Cox's earnest, functional prose.
He reviewed recent events briefly and without significant error. He
summarized issues dispassionately. His conclusions were reasonable
as far as they went.

"We are convinced," he wrote, "that ways must be found, beginning
now, by which students can meaningfully influence the education
afforded them, and the other aspects of the university activities."

On the other hand, "Resort to violence or physical harassment is never an acceptable tactic for influencing decisions in the university." Finally, "the vital decision rests with liberal and reform-minded students. They can save or destroy the institution."

It is unfortunate, I thought, to put so much on the students. Doesn't the future depend more heavily on faculty, on administrators, on trustees than on the transient young? Spotlights distracted me. Professor Fred W. Friendly was making his way toward a microphone. He was followed by four members of the commission. They marched to a small dais and sat, facing an audience that had grown to about two hundred, and included a crop of journalism students. Cox is a tall man, spare, crew cut, graying. To his right sat Dana Farnsworth, a jowly, psychiatrically oriented physician of sixty-three and director of health services at Harvard. On the other side Simon Rifkind, sixty-seven, Columbia law graduate, former judge and a lawyer of enormous wealth, glowered at a bank of television cameras. Anthony Amsterdam, a professor of law at the University of Pennsylvania, sat on the extreme left; he was the only commission member under the age of fifty-five.

"In case you're wondering how we'll work," Friendly said, "I think we'll take questions from the press for a half hour or so and then we ought to give the students a chance."

Archibald Cox began speaking in mild and diffident tones. "I want to make clear," he began, "that after our initial charter, we were left entirely alone. No one not on the commission staff has seen this report until this morning." He seemed comfortable facing the television cameras, the press, the students and a number of noteworthy professors who had come to audit.

"We have achieved a high degree of unanimity in discussing complex issues. We are, in fact, in virtual unanimity."

The diffidence fled before questions. Once someone asked the late Robert Frost what a certain line meant and Frost answered: "Do you want me to state it in worse English?" Cox took the same approach. When asked to clarify points in his long text, he fell back on the poetic imperative. "Read the report. The report speaks for itself."

"But I haven't read your report, Professor Cox," someone said. "Do you recommend changes, and if not, why not?"

Cox gazed. "If I were to read the report," he said, "I clearly would draw conclusions."

"Apparently, sir, you did not attempt to investigate the police role."

"The police action," Cox said, "seemed to be off the point."

"I notice, Mr. Cox, that you have some criticisms of Columbia administrators, but none of Columbia trustees."

Again a gaze. "Of course the trustees are part of the administration. In many cases when we mention the administration we are referring both to trustees and to central administration."

"Who wrote the report, Mr. Cox?"

"Well, let's say we all did. I mentioned the unanimity on issues. There was a unanimity about the report as well."

"Who gets the royalties from the book?"

"A charity," Cox said smoothly, "as yet undesignated."

In a few minutes, Fred Friendly walked to a microphone and said, "I think it's only fair now that we turn this over to students." The professionals began to file out. "What the hell," a *New York Times* reporter said. "What was the sense of asking us to read the damn report if he wasn't going to answer any questions on it?"

Whatever the sense, the effect of the conference and the report was to win for Columbia what it wanted most: the lead story in the Sunday *Times*. In addition the *Times* devoted two full inside pages to Cox's conclusions and saluted them in an editorial. The reporters' protest about the contrived press conference did not find its way into print.

By his own description, Archibald Cox is an optimist. He is a successful man, John Kennedy's choice for solicitor general, a professor, an active lawyer. But his work at Columbia all but overwhelmed the optimism. Since his study of the uprising, he has begun to fear for the future of "the liberal democratic enterprise." Although there is no hint of this in the final published report, there may have been before it was rewritten.

Cox composed the report himself, working in pencil on long yellow legal pads. The beginning was "fun"; the end was "extremely hard." He showed his work to his colleagues for comment, and late in September, another commission member startled him with the assertion that "it would be a catastrophe if the report came out as written." Cox refuses to identify the man; other sources say that it was Simon Rifkind.

Rifkind is a man with iron links to the American establishment. During the William Manchester book dispute, he was counsel for Mrs. Jacqueline Kennedy Onassis. This is no boat-rocker. Precisely what Rifkind excised from Cox's longhand is something neither will reveal. In Cox's words, the other commission member "sat up all night writing and rewriting and delivered the revised report to me at six fifteen in the morning. Then I went over it again and we delivered it to the publishers at five or six that afternoon."

Was there a sharp direct attack on faculty passivity? Was the administration assaulted as feudal? Were there words for the businessmen-trustees? Did police violence come under extensive criticism? Was the burden placed heavily on others besides Mark Rudd? These questions are moot, because no one will answer them. All we can know surely is that the published report is watered down, as best a prudent legal workman could do it.

Whatever was lost, the published Cox document does project a sense that Columbia, which had been in serious trouble, is coming to grips with itself through traditional and respected academic means: dispassionate inquiry and the application of reason. This view and the report itself drew torrents of praise.

Then on October 15, the Students for a Democratic Society printed their new newspaper, *The Hard Core.*

In the lead position, Stu Gedal, a fluent SDS leader, commented extensively on the Cox report. For the commission and its 21 days of hearings, its 79 sworn witnesses, its 3,790 pages of transcript, its 222-page $1.95 book, the SDS offered a terse headline: ARCHIBALD AND THE FACTSUCKERS.

Clearly, rational discourse at Columbia had limitations.

I walked the Columbia campus in spring, summer and fall, watching, listening, questioning. I talked with radicals, blacks, rightists and centrists; students, teachers, parents, policemen, administrators, librarians and hangers-on, people attracted to Columbia as a place of action. The sense I took away was overwhelmingly a sense of trouble—trouble with a university, trouble with a society, trouble with individuals.

Away from the World Room, beyond the television cameras and the carefully arranged releases of fact hyphen finding commission documents, spring, summer and autumn were desperate, wounding times. The sense was everywhere. Ambling on College Walk or across the Van Am Quad, going from the graduate sociologists gabbling in Fayerweather, to frosh reading in Butler Library, its portico carved with the names of ancients; from the commodious green office of President Cordier to the narrow apartment of the radical Tony Papert, the profound mood was one of time running fast.

Time (to some) is running out on American society. "Ah," says the historian, putting suavity over his concern, "you and I are liberals living in the Age of Metternich. But revolutions kill indiscriminately and just ahead of us is 1848."

I walk from the bar on the ground floor of the men's faculty club to tall drab Pupin Hall. Twelve stories high in Pupin, a young physicist is working with batteries of electronic equipment. "Unless," he says, "my particle analysis gets classified as essential work, I'm going to have to fight in a war. Vietnam. Korea. Bolivia. Who knows where?" The physicist is thin and intense. He wears the beard one sees in illustrations of Odysseus. Suddenly he looks vacant and touches the beard absently, and I wonder if the thin young scientist is measuring his own life expectancy.

I make a short march to meet a Maoist in a dirty restaurant on Amsterdam Avenue. The Maoist, a graduate student, is short, bespectacled, clean-shaven. "What you want to understand," he says over the chipped coffee cups, "is that the campus movement has gone as far as it can. Now we have two years in which to form a coalition with the working class. Otherwise, fascism wins."

I cross the campus toward Broadway. Along the center mall, College Walk, new grass sprouts through a gauzelike covering. Columbia looks after its grass. I meet a philosophy teacher, a friend, in a Broadway bar. He nods, reserved and silent, and we both stand listening to the bartender lecture at an off-duty patrolman. "We're up against it," the bartender says. "In ten years these Commie kids will be taking over."

"Oh, I don't know," the man in plainclothes says.

The bartender glares at the philosophy teacher, who wears his dark hair long. "You'll know when *they* take over," he says. "Jesus, you'll know. Your tongue will be stickin' out after they hang you from a lamppost, that's how you'll know."

I walk to Ferris Booth, the student center, and wait to meet a young journalist in the student lounge. Nearby a black undergraduate, wearing sunglasses, is smirking at a slim white girl, whose hair is stringy brown. "I say you already fucked," the black student is saying. "Your society fucked you and we goan' fuck your society and tha's where it's at."

She looks at him patient, wide-eyed. She wants to hear a credo. She wants to be stirred.

"You see where it's fuckin' at," he says. "Or you too fucking ofay?"

"Oh, no," she pleads. "I'm not. I swear I'm not."

I have gone home. Our apartment sits high over Riverside Drive, commanding a view of the Hudson River, gone foul with sewage, and the Palisades, being gouged to death by builders. It is a spacious apartment, and the graduate drama student here to visit looks about hungrily. "Ten people could be living here," he says.

"We only have two bathrooms."

"So what," the student says. "What the hell's wrong with pissing on the floor?"

He wants a drink. The white walls and the black fireplace and the glass-topped cocktail table make him uncomfortable. I give him a light Scotch. He pours himself two more. I ask about his quarrel with Columbia. He starts to shout. He knows karate, he says; the drama student is stocky, sandy-haired and handsome underneath a flaring moustache. "Hah," he roars, "hah-hee. Punch through. I could drive your nose out the back of your head."

"I'm asking about Columbia."

He calms himself there on my blue couch, close to the windows fronting on the river. "It's a stinking, racist, warmongering dump. It's real estate, not books. How would you know? What could you know, living in a place like this?

"It's like society," the student says. "Plastic and white and glass and dead. A sperm couldn't live in this place." I almost laugh. I tell him I have three children.

"Well good for you," the student says, rising. "I'm going to save your kids from the life you have in this lousy sterile society. I'm going to teach your kids how to fuck."

I stand up. We are about the same height, but he is broader. I wonder about the karate. I tell him, "All right. I think you better go."

He glares. "Yeah. You can have this big plastic apartment and the stinking society, and if I quit fucking Columbia, I go to fucking Vietnam. You can have that and the bomb and all the goddamn rest, and you think I better go."

I throw an arm over his shoulder and start him toward the door. "Look, Sean. You live your way and I'll live my way and we'll both respect that. Okay?"

He springs back. "No. I don't respect your way." He makes a fist. He grimaces. "But I love you," he says, and kisses me on the cheek.

2 SEASON OF MELLOW MISTS

MOTHER (AND DAUGHTER) OF REVOLUTION

"So, you've met him," Josephine Drexel Duke asks, after I describe the raging drama student. "He's exciting, isn't he?

"We have a lot of people like that in the Movement. They were lost, and now they're finding themselves." Josie's face, part dead end kid, part pixie, softly lights. "That's one of the satisfying things, people like that."

Josie Duke believes that she has found herself in the Movement, and she enjoys introducing me to other young people who have had problems. One boy talked longingly of suicide. Another was a drifter. The Columbia Movement brought them a purpose; now the suicide is full of life and the drifter wants to build a better society. Both inflate Josie with maternal pride.

Josie is a paradox of a mother symbol. She is eighteen years old, small-busted, slight. She wears her hair cut straight and short. She favors sweaters and flowered miniskirts. Sometimes she giggles. But Josie, the gamine of eighteen, is a willful woman, unyielding in her principles, even as the principles are developing. She looks after new leftists, who seem to need help, giving them chores and assignments. She is an extremely confident girl. She comes to radicalism from generations of money.

Josephine is a daughter of the Carolina Dukes, who made a fortune in tobacco. "I'm not specially proud of that," she says. "All it means really is that my family was one of the biggest slaveholders in the South. They were fascists." So much for the Dukes. Josie is also related to the Biddles, a family with a certain Quaker pacifist strain. This did not dissuade her from throwing a bag full of blood during a Vietnam protest.

I telephoned Josie one summer afternoon, after a mutual friend gave me a number where she could be reached. "She is a highly serious young woman," he said. "Don't take her lightly." When I introduced myself by telephone, Josie was cautious. She asked about the mutual friend several times. The conversation proceeded haltingly.

"Well, how will I know you?" Josie said at length.

"I'll be wearing a blue sports jacket and a white sports shirt."

"I'll be wearing nothing," said Josie, suddenly the eighteen-year-old tease.

I found her at the front desk of the Liberation School, manning a telephone, issuing orders, very efficient and contained.

We went across the street and into a student lounge at Ferris Booth Hall. When I mentioned that she was really wearing clothes, Josie brushed aside the remark. She was annoyed to have let flirtatiousness interfere with serious business, explaining the Left.

She has strong legs and thighs, not slim. Her face is triangular. Birdlike, she often cocks her head. We sit in the lounge and Josie crosses her legs, tugs at a print mini-dress and waits pleasantly for me to begin.

"I hear you looked different before the uprisings." Someone described the prerevolutionary Josie as washed out and unhappy. Now she glows and wears large circular earrings.

"Well, I feel a lot better about myself."

"Where would you be now, normally?"

"Normally, I'd be in South Africa. My mother wanted me to go with her. She's there now. She thinks it's a nice place. There are people in my family who think apartheid is a good policy. They approve. I told you. We're fascists."

She averts her eyes when she speaks, and she smokes cigarettes very hard, the way you do when you have not been smoking long. There is a shy-child quality to her; when she speaks about her fascist family, it sounds awkwardly like any young person turning against his parents for disappointing him.

Josie grew up in Florida, with intervals on the North Shore of Long Island. Josie dislikes describing the details of her upbringing. She is bitter but does not want to hurt individuals. Her mother, she feels, is a hard-line right-winger without sensitivity to the causes of peace or justice. Her father is a compassionate man. He is teaching on Long

Island; her parents are divorced. Josie was sent only to carefully
tended private schools. In 1962, when she was twelve, and attending
the Everglades School, near Coral Gables, the Cuban missile crisis
terrified her. Afterwards, Josie, very bright and very vital, found herself considering doom, and horrified by the contrasts in her life. She
had these thoughts of Armageddon, but whenever she came home
from school, she lived amid what Peter Babcox calls "the power and
self-indulgence and cynicism of the hereditary rich." What to wear to
the ball before the Flamingo Stakes? Whom to pinch at poolside? How
is the Lafite-Rothschild '47? The homes in Josie's Coral Gables en-
clave are ornate and sprawling models of Spanish manor houses. The
gardens flower with hibiscus and bougainvillea. Scions of old families
gather with their ladies for the gossip that invigorates the very rich.
Here Josie, who worried of doom, was welcome everywhere.

In the autumn of 1967, she entered Barnard, one out of 500 entering
frosh. She was social, like a few other girls, and alienated, like many.
But the established cards of identity no longer mattered. She was a
number to the Columbia computer, a seat in a Barnard lecture hall, one
clean face among many. She was unhappy. "What they were teaching
wasn't relevant," she says, "but most of the other students were very
smug and sort of passive."

Josie had never heard of SDS. When she did hear, she began attending meetings. At first they bored her. She did not care for dialectical
analyses. She wanted action, confrontation. Miss Josie Duke, of the
Carolina Dukes, became an early impassioned supporter of Mark
Rudd of Maplewood, New Jersey. After the uprising, she dropped out
of Barnard, against the opposition of her family. She could have
stayed. She can go back. But Josie is a member of the Movement now.
The Movement is her life, and, she says, her future.

As the miniskirted girl, her thighs crossed, tells me these things on
a sofa in Ferris Booth lounge, disbelief chokes me. It is hard to accept
this willful little daughter of the Dukes as Madame La Farge, or
Lenin's beloved Inessa Armand. Josie's mention of Marcuse and Marx
may be name-dropping. All right, little lady. If you want to play the
radical, very good. But, little lady of the hibiscus and bougainvillea,
and the Everglades School, you are not going to fool me. I grew up
knowing real radicals. My grandfather was a Stalinist.

The next time I see Josie, she is press secretary of the SDS. This is
a meeting from which the press is barred. Someone spots a red-headed
woman in a light green dress taking notes as Mark Rudd talks.

"She's press," someone shouts. "She's got to go."

"I'm *with* you," the red-haired woman says. "I'm a radical. I work for Canadian Broadcasting."

"Well, I don't know," Rudd says. He is puzzled, a radical from the middle class, having trouble being rude to a woman.

"I'm not long out of school myself."

"Well, uh, I guess it's all right," Rudd says.

Josie has been shaking her head. "Mark," she calls sharply, "Mark. It is *not* all right. We have a rule."

The redhead, recognizing the adversary, ignores Josie and continues to plead with Rudd. "I won't take any more notes. I'm not going to report. I just want to be on your side."

"She has to go, Mark, really," Josie says, firmly. "We made a rule. No press and no exceptions." A chant begins. *"Get out; get out; get out."* The redhead gathers her things slowly. Rudd resumes speaking. Josie never takes her eyes from the other woman. The redhead pauses near the door. Josie leaves her seat and walks toward her. The woman leaves. Revolutionary discipline is maintained.

A month or two later, Josie joins a group protesting the appearance of the South Vietnamese UN ambassador at a forum in New York University. After someone throws water at the ambassador, Josie marches up to him, sticks a small finger in his face and says: "Why don't you give up, little man? The FLN is going to win." After that she becomes a full-time revolutionary, a full-time traveler for the Movement. She visits women's colleges bearing the message, rebel, through the Northeast.

It makes no sense. If a Duke is in rebellion, let her marry eight times, or gamble, or drink or embrace cocaine. That is the kind of rebellion of the very rich that people with Stalinist grandfathers accept.

But the old signposts are overturned, the old shibboleths, the old clichés are dying. The country is rent, the world is at war and Josephine Drexel Duke is a real revolutionary. When I finish talking to her, a slip of an eighteen-year-old girl, I have learned. A radical in this Movement is not a grandfatherly intellectual Russian dentist. A radical is every man and woman who sees the world as the premature sepulcher for us all, unless the left rises up and saves it. That is what Josie sees and what she believes.

Things are changing fast, and what Josie, in her miniskirt, teaches is the speed of change. The only limit to that speed is the ability of you and me to comprehend that Josephine Drexel Duke, of the Carolina tobacco Dukes, is every cell as radical as she claims.

The charged autumn followed one of those sweltering, sooty summers that make New York feel pestilential. June was hot. There were
no thunderstorms to stir the air. In Riverside Park, along the Hudson,
leaves curled. Their green was dimmed before summer began.

July was worse. Ninety-degree days followed one another until
everyone's vitality was sapped. Even the children moved slowly. As-
phalt pitched and bubbled. Cars stalled and spurted steam. The city
baked.

At the Morningside campus the Students for a Democratic Society
were shielded by their own belief. They rented a venerable fraternity
house on 114th Street, and there proclaimed the opening of Liberation
School. Workers, blacks, even capitalists were welcome. There was no
tuition. "Right alongside imperialist Columbia," one radical said with
shining eyes, "we are introducing the first free university this country
has ever seen."

The frat house was bare and ill-kept. Paint peeled from walls and
the floors needed scraping. But in this building, with its sense of
rooming-house despair, the young radicals poured out enthusiasm.

In the lobby, a table overflowed with the so-called underground
publications: *The Rat* and the *New York Free Press*. Nearby, a bulletin
board was crowded with messages: call home, radical meeting, where
were you last night, great world a-comin'. On another wall, you could
read the weekly schedule of classes:

Monday, Wednesday, Friday
Elementary Marxist Economics
Decline of Bourgeois Culture
Imperialism
Tuesday, Thursday
The Capitalist Media
Health and Hospitals under Capitalism

The classes drew few blacks and no obvious capitalists. There were
mostly young perspiring radicals who sat in the dreary heat and participated. A basic idea was to continue the spirit of communes born
in the occupied buildings of spring. No individual led; instead classes
were conducted in a communal way, with two teachers or three or
even more. At Elementary Marxist Economics, the instructional duties were spread between a Mr. Davis and a Mr. Marcus. Perhaps forty
young people sat on the floor and in chairs on a second-floor room.
Mr. Davis began by stating premises. He described maldistribution of

wealth, exploitation of individual workers and the tyranny of the American profit motive. Mr. Marcus talked about a new American society, in which class boundaries would be eliminated. "The country," Marcus said, "is clearly in a prerevolutionary stage. Nixon and Wallace are going to run for President. When they do, the people will revolt."

Marcus excited the students. A boy stood. "It seems very clear that there is a great difference in the world views of these two gentlemen."

"I wasn't aware that I had stated my world view," Davis said. "This course is Elementary Economics."

"What we have here," someone else shouted, gesturing toward Davis, "is plain enough. A bourgeois economist."

The course on the Decline of Bourgeois Culture was wide in scope, but uncertain in thrust. Before it was very old, a young man stood up to make a pronouncement. "I feel," he said, "that I have begun my personal liberation. For the last two weeks I haven't read *The New York Times*."

These were involved young people, serious, concerned, desperate to escape old parents and to find new ones, to flee both their backgrounds and their misfortunes. Many had real understanding of real inequities in current America; many did not.

Four hundred enrolled in Liberation School during its first weeks. But soon the heat, a sense of absurdity, varieties of disenchantment and general ennui took hold and most drifted away.

By August the school was waning, but Josie Duke felt that lines were firming up. "We're really learning who we can count on," Josie said.

"Like who?" I said.

"Like not too fucking many," Josie said. "Here or anywhere else."

She had been to a party for the SDS at Norman Mailer's home in Brooklyn Heights. Mailer told the radicals, "I approve of your methods, but not your aims." It was a contrary, arresting thing to say, and characteristic.

"We went," Josie said, "and did our thing, because he said he'd have friends there and raise money. We trusted him; his daughter had gotten busted in Mathematics. And he had his party and showed us off, and at the end of the evening the son of a bitch gave us a lousy hundred dollars."

In hot and hostile August, the radicals let slip some plans and boasts for fall. They would assemble a world conference of students at Morningside Heights. They would block autumn registration "with our bodies." They would feed magnets to the Columbia computers. The hope of several SDS members was to drive the Columbia computers crazy. They imagined computers, gone insane through random magnetic impulses, suddenly issuing pay checks to cafeteria employees for $10,000 a week, writing a check for one kopeck to Zbigniew K. Brzezinski, the director of Columbia's Institute of Communist Affairs, and, the young radicals believe, an agent of American imperialism. There was no end to the fantasies: threatening letters rather than fund appeals telegraphed to alumni; class cards belched forth in such numbers that every New York subway worker and every black militant attended Jacques Barzun's History 4166y, "European thought, science, art and social life between Renouvier and Bergson, Huxley and Heisenberg, the Decadents and the Dadaists, the Dreyfus Affair and World War I."

Various university observers audited at the Liberation School and perhaps one or two plainclothesmen infiltrated. In July, with no announcement to the press, the administration replaced the windows of Low Library with plexiglass, shatterproof panes of the sort used in the turrets of World War II bombers. Similar changes were made at the president's house. Private detectives from the Wackenhut Agency were installed in a number of buildings. Still Columbia administrators clung to the fiction that the situation was nearly normal.

On August 23, after a meeting of trustees at the Columbia Club, on 43rd Street just off Fifth Avenue, Grayson L. Kirk, Ph.D., LL.D., the president of Columbia, was forced out of office. Kirk had become a focus for radical hostility, somewhat in the way that Lyndon Johnson became a focus of hostility to the war in Vietnam. As Johnson left political life feigning grace, so Kirk left his presidency in a "resignation."

According to Columbia spokesmen, Kirk retired voluntarily with a letter to William E. Petersen, chairman of the trustees. Kirk wrote:

> The campus events of the past few months have made it impossible for me to devote as much time to the [200-million-dollar fund raising] campaign as would have been desirable. In consequence, I have concluded that in the interests of the successful completion of the campaign, I should propose my retirement from the duties of the presidency and as an active Trustee, becoming effective at the earliest practicable time and if possible before my sixty-fifth birthday, on October 12, 1968.

The insignificance of becoming sixty-five was exposed at once. Kirk's successor, Andrew Wellington Cordier, Ph.D., LL.D., was a

man of sixty-seven. Trustee Petersen, baby of the trio, was sixty-two. Petersen is a man with great respect for form—president of the Irving Trust Company and a member of the Union League Club. He lists himself as a Republican in *Who's Who*, and he resides in Bronxville, probably the last suburb of New York in which a Jew was allowed to buy a home.

Form was carefully observed, but the fall of Kirk could not be disguised. Liberal professors had grumbled about him for years. Conservatives found him remote, aloof. But it was the radicals who roared in spring and summer: KIRK MUST GO, KIRK MUST GO. It is because of the radicals that he went (although he did not move out of the president's house, with its new plexiglass windows, until almost Thanksgiving).

Predictably the new chief executive was a diplomat, a man whose trade is to avoid confrontations. Andrew Cordier, dean of the faculty of international affairs, had served as executive assistant to the secretary-general of the United Nations from 1946 to 1961. He had represented the UN on special missions to Korea, to the Middle East ("the most complex of all") and to the Congo. Earlier, he had been a historian. His academic credentials included twenty-one honorary degrees. Gray-haired like Kirk, a product of a small town in Ohio, like Kirk, Cordier began by reading a statement at the Columbia Club that conceded errors.

"It is not uncommon," he said, "in the modern university that research has tipped the balance away from instruction. This has been one of the vital factors contributing to student unrest." He spoke of "preoccupied" administrators and suggested "that all of us having duties in the field of student interests, as well as the heads of schools and departments, reserve a specific time every month or week to receive any student without prior appointment.

"The change," he said, "aims at the assertion of human values and participatory possibilities of university life and at the elimination of the impression that [Columbia] is a large impersonal bureaucracy."

All through August, while the young radicals debated the courses of confrontation, Andrew Cordier issued statements of conciliation. He thought it would be a good idea for the university to have a Negro trustee. He would like to see charges dropped against most of the arrested radicals. He would like Columbia's disciplinary processes reviewed. He could not endorse all of Columbia's past administrative actions. He hoped for rapid and constructive change.

These statements were not issued all at once. Columbia engaged the public relations firm of Hill and Knowlton for counsel, and Cordier behaved like a man getting the best of Madison Avenue advice. On fully eight occasions, *The New York Times* ran stories about changes coming at Columbia. Dr. Cordier was milking the media. It was as if he were out to get one positive story into the press for each negative Columbia story that had run the previous spring.

Cordier is a round man, with a genial Santa Claus face, a genial Santa Claus belly and eyes of ice. He looks at you in conversation, but when he is pressed he looks at a point beyond your shoulder. The warmth, as with an undercooked potato, is on the surface. It is not really possible to press him very hard. He has the politician's knack of saying what he means to say, regardless of questions. When I interviewed him, he talked at length and I thought fairly well. But when I reviewed my notes, I found he had not said much. The presidency was a hard job. He meant to do well. There was no point in castigating others. Columbia was a great university. His time was very valuable. He hoped he had helped me. All these things were uttered with cordiality and, through executive alchemy, each was made to seem profound or at least meaningful.

It is in the nature of a diplomat like Cordier to give what he comfortably can. Cordier had not been in office very long before he gave recognized campus groups the right to meet anywhere. This backed away from Kirk's position against demonstrations within Columbia buildings.

It is in the nature of the SDS to test, to confront, and they immediately scheduled a general meeting for members and friends. A major topic would be Andrew Cordier. The radicals were assigned a spacious, acoustically flawed arena in Earl Hall, an architectural oddment that stands due west of Low Library. A long flight of stone steps leads to the main entrance.

The SDS issued flyers proclaiming the meeting, at eight o'clock at night. It was late summer, and the press was still covering the SDS with great hunger. The first indoor meeting since the spring explosion drew a platoon of reporters and a gaggle of television journalists.

Josie Duke stood at the top of the stone stairs. Her sturdy little legs were set wide apart. "No press," she repeated over and over. "Our meeting tonight is not open to the press." A CBS soundman, who had climbed to meet her, dropped a bag of equipment with an enormous thud. Josie jumped. "You couldn't tell me that before I climbed the stairs?" the CBS man said.

Josie shook her head. The soundman, swart and heavy, said, "Shit."

Someone standing behind Josie said, "We don't trust the fucking press, mister."

It was starting to rain.

"Can we go inside?" the photographer said. "Hey, here's Mark Rudd. Let's ask him."

Rudd was slouching self-consciously up the stairs. "Look," he said, "look. Josie Duke is press secretary. We met and we decided and she is implementing our decision. No fucking press."

The photographers, the reporters and the CBS men asked one another how did they like that, having to stand out here in the goddamn rain! Josie Duke looked past them, detached, as poised young ladies are detached in the presence of conversations they do not want to hear. But this was the night she caught the redhead taking notes.

The auditorium of Earl Hall, which seats about seven hundred, filled quickly. Racks of bridge chairs had been emptied, and young people sat in chairs and on radiators, and on the floor and on the stage. Most dressed conservatively, in open-collared sports shirts and slacks or in blouses and miniskirts, but a few opted for unorthodox appearance— bushy, uncut hair combined with round, steel-rimmed Ben Franklin eyeglasses. On the stage, one long-haired young man wore a bright red bandanna. It was a young crowd, white with one or two exceptions, intense and very enthusiastic.

Mark Rudd began the meeting, sitting on the stage. "Oh, fuck, let's start." A post-profanity smile cracked his face. "All right, can you hear? Can you hear?"

A few people shouted, "No."

"The loudspeakers aren't working," Rudd said. "They're giving us a hall. They're letting us meet inside. But they give us a hall with terrible acoustics and no public address system."

As he spoke, technicians worked to get the P.A. system functioning. In a few minutes, they succeeded.

"All right," Rudd said, "the purpose of the meeting. Hold it down. Stop the talking. All right." A babble continued. Rudd held the microphone close to his face and shouted, "Shut up." The words, amplified, startled the room to quiet. "Now," Rudd said, "will everybody who's been talking raise your hand—and then shove it down your mouth."

Nervous laughter, then the meeting began. Rudd, who retains the angularity of adolescence, stood on the stage and threw out an arm at people raising hands. Speakers came up and had their say. A dark-haired young man, Steve Komm, read a new position paper. Paul Rockwell, a fair, stocky graduate student, wanted three hundred dollars to publish a pamphlet called *Why We Strike.* Stu Gedal, wiry and bespectacled, rose to report on Dr. Andrew Cordier.

"I've watched him in action," Stu Gedal began.

Suddenly Gedal wheeled and pointed at the stage. He was indicating the man in the red bandanna, whose feet dangled over the stage. "You can go," Gedal shouted.

The man stood.

"He's a spy," Gedal said into the microphone. "A plainclothesman. He's working for the police Red Squad."

The man in the red bandanna said nothing. He slipped from the stage and began to make his way down the center aisle toward the door.

"Pig," came shouts. "Blue fascist. Pig."

The man stopped near the door and turned around. "We'll get you fuckers yet," he called. Then the policeman was gone.

The room rustled with sound; someone sitting next to me said, "The cop overdid it. He tried to look *too* hippy." But the sounds died quickly. Police spies are concomitants of radicalism.

"All right," Gedal said. "I want to report on President Cordier." He drew a deep breath. "If anyone thinks Cordier is a copy of Grayson Kirk, they're wrong. Cordier is a clever man."

Gedal had attended Cordier's first press conference. "When they asked Cordier about the student uprising, he asked the reporter if he was married. Then he told the reporter that what happened last spring was a squabble, like an argument between husband and wife.

"Cordier is nobody to laugh at," Gedal said. "Cordier makes this good impression. A real good impression. He comes on as a kind of a Dutch uncle.

"Well," Gedal said, "maybe he *is* a Dutch uncle, but his ancestry is American CIA."

Cheers.

Political action meetings, exciting in short stretches, wear abysmally. Like most meetings they are humorless, self-important and repetitious. The SDS leaders worked the crowd confidently, imposing sporadic abuse, establishing subcommittees. Rudd said "horseshit" or "make your fucking motion," reveling in the echoes of obscenity within a college hall. When someone accused him of manipulating the meeting, he laughed. "I'm determined that it will be manipulated, but in the right fucking direction." As the evening waned, so did the cut and bite and wit. Rudd left at ten thirty and Tony Papert assumed the chair. By eleven, Tony knew that the attention span of the young radicals was at an end. "All right," he said, "all right. Let's stop it now and meet again tomorrow. Everybody put away their chairs."

As Columbia needed a new president, the SDS needed a new issue and at the next meeting, Tony Papert offered a shocker. Andrew Cordier, he charged, the diplomat-scholar-academician, was also something else: accessory to a murder. While working as executive assistant to the late Dag Hammarskjold, Cordier had helped engineer the murder of Patrice Lumumba.

In theory, the issue was ideal. Lumumba, the man on the left in a three-way fight for the Congo, was shot while in protective custody, policed by UN forces. Cordier had been the UN's man in the Congo. Could there be a better prima facie case? The impact at Columbia could be staggering.

The weakness of the issue was practical. Cordier insisted he had not helped kill Lumumba. With inadequate forces in the Congo, he said, he had been unable to control the explosive nativity there. Some of his subjective decisions were questionable, but a few nights before the killing, Cordier increased the guard around Lumumba's house.

One September night, Rudd and his colleagues were promising to hold a memorial rally for Lumumba "right outside Cordier's fucking window." Then they either did more research or talked to lawyers. Quietly and without public announcement, the memorial to Lumumba was postponed.

The freshman class, 710 young men strong, Columbia College '72, was a worthy prize. Campus radicals and the university establishment struggled over these bodies in an uneven autumn battle.

Most of the frosh were impressionable—they had all heard of the romantic radical, Mark Rudd. Most were bright. They had gained admission, after fierce competition, to the smallest college in the Ivy League.

"We get an average of 3,700 applicants," reports Henry Coleman, now the dean of freshmen. "We accept about 1,300 and about 700 show up. But 700 out of 3,700 is not the real story. There is a terrific amount of weeding out before the 3,700 apply." High school advisors know that unless a senior is in the upper third of his graduating class, he wastes time and an application fee in trying for Columbia College. A number of athletes are accepted on muscle and a number of social types enter through caste. But both groups are small minorities; Columbia trails Yale, Harvard, Princeton and Williams in students listed in the *Social Register* and its football team seldom wins. Most students fit the description of a troubled, intense parent. After the violence of the spring, Mrs. Jeanette Cohen cried out in horror: "That the police should do this to such boys. They are all ninety percenters, A minus at the least."

To the SDS, capture of a substantial number of frosh would keep alive spring power. The radicals considered seminars, but first the radicals knew they would have to do something dramatic. To young freshmen, spring was medieval history. The radicals decided on a daring confrontation.

The administration wanted the freshmen too, and in late summer, Cordier set about putting the college in better order for them. David Truman, the university vice-president, had been the last college dean. He was popular, busy, charming, and he was replaced, pro tem, by Henry Coleman, who himself possesses considerable charm without having Truman's academic credentials (Ph.D., L.H.D.). Late in the summer, Henry Coleman himself announced that Carl Hovde was becoming permanent dean of Columbia College.

I had a pleasant talk with Hovde in his office on the ground floor of Hamilton. He is a tall man, bespectacled and fair-haired, who looks younger than his forty-two years. He holds a Columbia B.A., a Princeton Ph.D. and his father was president of the New School for Social Research. Hovde is a Thoreau specialist, a rangy man himself quite fond of walking. He brushes his hair across his forehead somewhat in the manner of John Kennedy and he is a hard man to distrust. Our conversation ranged from police to the fact that he had not sought the deanship to his horror of violence. Presently we were telling stories about books among the unlettered. Hovde recalled reading a Henry James novel, *The Wings of the Dove* I think it was, while an army private during World War II. The man in the next bunk interrupted to ask if it was a good book.

"Very good," Hovde assured him.

The man, who had never heard of Henry James, mused briefly. Then he asked: "Do they get laid?"

Now Hovde was occupied with a sophisticated task in a sophisticated ambiance. He had to write a welcoming speech, about which freshman orientation could proceed. He had to woo them without seeming to.

"Can I audit the talk?" I said.

"I hope you do," Hovde said. "Try to be there; the program begins at eight thirty tomorrow."

At eight fifteen on the night of September 17, I started into a side entrance of Low Library. Two uniformed security guards positioned themselves in the door. "No press," one of them said. "We don't have any okay for the press." The guard who spoke was a pleasant-faced Puerto Rican, who wore a thin moustache. His partner was black.

"Dean Hovde invited me," I said.

"We no know about that." The Puerto Rican was fingering a billy.

"You get many kids with that last spring?" I said.

The guard's mouth flew open. "Nevair," he said. "I nevair hit no student."

"Tell your boss," I said. "Tell him I'm a writer Dean Hovde invited."

"I no tell him. He tell me." The man looked at his partner. They both nodded, supporting one another.

"Look," I said, holding my green steno notebook in the air. "Let's not have a fight, I was with Dean Hovde yesterday. He said please come. You're telling me no."

The black spoke now. "No press."

Someone outside a heavyweight fighter's dressing room once blocked me but let Elizabeth Taylor enter. I protested, "Hey, she doesn't have to work." A security man kept me off Barry Goldwater's campaign Boeing 727. He said, *You have to ride the DC-6, with the other excess baggage.*

What the hell? What the hell for?

You're an Eastern internationalist.

Here at Columbia, I was not outside a fighter's dressing room or among the simple, vicious folk who surrounded Goldwater. Here was a university, civility, Carl Hovde, who loved books and Thoreau. But suddenly, what difference, what did it matter? In the end I was facing the same insensate behavior. All the radical talk of the dehumanized university became real. For that moment, facing two poor men who had been programmed to follow orders, I felt that I was a student at Columbia. And I was being cheated out of an invitation, a promise, from the dean.

I looked at the black and Puerto Rican functionaries, $86 a week from Old Inhuman U. and said loudly, clearly, "Fuck you both." Their faces went expressionless. They were programmed for this as well. They stood at attention and stared blankly at the night.

"Sir," a man in a brown suit called. "Sir." He was walking toward me from the innards of Low. "I'm sorry if there's been a misunderstanding. It's okay, boys. Let him through. The press is okay for this one."

Haunting music sounded from the chapel. The ceiling towers, a great dome, and under it, in a concealed balcony, musicians were playing Purcell. All the freshmen were gathered, listening. The Columbia Glee Club, at ground level, was resplendent in tuxedos. The Purcell ended with horn notes echoing long. The glee club sang rousing student songs. Full-throated voices rose up under the dome. An on-key college glee club is startlingly affecting.

> *Roar, lion, roar.*
> *And wake the echoes of the Hudson vaaal-lee.*
> *Fight on to vict'ry evermore,*
> *While those sons of Knickerbocker rally round*
> *Columbia. Co-lum-bia*
> *Shouting her name, forever . . .*

One had to be touched by the spirit. In this great hall of Low Library, the music and the marble spoke tradition. There was no arguing against tradition here. This was Columbia's true home arena.

Ritual followed fast on the music; the introduction of the deans. In turn, as their names were called, each dean of Columbia College rose solemnly.

Coleman, Colahan, Flanagan, Wellington, B.A., M.A. The freshmen responded with bursts of applause. These men, assistant and associate deans at Columbia College, were going to influence their lives for four years, perhaps forever. From the rear of the chapel, I watched the backs of freshmen's heads. On one I spotted a yarmulke, the skullcap worn by certain religious Jews. Well, why not? In pluralism, Low Chapel is as good a place as any to find yarmulkes. But it struck me how different were the names of Columbia deans from the names of Columbia professors. The professors are not Coleman, Colahan, Flanagan. They are called Lieberman, Breslow, Dorfman. There is nothing provable here, and at least six of Columbia's trustees are Jews. Still, there seems to be this sense at Columbia, as at big American establishments everywhere: let Jews do abstract thinking and financial manipulation. Leave real governing to Christians.

Carl Hovde looked very tall and very wasp as he rose carrying his speech. "On behalf of all of us who belong to Columbia College," he began, "I wish to welcome you to the two hundred and fifteenth year of this institution's history. It would be a great understatement to say that you had merely heard of the events of last spring. The 'bust,' as we call it, really put Columbia on the map."

Hovde had been chased up and down Broadway by mounted policemen. He did not tell the freshmen that. Instead he characterized events with professorial impersonality. "It is a good thing, to be sure, that your own lives were not disrupted last spring at Columbia, but you will find a fair number of people who think of the disorders in the way that Ernest Hemingway thought about combat: 'It was awful, but I'm glad I was there.' "

Hovde spoke quietly and evenly, interspersing long, well-constructed sentences with wry jokes. Pleasant laughter arose. The boys were interested in Dean Hovde. They were responding. He told them that emotions at Columbia were strong now and that while emotions were both inevitable and good, it was possible for emotion to interfere with clarity of judgment. A danger was that an emotion could lock a man into a "frozen point of view. I would be less than candid if I were to argue that none of us suffered from this malady last spring—we had a sufficient supply of what one might call frozen ideologies. In saying this I by no means intend to exclude myself—"

Confrontation came suddenly, just when it seemed that the security men, at all the entranceways, had succeeded in keeping out the SDS. A short, dark student came striding down the center aisle of the chapel shouting at soft-voiced Carl Hovde and waving one hand in the air. It was Stu Gedal. "We receive only a one-sided education here," Gedal cried. Dean Hovde stopped and waited.

"This man is defending one-sided education," Gedal shouted. "He is not speaking to the issues. He is defending racism and imperialism and war."

Security men moved toward Gedal.

The frosh were shocked. Most had not heard exactly what Stu Gedal had said. Instead they had heard noises that were inchoate and that disrupted a measured lecture by their dean.

"At least," a boy near me said, "you'd think those guys [the radicals] would have some manners."

The sense of tradition and order and caste was overwhelming. Stu Gedal had interrupted Hovde in the wrong place at the wrong time.

"Gentlemen," Hovde said mildly as Gedal scurried out, "I suggest that this man has shown contempt for all the audience."

The frosh applauded. "As we think about the situation at Columbia," Hovde said, returning to his speech, "we must make one the powerful minds we spend so much time studying. Aristotle and Spinoza. It is a first rule of intellectual life, gentlemen, that one should never underestimate the power of Aristotle.

"One might define your four-year enterprise at Columbia as thought upon the memories of our race. To have memory only is to be a pedant; to have thought with few memories is to be uneducated; to have emotion without either thought or memory is not to be a man at all, but only an animal.

"I do not want animals, or small children either, to be anything different from what they are, but one wants full potentialities developed. A kitten becomes a cat, but a small girl becomes a man— a man, that is, in Aristotle's definition—an animal that thinks. Cats, children and men are all filled with emotion, but only in man are mind and emotion coexistent. Think of what a testimony it is to your parents' care and dedication that when you entered this elegant marble hall you did not come in on all fours, howling and biting one another. . . .

"It is men we all must be. There are those among us who love Columbia College deeply—I am one who does. I came here to study a longer time ago than all but a few of you have been alive, and I look forward with the greatest anticipation to what we shall all be doing here to fulfill our promise." The freshmen rose and cheered.

The radicals had been soundly beaten. The university, computers, registration programs, faculty smokers, research, classes and all the rest of it, was functioning cohesively under new leadership. Cordier and Hovde had helped right Columbia. But so, too, had plainclothesmen, blustering and intimidating as they moved, and the New York criminal courts, which held two dozen radical leaders under indictment. Perhaps, most of all, order came with the time of the year. The autumn mood on campuses is urgent. We all feel a year older. We have had our summer fling. Time presses and winter is coming. The approaching cold reinforces a sense of inevitability. Some rules are necessary. Look to the hearth. Break open books. Let's go to class.

But the failure of the radical offensive did not mean that Columbia's positions on major issues were correct. Despite the appointment of new executives, Columbia was very much the same in the fall as in the previous spring. The final radical spasm of the autumn, one more calculated and impolitic confrontation, cut away sham and bared an ugly truth more vividly than any event before.

The night of September 26 was cool and clear. The SDS had organized a modest Lumumba Memorial rally. That same night faculty and students met in Wollman Auditorium and discussed Columbia and the American military machine. Carl Hovde had volunteered to chair the moderates.

The SDS had been tramping through the streets. Outside of Low,

Mike Golash told 150 people that Columbia's real estate department had evicted seven persons, several of whom were elderly, from the St. Marc Arms Hotel on West 112th Street. "They are doing this," Golash shouted, "to clear the site so that somebody can put up the Morningside House for the Aged. They kick out old people so that they can put up a home for the aged."

"Let's march," someone called.

The radicals moved, hurrying into Broadway. They turned east on 110th Street and headed toward Amsterdam Avenue. One student, who was stocky and blond, bore a red flag.

At the corner of Amsterdam and 110th, two police cars were parked in the center of the street, blocking the intersection. Three policemen stood in front of the cars, waiting. "Get rid of the goddamn red flag," a policeman shouted. He lunged and tore the flag from the blond student's hands. Other students surged. A siren wailed. Very quickly a column of burly plainsclothesmen appeared. The police waded into the students, swinging clubs, and the SDS marchers broke, amid howls.

"Wait," shouted Paul Rockwell, a stocky graduate student. "We can't quit right here. Let's march into that meeting in Wollman."

About seventy-five radicals broke into the Wollman meeting, as a leftist liberal woman, Mrs. Rusty Eisenberg, was announcing that she had important information. "The School of International Affairs runs a series of international institutes," she said. "I have seen evidence that the directors of these institutes have to be approved by the federal government before they can assume their positions at the university."

The radicals swarmed onto the stage while the woman was speaking. From the floor, Stu Gedal walked to a microphone and his recent adversary, Carl Hovde, approached him. "Would you like to sit and wait your turn?" Hovde asked.

"No," Gedal said. Hovde stood next to Gedal, frowning. Gedal ignored the dean and began to orate. He had urgent data on Professor Eugene Galanter of the psychology department, he said. Galanter, tall and smooth, was seated on the stage himself. He wore wraparound sunglasses and an impassive expression.

"Now about Professor Eugene Galanter," Gedal said. "We have information that Professor Galanter is working on a contract, amounting to $37,185, on weapons systems that make use of adjustable manual ranging devices."

Ranging devices are used to zero in on a target; a bombsight is a ranging device. "One phase of Professor Galanter's experiments on

behalf of the war machine," Gedal said, "were conducted in the psy-
chophysics laboratory in Schermerhorn Hall. Other phases involved"
—Gedal was reading from notes—"judgments by observers in an aircraft of a fixed ground target—that is, a strafing or a rocket approaching." He did not make the case very well, but the case was powerful.
A Columbia professor, claiming to be a friend of Columbia students,
was making a personal profit out of the Vietnam War.

Dean Hovde regained the microphone. "Professor Galanter," he
said.

Galanter moved slowly to the center stage, a man who carried
himself with assurance. He waited for the audience to quiet. He is a
Swarthmore graduate, who took a doctorate from Pennsylvania.
"First," Galanter said, bluntly, "I would like you to know that the
contract described here is a contract I wrote and transmitted to the
military. It was funded. It concerns trying to understand how people
see and how they act in terms of what they see.

"The work we're concerned with requires that we move people at
high speeds so that we can assess how it is that they see—"

Someone in the audience shouted, "From a B-52 bomber."

"No," Galanter said, "we don't use those."

The psychologist leaned close to the microphone and talked inti-
mately. "One of the important results of this work has been to produce
criteria for aircraft separation. If you move from one place to another
in an airplane, whether it's Vietnam or Kennedy Airport—"

Another shout. "Or Bolivia."

"Or Bolivia," Galanter said, "you will arrive where you are going
without intercepting another airplane, partly because of this work."
The audience broke into light applause.

"Another contract," Galanter said, "concerns the ability of people
to use information that is only *likely* rather than certain to make
judgments about what they will do." Galanter was starting to lecture.
"Suppose you are a soldier," he said.

"No," a boy called. "You be the soldier, Galanter."

"I am," Galanter said. "Now suppose you are watching a radar
display full of little pips."

"That's us."

Somebody giggled. Protected by his wits and the wraparound sunglasses, Eugene Galanter was softening the audience. "Now you have
these little radar pips and you're concerned with deciding whether
they are a flight of missiles or a flight of geese. The trouble is that radar
doesn't help you to make this distinction. You have to train yourself
to know how to do this, and having made this decision, you've got to

push one button or another. One button means it's only geese and the other means it isn't geese at all."

The audience was quiet now, intent.

"The principle that I've heard," Galanter lectured, "is that you want to make the majority of people happy. In cases, then, where the individual cannot make a clear-cut black-and-white decision, he tries to work out what majority opinion is and act accordingly. Now when you say that majority opinion should guide, you are right, because majority opinion *does* guide. As far as we can tell, you see, it is the majority of neural actions in the brain that makes you take the decision that you do."

Professor Galanter smiled. "The evidence," he said, "is that your own neural structure conforms to your idealism. Do you recognize the profound implications of this? You have reached down into your own actions and come up with the very nature of man."

It was a minute or so before a red-haired young woman stood up to be recognized.

"Well, mister—uh, I don't even know his name—" the young woman said.

"It's Galanter," someone called.

The young woman said thank you. She spoke in a soft German accent. "I am not a psychologist or a professor," she said, "and there are many things this gentleman said, we had fun because they were funny. But one thing struck me wasn't funny. I am from West Berlin."

She held the enormous room. "In Germany, we did the same thing with our professors."

"Herr professors," shouted a boy, courting attention.

The red-haired German nodded. "When we asked our professors, we didn't ask them about the Vietnam War. We asked them about Nazi Germany. We asked what they had done, and they told us what they had done, just as these people here are being told what these professors are doing now."

She turned. "When we asked our professors they reacted like this gentleman." She gazed at Eugene Galanter and his wraparound sunglasses. "They didn't yell at us," she said. "They were very polite. They walked around the room and gave us lectures. They lectured about experiments, like this gentleman, that were necessary to rid themselves of our enemies."

The handsome German girl shrugged her shoulders and tossed her red hair. She looked as though she were about to deliver a philippic. "But they didn't lecture us about what they had really made," she said. "They never lectured us about the gas ovens."

3 NOTES TOWARD A DEFINITION

LATE in the nineteenth century, under the winy influence of prosperity, an earlier Columbia president boldly defined the relationship between the university and the city around it. Seth Low, a vigorous, powerful, moustached man who was to leave Columbia and become mayor of New York, stood before the library named for his father and told dignitaries: "A university set upon a hill cannot be hid." The date was May 2, 1896. The Morningside campus was being dedicated.

"I count it as a matter of no little moment," Low continued, "that here, in its new home, Columbia cannot escape observation. The university cannot be indifferent to what is going on in the great city of which it is a part, and neither can the city forget, as it looks toward this hill, that there is in its midst, in this university a life, the watchword of which is truth." Low saw Columbia's visibility as an advantage. In the intervening seven decades, others have not been so sure.

Columbia is of New York; it is a prominent part of the City fabric. Yet during this century, it has held itself aloof, pursued private profit, practiced genteel anti-Semitism, rejected meaningful integration and, despite Seth Low's stricture, hid its books, its inner workings and its real aims as only a private corporation can. Describing Columbia in *The Closed Corporation, American Universities in Crisis,* James Ridgeway, late of the *New Republic,* maintains: "It would be difficult to find an institution of higher learning in the country so deeply and justly detested as is Columbia University in New York City."

One does not have to subscribe to Mr. Ridgeway's flat assertion—

Columbia is a place that many people love—to accept a part of his title. American universities are indeed in crisis. I think it is fair to say that no major university in crisis has handled itself as poorly as Columbia.

Columbia University, the eleventh oldest and eighth wealthiest educational complex in the United States, grew out of Columbia College, which in turn grew out of King's College in colonial New York. King's was chartered in 1754 under George II "to promote a liberal education" in the British province of New York, sparsely settled then and extending from the eastern tip of Long Island to the "Iroquois hunting grounds" in the north. The British had captured the province from the Dutch eighty years earlier.

New York, 1754, was polyglot and acultural. Most people spoke English, but many knew only Dutch or French or German. In one contemporary account, the populace is described as "having no interest but commerce and their owne gayne." The British believed that a college in New York would be a powerful force for unity. It would teach one language, English, and one religion, high Episcopal. No less important, it would "prevent the growth of republican principles which prevail already too much." From the beginning, Columbia and the people of New York did not perform as expected.

Because King's was sponsored by the Anglicans, it was attacked by Presbyterians, a powerful bloc in eighteenth-century New York. To pacify the Presbyterians, King's surrendered half its birthright—a £6,400 grant from the provincial assembly. With this money turned back to New York City, the presbytery was mollified and King's survived in a schoolhouse attached to Trinity Church. Its first president, Dr. Samuel Johnson, started at an annual salary of £250. For one year, he was the entire faculty.

In 1760, King's College, aged six, acquired a place of its own. The new campus was a fenced private park, situated near the Hudson, at the foot of what is now Park Place. The hall of the college was a three-story stone building consisting of twenty-four rooms. This was classroom space, living quarters and chapel. Soon after sundown, the gates to the campus were locked. There was no fear then of assault from without. The idea was to contain the students.

In March, 1761, King's College appointed a steward and students were ordered to "breakfast, dine and sup together in the College Hall." Breakfast and supper were unvarying. The days began with coffee or tea and bread and butter; they ended with bread and butter and cheese or milk "or the remainder" of the noon meal. Dinners were more interesting. One two-hundred-year-old menu "For Every Day in the Week" survives:

> Sunday, Roast Beef and Pudding
> Monday, Leg of Mutton, etc. and Roast Veal
> Tuesday, Corn'd Beef and Mutton Chops
> Wednesday, Pease Porridge and Beef Steaks
> Thursday, Corn'd Beef, etc. and Mutton Pye
> Friday, Leg Mutton and Soop
> Saturday, Fish fresh and salt in their season.

Considering the past from the safety of two centuries, Columbia historians report proudly that "the closely controlled environment at King's failed to produce the desired conformity." When the American Revolution erupted, three major rebel figures were King's College men. Alexander Hamilton and John Jay had attended briefly; Gouverneur Morris had been graduated. During the Battle of Long Island, King's people lent the college telescope to Washington. Soon afterward classes were suspended. The college was shuttered for the next decade.

When the campus reopened, with a charter from New York State, the legislature had decreed that "The College within the City of New York heretofore called King's College, shall be forever hereafter called and known by the name of Columbia College." Columbia was a new, extravagant word for the United States. It was popular with nationalistic, antimonarchist journalists and poets, just the sort of revolutionaries that King's College had been intended to suppress.

In 1810, another legislature passed an "act relative to Columbia College in the City of New York." This second act created the autocracy that later presidents and trustees were to exploit. Section I provides:

> Be it enacted by the people of the State of New York that John H. Livingston, Richard Varick, Brockholst Livingston, Abraham Beach, John Lawrence, Gershom Seixas, Richard Hairson, John Watts, William Moore, Cornelius I. Bogart, John M. Mason, Edward Dunscomb, George C. Anthon, John N. Abeel, James Tillary, John H. Hobart, Benjamin Moore, Egbert Benson, Gouverneur Morris, Jacob Radcliff, Rufus King, Samuel Miller, Oliver Wolcott, and John R. Romeyn, the present trustees of said college, and their successors, shall be and remain forever hereafter, a body politic and corporate, in fact and name, by the name of The Trustees of Columbia College in the City of New York, and by that name shall and may have continual success forever hereafter. . . . And be it further enacted, That the said trustees, and their successors, shall forever hereafter

have full power and authority to direct and prescribe the course of study and discipline. . . . No professor, tutor, or other assistant officer shall be trustee. . . .

Three things are notable in the 1810 law. First, the names read like a street map of New York. Livingston, Varick, Tillary and King are all the names of streets in long-settled portions of the city. Second, there is a sephardic Jew, Gershom Seixas, named trustee during years when the Episcopalian influence was enormous. Anti-Semitism had little snob appeal. Most important, the trustees are granted absolute power at a time when the country generally and New York State particularly were sensitive to the need for checks and balances. The great issues at Columbia then were academic standards, discipline, enlarging the curriculum and attracting students. (Between 1784 and 1810, the average graduating class numbered seventeen.) In its haste to create a prestigious university, the New York legislature erected a narrow oligarchy. Within a year the first uprising at Columbia disturbed the torpid peace of August.

As students saw things, the issue that precipitated "the Riotous Commencement of 1811" was free speech. According to administrators, it was discipline. A Columbia senior, John B. Stevenson, had prepared a commencement address on "The Duty of the Representative to Obey the Will of His Constituents." Briefly, the conservative view was that representatives, being brighter and better informed than most voters, should decide issues without necessarily consulting the constituency. Liberals, like Stevenson, saw legislators as lawyers to the people's will.

Dr. John M. Mason, the provost and most forceful executive at Columbia, disagreed with Stevenson's liberal view. He arranged for Peter Wilson, professor of Latin and Greek, to soften and edit Stevenson's text. But at commencement, in Trinity Church on August 7, 1811, John Stevenson reverted to his original script. Covering himself, Wilson explained to Provost Mason that this was not the speech as he had corrected it. Mason did not interrupt the address, but whispered a proposal of punishment to William Harris, the university president.

An hour later, Dr. Harris refused to present Stevenson with his degree. Embarrassed, Stevenson hurried off the stage. But his classmates were aroused. They pushed Stevenson forward, urging him to present himself again. When he did, President Harris ignored him. Down Stevenson tramped and then, among his classmates, borrowed courage once more. For a third time, he mounted the platform and, in a kind of inversion of Caesar at the Lupercal, was for a third time denied.

Desperate, he shouted, "I want my diploma." The audience burst into applause. Provost Mason ordered a city marshall to arrest Stevenson. Other seniors shouted "No, no." Hugh Maxwell, Columbia 1808, leaped onto the platform and called: "This young man is unwilling to express the sentiments of others as his own. And for that reason and that reason only, he is being deprived of his degree." Gulian C. Verplanck, a lawyer and an annotator of Shakespeare, demanded that Provost Mason explain his own behavior.

Mason replied briefly. Verplanck announced that the remarks were unsatisfactory. The audience cheered. Dozens of people pushed toward the platform, eager to speak. Faced with this wave of protest, President Harris, Provost Mason and the faculty fled Trinity Church through side exits. Students beat off a detachment of police. The church was loud with hisses and cries of tyrant. In the confusion, Stevenson left quietly without his degree.

After Richard Varick, chairman of the Columbia trustees, consulted with DeWitt Clinton, the mayor of New York, indictments were drawn charging riot. The two alumni, Verplanck and Maxwell, were fined two hundred dollars each. Stevenson did not get his undergraduate degree until five years later. Verplanck was bitter about his fine, but in 1835 accepted Columbia's offer of an honorary LL.D.

In the nineteenth century, educational goals at Columbia began to be defined in a way distinct from older traditions. At the same time, Columbia began to accumulate great wealth through the acquisition of Manhattan real estate.

A political struggle early in the century left Columbia with a valid claim against the legislature. The college had been excluded from the proceeds of a state lottery for education. The trustees hoped for a settlement of $80,000, but had to accept instead a tract called the botanic garden, which one trustee said, "would not upon a sale bring more than six or seven thousand dollars." Today it would. Still owned by Columbia, the botanic garden is the land underneath Rockefeller Center. The annual rental brings Columbia $3.6 million.

Columbia moved to the Rockefeller Center site in 1857, first occupying a building that had been a deaf-and-dumb asylum. In landscaping the workmen removed "the bones of the unknown dead" from a potter's field. At the time, Madison Avenue was paved only as far north as 42nd Street and ended at 49th, which is where the campus began. An old daguerrotype of the main building shows a long, rectangular three-story structure, distinguished by ten chimneys, a variety of shutters and the debris that, then, as now, builders leave.

But as late as 1872, Columbia was a small college with an uncertain future. That year, the total registration was 116 students. Frederick A. P. Barnard, a deaf mathematician from the Berkshire hills, rescued struggling Columbia and set it upon the course that led to success, ascendancy and riot.

Barnard, the tenth president of Columbia (1864-1889), had to use a long curved ear trumpet to communicate with faculty and students. But he had a fine grasp of statistics, and by the 1880s he had become convinced that the American liberal arts college was a failing venture. Taking a thirty-year period during which the population tripled, Barnard drew up tables that proved fewer and fewer "white Americans" were entering college.

In 1840, one of every 1,549 Americans attended a college.

In 1860, the ratio was one out of 2,012.

In 1869, it was one out of 2,546.

Clearly, Barnard reported, the liberal arts college was in decreasing demand. "There is not a state in the union," he wrote, "in which the number of colleges is not greatly in excess of the educational needs of the population." New York City, with a population of two million, needed one college. It had five. "Therefore," Barnard commented, "it would not be an educational misfortune if Columbia College should cease to exist, as a school for undergraduate students." The implication of the final phrase is important. While interest in undergraduate education lagged, the demand for specialized and technical education surged. Barnard's pragmatic suggestions for a successful Columbia swept into many areas. Most germane today is that he imagined Columbia as a university, rich in graduate, specialty and professional schools.

The Columbia School of Law was founded in 1858. A School of Mines, now the School of Engineering, was begun in 1864. Barnard worried about the original college. He advocated teaching modern languages there, proposed honors courses, suggested a national uniform college entrance examination and urged that women be admitted. "The presence of young women," he wrote, "is conducive to good order." But all this was to happen at a college within the confines of a great university. Columbia, the university, Barnard wrote, "has a mission of such dignity and grandeur that her original mission as a school for training boys shrinks into comparative insignificance."

His faculty meetings were memorable. The staff sat at a long table, with Barnard at the head holding a huge hearing trumpet to one ear. Tubes ran from the trumpet to each seat. The President could hear only what was shouted into the tubes. He was indomitable and he had his way.

During his tenure, the Graduate Faculty of Political Science was organized. He was the driver whose push created Teachers College (1889) and Barnard College (1889).

On February 3, 1896, seven years after Barnard's presidency ended, the trustees passed this resolution:

All the departments managed by this corporation may be designated collectively as "Columbia University in the City of New York." The School of Arts may hereafter be designated as "Columbia College."

Columbia's rise from boy's school to university was fact. Its new name was formalized in state Supreme Court sixteen years later.

As Manhattan expanded north, the 49th Street quarters became cramped and noisy. In the late 1880s, a trustee named John Pine called attention to several blocks of uptown terrain that housed the Bloomingdale Insane Asylum. The trustees bought an option on the land and in April, 1892, made the purchase, eighteen acres of rolling high ground, for two million dollars.

Columbia now had an ample site for large ambitions. Barnard's successors, Seth Low and Nicholas Murray Butler, made the most of it. Low, a powerful, vigorous rich man, supervised planning the new campus. Rolling ground was ingeniously transformed into a series of plateaus. Low Library rose, huge, neo-classic, domed, formidable. Daniel Chester French designed the statue before the main entrance of Alma Mater seated with a book in her lap and a hand extended, as if to see if it was raining. Few apartment houses had been erected then, and from Grant's Tomb on Riverside Drive you could get a clear sweep of the campus: brick buildings spread across six blocks, none distinguished in themselves, but in the sum impressive. At least sixteen buildings were completed in a decade.

Low also worked toward imposing unity on the expanding university. He arranged contracts with the semi-independent professional schools, law and medicine, bringing them under direct university supervision. He insisted that students at Columbia University be allowed to take courses under any faculty without extra fees. "Thus," Low wrote, "Columbia ceased to be divided into fragments, and took unto herself the aspect of a university, wherein each department was related to every other and strengthened all."

By the time Low resigned to become mayor in 1901, Columbia was a booming concern. The student body exceeded 2,600. The faculty numbered 400. The man who replaced Low, the most commanding leader Columbia had ever had, was able to accelerate the growth.

Nicholas Murray Butler, who presided over Columbia for forty-three years, from 1902 to 1945, was handsome, autocratic and arrogant. "It is literally true," he confessed in his memoirs, "that beginning with Gladstone, Prince Bismarck, Cardinal Newman and Pope Leo XIII, it has been my happy fortune to meet, to talk with, and often to know in warm friendship almost every man of light and learning during the past half century." He boasted acquaintanceships with Tennyson, Browning, Matthew Arnold, Robert Louis Stevenson and Kipling. He claimed to have known thirteen American Presidents. Once he remarked to Franklin D. Roosevelt, "You will never be able to call yourself an intellectual until you come back to Columbia and pass your law exams."

"That shows," F.D.R. said, "how unimportant the law really is."

Butler and Columbia were preeminent in the era of the university explosion. The colleges—Cornell, Chicago, Wisconsin, Michigan—were developing into universities. The universities, Harvard and Yale, were expanding. The times called for strong, enterprising university presidents and they appeared: Charles Eliot at Harvard, Andrew White at Cornell, William Rainey Harper at Chicago, David Starr Jordan at Stanford. "Captains of erudition," Thorstein Veblen called these people. None was a mightier, busier captain than Nicholas Butler. Soon after taking command, he employed a personal staff of two office boys, three secretaries and five stenographers. Apparently he kept them all busy.

In 1920, Butler ran for the Republican presidential nomination. His slogan was: "Pick Nick for a Picnic in November." He drew 69½ votes and the convention picked Warren Harding. Later, Butler became president of the Carnegie Endowment and toured the world, acquiring decorations from fifteen countries. In 1931, he shared the Nobel Prize for Peace with Jane Addams of Hull House.

Under Butler, Columbia added schools of business, dental surgery, library service, social work and journalism. He was unenthusiastic about journalism. He had to be persuaded that it belonged in a university teaching program; afterward he treated the school as a stepchild. Columbia attracted a memorable faculty. Famous names glowed in almost every discipline: anthropologists Franz Boas and Margaret

Mead; classicist Moses Hadas; philosopher John Dewey; physicist I. I. Rabi; chemist Harold Urey; historians Allan Nevins, Henry Steele Commager, Charles Beard.

In his time, Butler was indiscriminately acclaimed. (President Theodore Roosevelt insisted on calling him "Nicholas the Miraculous.") But the judgment of perspective is less generous. It was Butler, grasping for power, who established the Columbia president as dictator. He wanted no questioning and brooked none. It was Butler who downgraded the undergraduate college. He argued that a four-year program was a waste for future graduate students; it would "produce moral weakness" by postponing the time when they began to earn a living. It was Butler who kept the faculty in its low station. He regarded professors as bright enough to reach decisions on curriculum and tenure, but nothing else. The administration alone made the rules and enforced discipline.

In 1917, Butler fired J. McKeen Cattell, a professor of psychology with twenty-five years of service. Cattell had urged members of congress to support a bill that would have prevented the army from sending unwilling draftees to fight in Europe. Soon afterward Cattell observed, "It is desirable to speak in faculty meeting only so long as the policies and the prejudices of the president and dean are re-echoed." At the same time Butler dismissed an English instructor, Henry Wadsworth Longfellow Dana, who had delivered antiwar speeches.

The dismissals were applauded by the bellicose press. "Columbia," commented *The New York Herald*, "has washed her hands of [Cattell and Dana] and is well rid of them." But a week later Charles A. Beard resigned.

Late in life, Beard became an isolationist; he failed to recognize the danger of Nazism. But in 1917, Charles A. Beard was in his prime.

> Having observed closely the inner life at Columbia for many years [the historian wrote on October 9], I have been driven to the conclusion that the university is really under the control of a small active group of Trustees who have no standing in the world of education, who are reactionary and visionless in politics, narrow and medieval in religion. Their conduct betrays a profound misconception of the true function of a university in the advancement of learning.

Butler's own self-appraisal is ironic. He had built a university so large as to be inhuman. He had nurtured conformity and elitism, the belief that Columbia people, and white Protestants generally, were the chosen. All this was tested in the riots of April, 1968, and found questionable. Yet Butler, the complete autocrat, allowed for no doubts. "When you have served a university," he once said, "you learn the meaning of immortality. That university is not going to die. Your work is not going to be lost."

Butler did not go gently to his good night. Blind, ancient, he clung to office through the great changes of World War II. When he finally did retire, he insisted on remaining in the president's residence; it was his home until his death in 1947.

The thinking behind the selection of General Dwight David Eisenhower to succeed Nicholas Murray Butler remains mysterious. According to one hypothesis, Republican members of the Columbia trustees pumped for Eisenhower to demilitarize him. The Democrats had held the White House since 1933, and Eisenhower was the man who could most likely turn them out. But there are persistent popular objections to having a general as President. As Grant demonstrated, a military career is incomplete training, and there is a deeper concern about keeping the military under civilian control. The problem for ambitious Republicans was to get Eisenhower into civilian clothes. What better way than to install him in a university, where his outfit would include robes and mortarboard.

Another explanation is lighter. In this story the Columbia trustees are meeting in their paneled room. After long and thoughtful talk, they agree to the appointment of Eisenhower as "a man uniquely qualified to lead the university in a challenging era." The new president walks into the room and the trustees gasp. But it is too late. "How could we admit that there'd been a foul-up," one explains later, "that we wanted the other Eisenhower? Milton."

Dwight D. Eisenhower accepted the presidency of Columbia, after which he began to develop doubts. Unsure of himself with intellectuals, the general walled them out of his life. Unhappy with scrutiny, he became inaccessible to campus reporters. "When he first took office," a former *Spectator* reporter remembers, "he told us that his door would be open any time. Then I had to wait three months to get to see him. He gave me a couple of minutes and didn't say much."

The gap between the scholastic branch—students, faculty—and administration widened. Poking fun at Eisenhower, faculty people repeated someone's remark: "In a community of scholars, his best friend is the football coach."

For his part, Eisenhower made a show of unconcern. Stories persist that his principal pursuit in his office was perfecting his bridge game against General Alfred Gruenther, an expert.

Eisenhower took regular walks about Morningside Heights, but even here he felt out of place. Long-time residents insist that he seldom acknowledged greetings. A stranger's "good morning," aimed at Eisenhower, drew a stony stare. Before the general began walking in his new neighborhood, he applied for and received a permit to carry a pistol.

The official justification for Eisenhower's appointment was the need for fund raising. In the days after World War II, as education and educational costs increased, the universities felt they needed presidents capable of canvassing. Eisenhower, a national hero, could go anywhere, reach anyone and ask for anything. At the very least he would get a courteous hearing. In fact, he was able to convince the Harriman family to present Columbia with a large tract of Rockland County. But he achieved no comparable coups. He left Columbia after two years "on leave" to command the forces of NATO. He did not return. One professor is supposed to have said, "Columbia's loss is the nation's loss." Grayson Kirk became the fourteenth president of Columbia in 1953, the year in which Dwight Eisenhower was inaugurated as the thirty-third President of the United States.

Kirk was an essentially conservative man in radically changing times. The Columbia that Butler left was the realization of nineteenth-century ambitions. What Kirk was to leave, on his resignation, was an institution overtaken by the present.

Kirk's shortcomings, according to one generally sympathetic observer, have three sources. "They are," asserts George Keller, who formerly edited the alumni magazine, *Columbia College Today*, "personal, organizational and cultural."

He is a shy man, most comfortable in small groups. Under heavy pressure he stutters. At all times he tends to speak very deliberately. The timidity and curious speech contribute to an air of aloofness. In addition, he is not at ease with fiery intellectuals or innovative thinkers. "This was an Ohio farm boy," Keller says, "who became urbane without becoming urban." The license plate on Kirk's black Cadillac reads GK-1.

He generally shunned large parties and, as his work load increased, he mounted his Cadillac weekends and rode off to a country retreat. This removed him farther from informal dinners and smokers. He had few intimates, except for his wife, Marion, whose orientation went toward the aesthetic. He was a private man in a public position.

Kirk ran Columbia through a small band of colleagues whom he dominated. Despite the obvious urban crises, he hired no urbanologist for his cabinet. When Columbia began a $200 million fund campaign, he neglected to appoint a vice-president for development. Briefly, as Keller put it, "he failed to develop a staff that could gather facts, analyze trends, plan, project, persuade and press a variety of constituencies and media." He was both autocratic and poorly informed.

Finally, his own intellectuality, such as it is, runs exclusively toward conventional fare. He admires Aristotle and Jefferson, Oriental art and Mozart, and he automatically rejects new things. A culture gap spread between Kirk and his critics. To quote Keller again, "He was doing Mozart, James Madison and Ralph Bunche, while others were doing Bob Dylan, Che Guevara and Stokely Carmichael." The Wee Kirk was not a large man.

The dominant function of Columbia changed in the period after World War II. A university is no longer simply a perpetuator of caste, an educator of young men. While Kirk presided, but did not really guide, Columbia became what Clark Kerr describes, in an ugly but valid term, a multiversity. According to Kerr, a former president of the University of California, the multiversity is an academic colossus that supports what may be the largest of all fields in current America.

The knowledge industry [writes Kerr in *The Uses of the University*] is coming to permeate business and government. The production, distribution and consumption of "knowledge" is said to account for 29 percent of gross national product. What the railroads did for the second half of the last century and the automobile for the first half of this century may be done for the second half of this century by the knowledge industry: that is, to serve as the focal point for national growth. And the university is at the center of the knowledge process.

Veblen's captains of erudition are now captains of the knowledge industry. Their function is to manage corporations efficiently and to see that the corporations grow. Faculty men contribute to the knowledge industry. They run research programs and peddle knowledge for profit to themselves and to the university. The role of students is reduced: graduates help faculty complete projects, but undergraduate students, particularly, are impedimenta, nothing more.

The principal customer for the knowledge industry is the federal government. In the multiversity, student tuition fees have been dwarfed by grants and contracts from governmental agencies. Old economic laws are still at work. The multiversity, like General Electric, services customers in order of importance. Students now come fourth or fifth.

Kirk's Columbia is Kerr's multiversity. On Morningside Heights and beyond, there are sixteen "schools and faculties" and twenty-four "institutes, programs and centers." Each of the forty has a dean or a director. Each offers courses and undertakes research. Of the forty, thirty-eight are on the graduate level. In the prodigious Columbia complex, there are only two undergraduate schools.

Columbia's recent development has been particularly lopsided. Consider the chronological list of its postwar additions:

The Russian Institute, 1946. The School of International Affairs, 1946. The School of General Studies (formerly the University Extension), 1948. The School of Dramatic Arts, 1948. The East Asian Institute, 1948. The European Institute, 1948. The School of Painting and Sculpture, 1949. The Lamont Geological Observatory, 1949. The Center of Israel and Jewish Studies, 1950. The Institute of Air Flight Structures, 1953. The Near and Middle East Institute, 1954. The Program on East Central Europe, 1954. The Institute of Nutrition Sciences, 1958. The Institute of War and Peace Studies, 1959. The International Fellows Program, 1959. The Research Institute on Communist Affairs, 1961. The Institute of African Studies, 1961. The Institute of Latin American Studies, 1961. The Foreign Student Center, 1961. The Computer Center, 1962. The Southern Asian Institute, 1966.

With two or possibly three exceptions, these programs service the federal government. It is possible to trace America's overseas problems by the institutes Columbia established. In 1946, no one knew what Soviet policy would be; Columbia began its Russian Center. Twenty years later, with the country trapped in Vietnam, Columbia opened the Southern Asian Institute. Both run primarily on government support. To a large degree, Columbia has allowed itself to become a service agency of government.

The multiversity is not change but revolution, and Grayson Kirk was either unable to recognize the revolution or to cope with it. He was happier with the old revolutions, with Madison and with Robespierre.

The developing multiversity threatens stability in a bewildering variety of ways. Nationally, there are complaints that undergraduates are taught in overcrowded classes by underqualified men. The great teachers, when one finds them in a multiversity, prefer work on a graduate level. It is more interesting to most and more rewarding. Columbia administrators insist that they want to keep the undergraduate College small to retain "quality and individualism." Actually the

College has been dwarfed, and many members of its faculty devote their primary teaching time to graduates. The Columbia undergrads, impedimenta, felt ignored. That contributed to the climate of riot.

A second danger is the involvement of the university in question-able areas. Should a free and open university train people for espionage? Can it do so and remain open and free? The answer seems to be that it cannot. Columbia thinkers are important to the planning of American policy, but they do not make policy. They sell or rent their ideas without controlling the conclusions. What results then is not university dominance, but rather the university *being* dominated by the group that pays for its services, here the federal government.

One survey undertaken by a bright radical lists "individuals connected with Columbia who are also affiliated with CIA-related organizations." This table cites twenty-six prominent Columbia people, ranging from Kirk (trustee for the Asia Foundation and for the Institute for International Education) to emeritus professor Horace L. Freiss, director of the American Council for Emigrés in the Professions, an organization that has accepted CIA funds.

A third danger proceeds from simple economics. Is Columbia, run with government support, government controlled? The university drew $66 million from government sources in 1967. According to a statement filed during a litigation in Brooklyn Federal Court, Warren F. Goodell, vice-president for administration at Columbia, rejects that idea. "The [government] funds," he stated, "do not represent a subsidy. For the most part they are received by the university in payment for research or other programs undertaken by contract on a nonprofit basis." Even accepting Goodell's obtuse terminology, one still runs into the fact that more than twice as much money comes to Columbia from the government as from students. In 1967, the ratio was $66 million to $24 million. The question remains: Is Columbia, run with government support, government-dominated? Has this putative fortress of capitalism been socialized?

Certainly government money shapes Columbia. Washington gives few if any grants to study Keats. It underwrites studies of weapons and foreign policy. But according to one Columbia official, "Without the grants we'd be a third-rate place. These days our faculty depends on them. We couldn't get the good people we've got—we don't have enough—if they couldn't work in government research. Beside, without government help we would go broke."

Columbia people tend to delude themselves about the nature of their employer and the extent of their own freedom. "I'm a socialist,"

Sidney Morgenbesser, professor of philosophy, announces airily to the radical leader, Paul Rockwell. "You're a socialist, and it's irrelevant." But all Columbia faculty members must swear or affirm, as a condition of employment, that they will uphold the constitutions of New York and the United States. This oath, if followed, allows them only to be evolutionary socialists. They are also free to criticize, in a modest way, policy on China and to write letters to John B. Oakes, the choleric editor of *The New York Times* editorial page. But is there the deep freedom to attack the American system where it needs attacking and to teach ways to change the system, if that is what one really believes, through boycott, demonstration, even violence? The answer is no. Columbia has become a quasi-governmental institution. To indict government policy meaningfully is awkward for employees of a quasi-government agency. The blunt, astonishing reality is that Columbia already has been socialized—and by conservatives.

It is significant that Columbia made no effort to hire Herbert Marcuse after Marcuse left Brandeis, and just as significant that the Columbia faculty was not concerned. There is no search for people who make one feel uncomfortable. Columbia professors are paid at least $18,000, and many earn much more from the federal grants. Affluence makes men prudent, and at Columbia today prudence and comfort dominate. Columbia today would not be a convivial place for Tom Paine to teach political science or for Thomas Jefferson to teach the theory of revolution.

Like all entities that sell for profit, the multiversity becomes avaricious. The final damage is that avarice may override everything else. That may be why Kirk and Columbia became parties to a cigarette filter whose merit, as I write this, is uncertain.

The Strickman cigarette filter affair, James Phelan wrote in *The Saturday Evening Post*, "brought down upon Columbia such excruciating embarrassment that its president [Kirk] refuses to discuss it and has forbidden university personnel to talk about the matter." One university executive, a Ph.D. in chemistry, violated Kirk's order long enough to tell me, "Phelan got it exactly right." As Phelan recounted, Columbia was $163 million shy of a $200 million fund drive, when the trustees agreed to market a new cigarette filter developed by Robert Strickman, chemist and inventor, who had never graduated from college.

This was in 1967. According to Strickman, the filter would remove more tar and nicotine than any other without reducing the tobacco flavor, and the Columbia administration was immediately alert to the commercial possibilities. The scientific questions came afterward. Before signing a contract, Columbia did test the filter, but not at any of its own excellent chemical laboratories. Instead, Columbia leased the work commercially, under the supervision of Dr. Donald Tapley, an associate professor at the medical school. Tapley is an M.D. specializing in internal medicine. Cigarette filter technology is not his field. The chemical tests that he supervised seemed favorable, and on July 13, shortly after the trustees had given their approval, Grayson Kirk, standing between Strickman and Dean H. Houston Merritt of the medical school, announced at a press conference that Columbia would market the new filter. What he hoped, Kirk said, was that the filter might lead to a lessening of one of the world's major health problems. He did not mention the financial arrangements. They would lead to a lessening of Columbia's fiscal problems. Each large tobacco company that wanted the filter would have to pay a license issue fee of $2.5 million. In addition, there would be a royalty of a penny a pack for the first year. Slightly different royalties would obtain thereafter. Jim Phelan calculated that the potential annual Strickman filter royalty in the United States would be $180 million, of which Columbia would get approximately half. The Strickman filter, then, could bring Columbia an added income of $90 million annually. This would increase the Columbia budget by about seventy-five percent.

The impact of Columbia's name and scientific prestige are tremendous. After the Kirk announcement, stocks in all six major U.S. tobacco companies reached highs for the year. Soon Strickman's laboratory was crowded with delegations from cigarette companies. Talks on a number of deals began. Some time afterward, in the Senate Office Building in Washington, D.C., staff members of the Committee on Commerce were puzzled by the sketchiness of the data on which Columbia's claims were based. There was, for example, no information on "draw," the amount of inhaling force needed to pass smoke through the filter. One way to make a filter better is to pack it very tightly. Few tars will pass through; however, the smoker, trying to inhale, may suffer a hernia. Nobody at Columbia, Tapley conceded, "had ever heard of the draw problem." While there was no evidence in the Columbia data that the filter was tightly packed, there was also no evidence that it was not. Under pressure from Senate investigators, Columbia began to reconsider.

Grayson Kirk was called before the Senate Committee on Commerce in August and read a prepared statement. It was at odds with his original proclamation to the press. "Until a testing program—a very extensive testing program—is completed and the results prove entirely satisfactory," Kirk told the committee, "we will not license any cigarette company anywhere in the world."

Under gentle questioning, Kirk began to stammer, and the committee let him go. "We didn't want to embarrass him any more," one senator explained. Back in New York, Kirk designated Dr. Ralph Halford, a qualified chemist who had been dean of graduate faculties, to supervise additional tests. Dr. Norbert Bikales, a chemist who had worked on the filter for Columbia, said the Halford report supported Strickman's claim for his filter's superiority. But, according to Senator Warren Magnuson, chairman of the Commerce Committee, Halford's report indicated that the Strickman filter "is not by any stretch of the imagination the revolutionary development Columbia first heralded it last July."

Now Columbia sought to buy its way out. It faced $95,151.60 in legal fees for making and breaking contracts with Strickman. It was billed $35,168.61 by Sidney S. Baron and Company, a public relations firm. Baron has carried among his clients the Latin American despot, Rafael Trujillo. Presently, Wesley First, Columbia director of University Relations (publicity), resigned.

A number of the errors are understandable, if not excusable. Tapley, the internist, was naively enthusiastic about the filter. Kirk went along with the people from his medical school. But ultimately the avarice of Columbia's administrators surpasses understanding. As Phelan asked, "If Columbia had indeed acquired as a gift a revolutionary filter that was a boon to the nation's smokers, was it proper for the university to levy a multimillion-dollar tribute for its use?"

4 THE GATHERING STORM

THE VICE-PRESIDENT WHO
HAD TO GO TO THE COUNTRY

I AM very late, later than a reporter should be, and David Truman's secretary shakes her head. "He's been waiting, you know." It's been hot. I lost track of time playing tennis. In the air-conditioned efficiency of Suite 202, Low Library, there isn't any way to explain.

David Truman seems to understand. He emerges from his office, waves and, as I follow him in, points to my racket and says, "I admire anyone who can play tennis in this heat." The awkwardness of the instant disappears.

He is a spare, neat man, contained and dignified. He motions toward a French period chair in his long rectangular office. It is a comfortable room, with walls of neutral green. Sixty nervous rebels slept in here last April. "How is your research coming?" Truman says. "It must be difficult figuring out where all the pieces fit." He is turning gray and has lost some hair. There is gray, too, in his brows. He has a pleasant and unmemorable face. The place to begin, he suggests, is with a description of how Columbia runs. He knows that well. He often runs Columbia.

"Fine," I say, and the lecture starts.

"The university," Truman says, "is divided among institutions which are a part of the corporation, governed by the board of trustees of Columbia University in the City of New York and a number of affiliated institutions, the nature of whose affiliations varies somewhat.

"Barnard has its own board of trustees and its own president. The president of Barnard College is a dean in the university. The university awards degrees to Barnard students, and there is a legal agreement that makes the university responsible for educational quality at Barnard. The arrangement with Teachers College and the College of Pharmacy is similar. The arrangement with Union Theological Seminary is looser. Their students can pursue Ph.D. programs in the university and there is a certain informal exchange of faculty. But technically, the seminary is not an affiliated organization."

He is a lucid lecturer. He taught political science for more than twenty years. "Now within the university, we have a division of the arts and sciences into a series of separate faculties. Columbia College has its own faculty under its own dean. The graduate program in arts and sciences is divided into three separate faculties going well back into the last century. There is a School of General Studies, which has its own faculty and dean, and finally, there is the School of International Affairs, which, in turn, has its dean and its faculty.

"Now all of these faculties that I have just mentioned are served by essentially the same *departments*, that is, the Department of History, the Department of Economics, the Department of Philosophy.

"A member of a department may be a member of more than one of these faculties. It's very common for a man to be a member, say, of the college faculty and one of the graduate faculties. There is decentralization in structure here, which, particularly in relation to the graduate level of the university, places heavy responsibility on the departments."

It is a good rundown of a complex conglomerate and I ask what he thinks of the structure.

"I tend to be somewhat critical," he says. The problem, of course, is the appeal of graduate teaching. Only one of Columbia's four Nobel laureates stoops to instruct undergraduates.

"How much do you think this contributed to the riots?"

"I tend to think first of other factors," he says. "I'd say the student climate here, at Columbia, began to change in 1964."

"In response to Goldwater?"

"In response to escalation in Vietnam." He pauses to light a pipe. An air conditioner whines faintly.

"If you consider student activities around the world, you find a pattern of unrest. You have student protest in Germany and in France and at a number of other campuses in the country. And even on the other side of the Iron Curtain in Warsaw; and in China, too.

"Now you ask yourself what is the common factor?

"Certainly in the Western World, there is affluence. Not everywhere equal to American affluence but great affluence in terms of the particular country in question.

"Then there is something else. The young people on both sides are the first generation to have known only the atomic world. These young people have lived with the atomic bomb from their very beginnings. All of us *learn* to live with it, or try. We make an effort to adjust to the idea that the world can destroy itself by design or miscalculation. But the atomic world is the *only* world these young people have known, which is a vastly different condition of growing up than either you or I knew."

He grew up in Illinois and his own academic career had been a model of success. He studied at Amherst and took graduate degrees at Harvard and Columbia, majoring in government and concentrating on the American scene. While teaching at Harvard, he published *The Governmental Process,* a look at how decisions are reached in American government. Columbia lured him to New York in 1950. He became full professor of public law a year later and dean of the College in 1962. He was a busy, driving, efficient executive. Where Eisenhower had been absent and Kirk was remote, Truman practiced accessibility. His door was open to college students. He greeted them on the campus, remembering names. He appeared to care about their problems. He was dignified without being stuffy. By most testimony, he was the most popular college dean in fifty years.

In 1967, Grayson Kirk and the trustees promoted Truman to the vice-presidency. After that he was the most likely successor to the presidency.

In the narrow office, he speaks remotely of what the riots meant. "Some good came from them, you know. There is talk of change now. I suppose changes would have happened eventually anyway, but the students have hastened them and some were needed."

He insists that the violence has been overstated. "One has to be careful about a term like police brutality. There is a difference between a brutal act and a professionally administered blow on the head that causes a lot of blood but can be closed up with two or three stitches."

"Are you defending the police?"

"They broke their word on two points. They moved their vans on the campus, in violation of an agreement, and they provided no medical help for the injured. They said that they would."

What he is defending, really, is David Truman. He personally sympathizes with student opposition to the Vietnam War. He insists that he is opposed to the war himself. He thinks that riots may happen again, there is no predicting, but Columbia will be better equipped to cope with them.

"By taking a hard line?"

He smiles and doesn't answer. It is entirely possible, he says, that Columbia will have to leave the city. The Lindsay administration is difficult to work with. The city itself is in doubt. Columbia will move rather than be overrun. "We've moved twice before in our history."

"That could devastate part of New York."

He nods. "It could, and that would be unfortunate. But Columbia has not been established to look after the city. There are other agencies for that."

What is most remarkable is the poise. This is a man who spent his prime years at Columbia, who identified himself with Columbia, whose life, in a sense, was Columbia, and whose reward was to be the presidency. The prize hung there a season or two away and then, with no clear warning that he could read, the presidency was snatched from his reach. The grapes of Tantalus. The presidency was gone and soon Columbia would be gone, and he would have to retreat from pulsing city into rural Massachusetts. All his plans have come undone, but in the interview there is no rage, no bite of bitterness, only a kind of minor sadness.

One begins to understand him then. He is a good campus executive —civil, controlled, fluent, eloquent, liberal. But none of that mattered in the uncivil spring. He had been confronted with a march of radicals crying motherfucker, and he simply did not know what to do. He knows faculties and departments and affiliations, but he does not understand about the radicals or the police.

He is generous with his time. As the interview closes, he says he hoped he has helped me, and if I want to talk again, to call.

Riding downtown, I wonder briefly why he cried after the police had come: was it simply at the horror of it, cops trampling on his campus, or was it another horror, the sudden sense that these police were grinding his Columbia career into spring mud.

In the end it does not matter. I have other victims to see.

*   *   *   *   *   *

Dr. Ralph Halford, the chemist who correctly evaluated the Strickman filter, walked up to me one morning as I sat reading testimony solicited by the Cox commission. Most witnesses were prolix, and the cross-examination was often vague.

"Do you have any tips?" I asked Halford, gesturing toward a dozen bound volumes. "Anything to look for in there?"

Halford grinned slightly. "I think you'll find the quality of self-righteousness consistent."

The most popular way to explain the Columbia disaster, among Columbia faculty and administrators, is to point beyond the campus at a world gone mad. *The time is out of joint, O cursed spite/Columbia alone can't set it right.* If one accepts this overview, Columbia becomes victim rather than victimizer, and the great leonine multiversity is transformed. Suddenly, she is a white lamb beset.

Within the last decade in America real radicalism has appeared and black power has arrived. Without each, Columbia could hardly have been devastated. However, Columbia administrators fought both movements. They pitted the university against the times. Partly, Columbia was devastated on merit.

An essence of the new American radicalism has been distilled by Herbert Marcuse in his *One Dimensional Man*.

> We submit to the peaceful production of the means of destruction [he writes], to the perfection of waste, to being educated for a defense which deforms the defenders and that which they defend. . . .
>
> The defense structure makes life easier for a greater number of people and extends man's mastery of nature. Under these circumstances our mass media have little difficulty in selling particular interests as those of sensible men. . . .
>
> And yet this society is irrational as a whole. Its productivity is destructive of the free development of human needs and faculties, its peace maintained by the constant threat of war, its growth dependent on the repression of the real possibilities for pacifying the struggle for existence.

In other words, we are living an absurdity. We talk of peace and construct missiles. We invest billions in weapons that quickly become obsolete and that are too horrible to use anyway. We perfect the mythology of anti-Communism and stumble into endless war in Vietnam. But we are making a living, provided we are white. NBC and *The New York Times* and *The Ladies' Home Journal* ceaselessly instruct us in our prosperity. The washer-dryer works, if the color TV doesn't, and if we pay Saks this month, surely Gimbels will wait till next.

Marcuse is a refugee from Nazism alive in the time of the hydrogen bomb and both are central to his thinking. In a sense his philosophy proceeds from Auschwitz to Hiroshima to Vietnam. Mankind's recent record is execrable, and Marcuse reviews it mercilessly.

One Dimensional Man, first published in 1964, has gone through six printings. Marcuse's chilling dogma swept American campuses, although certainly a significant number of students who bought his work dropped out without finishing, defeated by the prose style, which is pure lead. But if the going was hard, the message was compelling, and it was reinforced by current events. Marcuse had the good fortune to publish his attack on irrationality when the irrational Vietnamese War was being intensified.

During the 1964 presidential campaign, Barry Goldwater ran as the war candidate. He spoke of defoliation, escalation and of dropping bombs until late in his campaign, when his own essentially forthright nature was twisted by his aides. After that he said very little. Against him ran Lyndon B. Johnson, peace candidate. Johnson Democrats preached peace and created a peace commercial for TV. A little child is shown picking the petals from a daisy. A man's voice counts slowly backward. Six, five, four, three, two. At zero, flower, child and all the screen explode in an atomic blast. To avoid this, one is urged to vote for Johnson.

In unprecedented numbers American voters responded. Goldwater, the war candidate, was rejected by the largest margin in history. Then within three years, Johnson put half a million Americans into Vietnam. No more naked defiance of the American popular will comes readily to mind.

Campus people were particularly quick to recognize what had happened. Since campuses gather people of draft age, the consequences here were profound. As the draft worked, a young man had to keep up with his class and maintain passing grades or lose his deferment. Suddenly college students could not safely drop out for a time to travel, or loaf, or think long thoughts.

The Vietnam War and the policy of selective service turned American universities into prisons. However frustrated one was by an unimaginative educational system, one had to remain inside it, or face patrol duty against the Viet Cong and death in a purposeless war. It was in this climate that Marcuse was acclaimed prophet. It was against this background that the Students for a Democratic Society was able to grow with such astonishing speed.

In the beginning, the SDS, founded during 1960, was a young people's version of the League for Industrial Democracy, a small organization of anti-communist democratic socialists. Norman Thomas was a member of the league; so were Bayard Rustin and Michael Harrington. Technically, the SDS traces to the 1930s; the League for Industrial Democracy opened a student division then, as a haven for the young non-communist left. But actually it is an organization of the present. It lay moribund until 1960 and mute until 1962 when Tom Hayden of Michigan began a passionate declaration called The Port Huron Statement: "We are the people of this generation, bred in at least modest comfort, housed now in universities, looking uncomfortably to the world we inherit."

The Columbia SDS chapter was organized in 1961 by the group that included Marcuse's stepson. As one experienced Columbia radical reports, SDS began as "just one more of the groups coalescing around the issues of the day: race and foreign policy. There was nothing to mark Columbia SDS for future prominence, as opposed to, say, Columbia CORE."

Indeed the national SDS at first was not notably radical. The Port Huron Statement, reread today, exudes a dreamlike quality. Hayden agonized over student "isolation and indifference." He wanted students to state a vision. "What," he asked, "is the perimeter of human possibility in this epoch, and what role have we [students] to play as a social force?"

Hayden conceived a democratic, open new left gathering at university communities. It would be possessed of intellectual skills, and would welcome liberals "for their relevance" and socialists "for their sense of thoroughgoing reforms." This new *Front Populaire* would transform "modern complexity into issues that could be understood," and give form to "feelings of helplessness and indifference."

But students would not go forth as an intellectual elite, any more than they would go forward throwing grenades. There was to be a great egalitarianism, in which students taught one another and in which no one really led and no one really followed. At most, there would be a *primus inter pares*, first among equals.

A history of the SDS is a story of the increasing disillusion and consequent violence of the young. The SDS may be a kind of Willy Loman of radical groups, wanting to achieve something it did not understand, but it had a respectable neo-liberal dream. At first, working toward the vague goal, it intended to proceed through existing institutions. Then it found it could not; existing institutions did not want to contribute to their own demise. First it would have no permanent leaders. Then ambition stained its people. What charged ambitions with a sense of power was the successful eruption at Berkeley, California, in the autumn of 1964.

The Berkeley division of the enormous University of California traditionally excluded non-campus political groups from meeting on its grounds. As one result, some political activity moved adjacent to the campus, often on a strip of land that most of the students and faculty assumed belonged to the City of Berkeley. In September, 1964, campus officials issued a statement that the land—a twenty-four-foot strip—was theirs. No further political meetings or speeches there would be allowed.

A student protest developed rapidly. Throughout the semester, the so-called Free-Speech Movement battled the administration. Before the dispute ended, faculty was involved, Governor Pat Brown was drawn in, legislators took sides, and, after a series of sit-ins, eight hundred students occupied the central administration building. It took eight hundred police to remove them.

The practical lesson was clear enough. Students by themselves had power. They could not threaten the Pentagon, but they could, all by themselves, paralyze a university. They could be more than vague radicals. They could become active revolutionaries.

"What we are witnessing and participating in," Carl Davidson, an SDS member who had majored in philosophy at Penn State, wrote after Berkeley, "is a revolt of the trainees of the new working class [students] against oppressive conditions of capitalism. A spectre is haunting our universities—the spectre of a radical and militant nationally co-ordinated movement for student power." Davidson called his work *The Multiversity: Crucible of the New Working Class.*

"We should remember," Davidson continued, "that we cannot liberate the university without radically changing the society." But the university was a kind of mirror and "every effort should be made to connect campus issues with non-campus issues." In essence, Davidson urged an attack on society through the universities. The university would become a vehicle in the student radicals' ride to the larger battles of the larger revolution.

He suggested specific tactics. One must never accept campus reform. "These come in the form of giving certain 'responsible' students a voice in certain decision making. But a seat should be seen as a soap box. We are not trying to liberalize the existing order but to win our liberation from it." Each issue raised by revolutionaries was a means to "desanctify institutions." Desanctification became absolutely critical. No one was likely to march against a university whose anthem made him weep with awe.

Davidson proposed burning deans in effigy, the way losing football coaches had been burned for years. At student meetings, SDS members were to mock the proceeding. At sessions of university disciplinary committees one good disruptive device was cursing. Another was to sing, quite loudly, the song of the Mickey Mouseketeers.

Davidson distinguished between faculty allies and faculty finks. The "younger, teaching" faculty might join the radical students "if we can get them to organize among themselves around their own grievances." Research people and the administrators were enemies. "We should set both ourselves and the teaching faculty against them."

Pragmatically, put as many people as possible on campus newspapers to work from within. Take the poorest courses and disrupt them. Study under the worst professors and disturb their classes. Dialogue was nonsense. The gap had grown too wide. The time for words was done. "We may be instrumental," Davidson proclaimed, "in forming a new International Union of revolutionary youth." By this time, Hayden himself, no longer the dreamy bourgeois, had been swept into the turbulent current.

In what has become a famous quotation from the left, Tom Hayden is supposed to have said of Columbia, "The one thing we knew we could count on was the continuing stupidity of Kirk and Truman." The judgment is harsh and incomplete. What the SDS could really count on was the irrationality, not of men but of a structure.

To make their revolutionary impact on campus, the radicals required prerequisites. The student body would best be disorganized. Unified students, with a real voice in running a university, tend to trust the democratic processes and shun radical action. The university authorities and faculty ideally would be involved in planning the Vietnam War. It would be difficult to focus Vietnam protest against, say, the peaceful faculty of Haverford. The university administration should be insensitive to the Negro drive for equal status. Arrogance toward blacks, and the underprivileged generally, is a model of an elitism. It can be called fascistic in debate.

Columbia met every prerequisite surpassingly. Its students were disorganized, its faculty did help with war planning and its administrators were insensitive to the poor people living near the campus. Beyond that, it was a weird autocracy. The president ruled without the advice and consent of a university senate. The faculty was passive. The trustees, under venerable law, could not be professors: educators were excluded from the management of Columbia. It would be difficult to find a purer kernel of irrationality among the great institutions of the American society.

According to Tomec Smith, past president of the Columbia University Student Council, the CUSC was organized shortly after World War II, when war veterans on campus wanted "to have some say" in their lives. "They were able to make a deal," Smith says. "The university agreed to consult them on matters pertaining to student life.

"A little while later, the university raised tuition. The students were informed.

" 'All right,' they said. 'That pertains to us. We want to consult. Let's see your books.'

"As far as I know the council was not consulted for the next fifteen years."

A powerless council was tolerable during the Silent Fifties, when the torpor of Eisenhower's White House infused the country. But with the sixties, sleepers awoke. Now the student body became receptive to groups that, unlike their council, got things done. As politics grew strident, new political action organizations formed. CORE reached Columbia in 1963. An Independent Committee on Vietnam followed soon afterward.

Columbia's alliance with the American military, firm under Butler, the president who dismissed a pacifist, was reinforced under Eisenhower. Then, as the military needed more and more intellect, Columbia and her faculty profited nicely. The university was awarded $16 million in defense contracts during 1967. Although this does not approach M. I. T. ($92 million), it is better than the defense business of all but four other American universities. But Columbia, the ally of the military, had to pay a price.

Among the twenty-nine instructional departments at the college, one is openly devoted to war. The Department of Naval Science and Tactics, currently under Commander Julius M. Larson, U.S.N., teaches amphibious warfare, weapons analysis and seven other courses in bellicosity. Students who complete a four-year program win commissions in the naval reserve. Following tradition, the 1965 awards to outstanding N.R.O.T.C. students were to be handed out on College Walk in May.

The radical, or at least anti-war, movement at Columbia surfaced on a rainy spring afternoon in 1965. Because it rained May 7, the ceremonies were moved into the rotunda of Low. Vietnam was worsening, and, protesting "campus militarism," a mixed group of students staged a rally in front of Ferris Booth, the student activities center, 200 yards southwest of Low. Despite the rain, the rally drew 200 people.

Three representatives of the Independent Committee on Vietnam and two whites from CORE spoke. When the rally was over, about 150 of the demonstrators marched through the rain toward Low. Fifteen campus police, in gray uniforms, waited in an uncertain line. When the students charged, the outnumbered police stepped aside. The students swept up the thirty steps of Low, but there they stopped. The glass library doors were locked. Locked glass doors were sufficient to stop Columbia radicals in '65. The group was standing, indecisive, when twenty-three patrolmen from the 26th Precinct appeared at the bottom of the steps.

The city police formed a double file and marched up the steps toward the demonstrators. The blue of cops and the plaids of students merged. Some students shouted. A policeman threw a punch. The scuffling grew rougher. A policeman slammed someone into a glass door, which shattered. Inside Low, Grayson Kirk was watching the fight. He ordered the Naval R.O.T.C. ceremony stopped, and with this announcement, police and rioters dispersed. For only the second time since the riotous commencement of 1811, student protest had interrupted an important university function.

Kirk first wanted to discipline the protesters. They could be placed on probation, suspended or even expelled. But when hundreds of students and faculty petitioned for an investigation, Kirk settled for a fact-finding commission. In the immutable manner of commissions, this one proposed the creation of another commission. The second group was to investigate "the quality and nature of student life" at Columbia.

As SDS grew at Columbia, the Independent Committee on Vietnam waned. Many of the same people were in each, and SDS had a broader appeal. The developing SDS met often, talked long, planned avidly and, in the autumn of 1966, organized a peaceful protest march when recruiters from the CIA came to Columbia. But mostly in 1966, SDS, like the clock as the hour approaches, was collecting its energy to strike.

CIA was a rather diffuse issue; the Columbia connection appeared shadowy and undramatic. Immediacy was more than ever the key: relating outside problems urgently to the campus. Looking elsewhere, SDS found a stronger case in Columbia's intercourse with a comparatively obscure body called the Institute for Defense Analyses.

The IDA was established by the Department of Defense and by the Joint Chiefs of Staff in 1955 to obtain organized research from university sources on the technology of making modern war. Clemenceau's remark that "war is too important to leave to the generals" is obsolete. Modern warfare is now too *complicated* for generals. Preparing is a business for physicists and chemists; it has been since weaponry exploded into the atomic bomb. Today's generals are tacticians and executives, administering programs conceived by Ph.D.s. IDA contractors plan weapons, such as the ABM, evaluate weapons systems and devise stratagems for global war. This highly secret agency is housed in a faceless modern building, 400 Army Navy Drive, in Arlington, Virginia, which it shares with a bank. To one side stands the interminable Pentagon. To another are the crowded airlanes approaching Washington National Airport.

The IDA runs on an annual budget of about $15 million and exists principally but not exclusively on government contracts. Technically, it is a private corporation. Five universities, M.I.T., Case Institute, Stanford, Tulane and California Institute of Technology, served as the original institutional sponsors. Seven others came later. Columbia joined in 1959. What finally made the IDA immediate to Morningside Heights was that President Grayson Kirk became an IDA trustee and a Columbia trustee, William A. M. Burden, became IDA board chairman.

In 1967, the SDS leaked information to *The Daily Spectator*. The SDS charged accurately that a number of Columbia professors possessed IDA contracts. The radicals also asserted that the IDA had "a facility" on the Columbia campus. Norman Christeller, the general manager of the IDA, is still furious about the second charge. Christeller smokes a pipe and wears spectacles, and works in shirtsleeves. He is an executive, rather than a scientist, and his manner is forceful and informal. As we were sitting in his Arlington office, with shuttle planes shrill beside the window, he was a man with paternal pride in IDA. The *Spectator* had lied about his baby.

"I want to point out," Christeller said, "that a *Spectator* reporter telephoned and asked point-blank if we maintained a facility at Columbia. We did and I described it to him."

Behind the spectacles, Christeller's mild eyes showed anger. "The facility is a small safe, two feet across by three feet deep by one foot high. It's used to keep classified papers. I explained this to the *Spectator* reporter. Then he wrote there was a secret IDA facility at Columbia, without stating what it was, so that it looked as if we had a building up there, a major installation, possibly performing secret work. The reporter never wrote that all we had was this small safe."

Norman Christeller emphasizes the non-defense work, which forms a certain portion of the IDA program. "For example," he says, "we studied the feasibility of the supersonic transport plane, looking at it from a number of angles, including the U.S. balance of payments. Our study was not encouraging." He argues that war planning can turn out to be anti-war. "A projection of nuclear casualty rates makes a brilliant case for permanent peace."

"But before you do any study, you have to get it funded."

"That's right."

"Well, could you fund a study on the long-term effects of the Vietnam War on the American economy?"

Christeller shakes his head. "I wish we could."

Someone prominent in the defense complex points to the IDA as a force for moderation. "You have thinkers there, men of sense and moderation. A helluva lot of their work is putting a check on the hawk-nuts in the Pentagon." Others suggest that attacking IDA is just one more irrationality. To assault the IDA is to assault armorers. Why attack the men who forged the breastplates that cloaked the hearts of warlike Gothic kings? It is not they, but kings, who make the wars.

These are fair areas for debate, but the SDS needed a disruptive issue. By planting a story in *Spectator* and getting an overstated account as a bonus, the SDS was successfully using the liberal press to oversimplify a complex issue. Columbia stood with the war lords. That was that. The pace on campus was quickening every spring. Kirk needed help. He soon would shuffle his staff, demoting Jacques Barzun, promoting David Truman from Dean of Columbia College to Executive Vice President. But not Barzun, not Truman, nor anyone else in administration recognized the severity of the gathering storm.

In late April, 1967, four U.S. marines set up tables in the lobby of John Jay Hall, an undergraduate dormitory at the southeast corner of the main campus. The marines were there to recruit.

Ted Kaptchuk, Columbia '68, chairman of the SDS, was preparing leaflets urging a powerful protest. While the marines were inside John Jay, a few hundred pickets would surround the building. The marines would then be trapped. The pickets would keep them trapped until the university administration agreed to terminate campus recruiting for "war-related" groups: Army, CIA, Air Force, Dow Chemical.

Kaptchuk won limited student support, but at the same time a group of about fifty other students decided that SDS activity on campus had gone too far. They prepared a counter-strategy.

On schedule, the marines moved into the lobby of John Jay Hall. Then fifty conservative students formed a protective cordon. When the radicals closed in, they could not reach the marines. The SDS

people set up a picket line and chanted, "Marines must go."
The conservatives, the so-called jocks, set up a counter-chant. "SDS
must go. SDS must go." The four marines, splendid in dress uniforms,
looked edgy.

It was a hot afternoon. Radicals and conservatives closed on a
narrow patch of lawn in front of John Jay. The crowd milled rather
than scuffled at first.

"War-lover!"

"Go cut your hair!"

"Jocks must go."

"You guys only believe in free speech for yourselves."

And then a crusher. "Ah, fuck you."

"What did you say?"

"I said, fuck you, Mac."

The crowd was so heavy and so boisterous under the hot sun that
no one could say for certain who was shouting what. The last expletive
is significant because immediately afterward, a stocky, well-built radical and a blond jock in white shirt began punching one another. There
were four other fist fights. Then a Columbia official announced that the
marine recruiters were leaving for the day. "Recruiting will be
stopped," he said. "It will be resumed tomorrow."

On the following day eight hundred students peacefully picketed in
the Van Am Quadrangle, before John Jay, Livingston and Hamilton.
About five hundred others marched in support of the marines. There
was no further violence; the marines finished their business, attracting
few volunteers, and left. The day was done, but the question of campus
demonstrations had risen clearly as the moon. Then Kirk, demanding
a solution, ordered: No further demonstrations inside buildings. His
thinking proceeded straight from the philosophies of King Canute.

The SDS did not have to contrive a second issue with impact
beyond the campus. A second one was offered by Columbia, one of
the largest and most aggressive landlords on earth.

Only the Roman Catholic Church owns more property within Manhattan than Columbia. Including the land underneath Rockefeller
Center, Columbia's off-campus real estate exceeds $70 million. In
addition, Columbia holds mortgages worth about $80 million. Accord-
ing to published figures, Columbia assets at the end of 1967 were $425
million. "Land and buildings being used," that is, the campus, had a
book value of $130 million. Arithmetic demonstrates that more than
half the university assets—$280 million—were land, buildings, mort-

gages. No other American university has a comparable commitment to real estate. Harvard, with an endowment of more than a billion dollars, does not own one parcel of investment real estate. Almost sixty percent of Harvard's money rests, or grows, in common stocks.

Columbia came into its fortune because Manhattan real estate appreciated. The historical pattern has continued. Columbia, the multiversity, is first a real estate holding company. At least five of Columbia's trustees are prominent in real estate and building finance. Three collaborated in erecting an office building in the Wall Street area, with a timely opening loan from Columbia. There is no evidence of anything illegal, just the time-honored business practice of people using contacts to find financing, tenants and profit. The men who run Columbia, the trustees, think like realtors. Their attitude, and the attitude of administrators, is often that of the realtor; above all, what is going to happen to property values.

In late 1966, Percy Uris, a chairman of the Trustees Finance Committee, assembled an entire block (Front Street, South Street, Gouverneur Lane and Wall Street) in the financial district of Manhattan. Columbia (Percy Uris, trustee) then leased the land to Uris Buildings Corporation (Percy Uris, chairman) at an annual rent of $400,000 until the year 2009. Uris Buildings planned to erect an office building, but to help obtain financing, it needed a committed tenant. An early committed tenant was the First National City Bank (Alan Temple, Columbia trustee, vice-president). Financing was eased by a $22 million loan to Uris Buildings from the Irving Trust Company (William Petersen, Columbia trustee, president). One real estate deal. Three Columbia trustees. Of such is the kingdom of academe.

In the cyclic nature of Manhattan development, the West Side began a decline after World War II. Despite excellent transportation and commanding views, the region twenty-five blocks north of the theater district slumped. "The only time I go west of Fifth," says the East Sider in one recent story, "is when I'm going to Europe. I take a taxi straight to a Hudson River pier."

When West Side real estate values declined, Columbia's institutional approach was not, what can we do to help the city that harbors us? Instead it was a furious determination to help Columbia.

In the days after World War II, a Puerto Rican immigration to New York began. The Latins jammed into Eastern Airlines coaches—federal subsidy kept the fare low—and settled in pockets on the West Side. Old residents were moving to the suburbs. Now venerable brownstones became slum roominghouses. One four-story building on West 75th Street, once a two-family home, came to house eighty people and a brothel. Puerto Ricans in New York found menial jobs or none, but apparently Manhattan poverty was more bearable than whatever had been left. They remained. On summer nights on the West Side, once-quiet streets resounded with dull drums and moaning songs.

A few years after the Puerto Rican influx, Negroes began overflowing Harlem. Birth rates in Harlem were high—so were death rates—and there was also a tide of mankind rolling up from the dirt farms of the South. When Harlem overflowed, the current ran west.

During the fifties, the Puerto Rican population of Morningside Heights nearly doubled. It rose from 1,650 to 3,014. The black increase was almost seven hundred percent, 470 to 3,133. Stated differently, whites were ninety-one percent of the Morningside Heights population in 1950. Ten years later, they were seventy-three percent. What was happening to American cities everywhere was happening in miniature around Columbia. As one instructor remarked in a letter, "What a wonderful opportunity for Columbia to research something more important than new weapons systems. What a chance to research how the American city could survive integration."

But the trustees and executives of Columbia, the real estate holding company, had a prior and overriding commitment. They had to protect real assets. Their method was to drive off the underprivileged.

According to one researcher, "The Columbia exclusionary process that developed is a kind of cultured racism. We are not talking about men with a redneck hatred for niggers and spics. What is involved is a 'distaste.' "

Columbia's earliest effort to preserve its neighborhood dates from 1947. In that year Morningside Heights, Incorporated, was organized. Dominated by Columbia, MHI also included Union Theological Seminary, St. Luke's Hospital, the Jewish Theological Seminary and Riverside Church. Its announced purpose was "to promote the improvement" of the neighborhood as "an attractive residential, educational and cultural area." It was also to prevent squabbling among members about who bought what parcel of land. David Rockefeller was the first president.

MHI is an example of private enterprise falling flat. The ultimate problem was conflict of interest: public good versus private gain. "Whoever owns the land has the leverage," says Warren Goodell, an important Columbia vice-president. Playing for leverage and saving a community are inimicable, and in the end Columbia grabbed land. When MHI built a middle-income development in the early 1950's, many indigenous residents, put out of their homes, were bitter. *Fortune* Magazine reported that "the whole community has experienced a psychological and physical turning [against MHI and Columbia]." By 1959, MHI decided that its job was just too large. The directors signed a report attesting to neighborhood change and asked for an urban renewal plan. That would have brought city officials and federal funds into the area.

Why did Columbia and MHI wait too long to call for help? The answer seems to be that to Columbia trustees, MHI was part of an enormous private plan for private gain. After decay depressed realty values, the West Side of Manhattan was to be turned into an upper income area. Property values would then increase like an algebraic progression. Columbia's endowment would sextuple. So, incidentally, could the fortunes of trustees with investments and careers in Manhattan real estate. The master scheme would proceed between cultural redoubts: Columbia on the north and Lincoln Center on the south.

Grayson Kirk and the multiversity trustees wanted a Columbia complex running from 110th Street to 123rd, and from the handsome buildings of Riverside Drive to the cliffs of Morningside Park. The projected plan would double space for classes, offices and laboratories. Faculty and student housing would be constructed. The new Columbia tract, three-quarters of a square mile in all, would be the largest urban intellectual hegemony in history. At the time of the riots, Columbia trustees were considering schemes to press clear up to 135th Street and the river.

At the south end Lincoln Center, an uneven mix of white stone and glass, stands completed. The center includes a glorious opera house, an acoustic enigma of a concert hall, theaters, the Juilliard School of Music, a bandshell. Around it one finds more than a dozen new apartment buildings, charging rentals of $100 a room. They have replaced old buildings where $100 was the rent for two or three *floors*.

Between Columbia's projected southern border at 110th Street and Lincoln Center lies an area approaching four square miles, Much of it is rundown and ready for renewal. The potential developers' profits could reach billions.

One cannot draw absolute lines. One cannot say here, this is how much Columbia wanted a better neighborhood for a university park, and here, this is how much Columbia trustees wanted a West Side boom for private profit. What one can say is that the lines of interest intersected. The policy that emerged was inhuman.

In all, Columbia had acquired only twenty-seven off-campus buildings in the Heights by 1934. Twenty-two buildings were added in the next twenty years. Then Columbia expansionists went wild: eighteen new buildings between 1955 and 1959; fifty-three new buildings between 1960 and 1964; sixty-two more in the years before the strike. In nonarithmetic, human terms, the story becomes an assault of Columbia, the immense institution, on underprivileged human beings, living in Manhattan's SROs.

The SRO, a single-room-occupancy building, is the foul essence of the New York slum. It was once an apartment house. Now it has been broken into single rooms. Each is equipped with a sprinkler to prevent death by fire. Few other precautions are taken.

One social worker, Joan H. Shapiro, pictures SRO life like this:

> Physical idleness and passivity, enforced by debilitation and limited life chances, create a vacuum. The future, over which one had no control and for which one could not plan, held no promise of change. The passage of days was marked rhythmically in two-week cycles by "check days"; when welfare checks arrived, the rent and money owed to the manager of the building was withheld, and the rest given to the tenant. Over the remaining thirteen days, tenants eked out an existence on an average of $19.80 for food and personal items for one person. Sporadic violence was the only form of excitement.

In *The City in History,* Lewis Mumford describes the slums of Rome with a graphic horror that makes a man rejoice that he was not truly born into the Augustan age. In New York today, the Roman slum has been reborn. Rome tenements had no plumbing. In the SROs ten men share a toilet. Rome slum dwellers lived in fear of death by fire. In the SROs there lurks death, by hopelessness, hastened by drugs and whiskey and varieties of insanity.

One recent day a tenant in a Manhattan SRO went out and bought a rifle. Later, high on narcotics, he began shooting birds. Or he thought he was shooting birds. Actually his rifle was pointed, from his sixth-floor window, down and across the street. On the opposite sidewalk, a man fell over, a bullet through his chest. He gurgled briefly, bled and died. He had been a hard-working man, the superintendent of several buildings. The killer told the police over and over again, "I was just trying to kill some pigeons."

The cruelty of the SRO is profitable. Occupying the same space, eight derelicts pay more rent than a single family. New York officials have plans for outlawing the SROs. Even now children are barred. But hundreds of SROs continue to rot on the West Side of Manhattan. There is no more frightful testament to a failure of the American society.

Columbia did not approach SROs as a civic helper. Stanley Salmen, coordinator of university planning from 1956 to 1967, articulated the attitude. "Some SROs are well run, but about half are pits of degradation, a disgrace to the city and *impossible neighbors to institutions attracting students from all over the world.*" Salmen uttered the limit of Columbia compassion. SROs were first a logistics problem. They had to be cleared quickly, or to be captured.

During the last decade, Columbia removed 6,800 SRO tenants from its environs. For the victims, Columbia created a new division, called, ironically, the Office of Neighborhood Services. Bertram Weinert, the first director, was fired. He failed to remove tenants quickly enough. Weinert's successor, Ronald Golden, "placed more emphasis on meeting deadlines."

In clearing the buildings, Columbia employees varied technique to meet the obstacle. A number of middle-class apartments "had to be" demolished to allow Columbia expansion. Here the university reduced services: dumbwaiters were sealed so that garbage would be carried by hand; heat was withheld in winter. Marie Runyon of 178 Morningside Drive, who has fought Columbia eviction for ten years, reports, "We do get plenty of heat in summer. When the thermometer hits ninety, they send heat." Only six tenants are left in Miss Runyon's apartment building. It has all the geniality of a ruin.

People like Miss Runyon understand law and lawyers. Harassed beyond a certain point, they take Columbia to court. Occupants of SROs are afraid of the law. Many have criminal records. A representative case of Columbia's neighborhood services took place at an SRO calling itself the Oxford Hotel.

A tenant of the Oxford, a woman named Yvelle Walker, tried to pay her rent after Columbia had purchased the building.

"Keep the rent," said a Columbia agent. "Columbia is going to use this place for offices. Everyone has to get out." He offered her $25 to move. Miss Walker, within her rights and the law, refused.

A week later, Columbia refused the rent again. "Just hurry," the agent said, "and find a place to move."

That night, the lock in the door to Miss Walker's room was plugged with a sticky substance, possibly wax. She could not get into her own room. She spent the night with friends. She left the Oxford Hotel soon afterward.

Another tenant of the Oxford, Bernard Moore, charges that a Columbia agent persuaded the police to harass him. Once, after attending a meeting of the Riverside Democratic Club, Moore returned to his room and found that it had been searched. Soon he moved out. The last tenants in the Oxford fled in 1967. It now houses the Goddard Institute for Space Studies.

Neglect is as effective as harassment, and Columbia perfected neglect in its stewardship of 609 West 115th Street, an SRO known as Conhar Hall. A building inspector found sixty-three violations in Conhar Hall during October, 1966. Conhar Hall tenants were without heat or hot water. The elevator was not functioning. Windows were broken. Garbage went uncollected. Doors had no locks. Toilets leaked. Roaches crawled. Rats prowled. Several months later, Conhar Hall was ready for demolition. All of its tenants had gone.

Columbia's treatment of other SRO tenants followed a three-stage pattern. First buildings were neglected. Then the occupants were harassed with door pluggings and police pressure. Finally, if this failed, rent checks were refused and eviction proceedings begun. There has probably never been a more efficient removal of people by a university, nor one as kindless. The numbers are cold testimony: within four recent years, nine SROs were demolished. Three were converted to university use. More than a thousand people literally were put into the street.

Columbia, the multiversity, wanted land, buildings, power. That policy overrode all others. The academic compassion of the sociology instructor was only incidental; the sociologist's employer had created grief.

Seen in the light of this history, Columbia's unbuilt gymnasium is more than a mixed facility for black and white. It is an outpost to the barony, keeping the blacks in place, nine floors below, and discouraging crossings from the neighborhood of Harlem to the neighborhood of Morningside Heights.

The gymnasium issue was as real as prejudice.

5 JUMP GYM CROW

THE COMMUNITY RESIDENT
WHO SAID WHO'S JIM?

HE will tell me only his first name, Wes. Where he comes from doesn't matter and where he is going is uncertain. He is settled down right now with a woman, but he has a hard time finding acceptable work.

"Dishwasher," he says, out of a smooth brown face. "Busboy. Stuff like that I ain't gonna do. I drive a truck, a rig they call it. That's what I do, and, man, it's harder than it looks. You ever drive a real rig?"

"Nothing bigger than a pickup."

"That ain't nothing." He squints at me and wrinkles appear.

It is four o'clock in the afternoon and Wes has been leaning against a fire call box near St. Nicholas Avenue, talking busily with three friends. No one is working. If you live in Harlem, it's hard to find a job unless you wash dishes, clear tables or sweep basements. Wes has a pride in his skills. Truck driving, he feels, is his profession.

"You in a union?"

"Nah. I ain't in no union. I don't believe I could get in no union."

"Then how did you drive?"

"On my own, and for a boss who don't like unions. Stuff like that."

"Want a beer?"

"What you want from me?"

"Nothing. It's hot."

We walk into a bar in the bottom of a red, old tenement. Hand-inked signs advertise three-fers, supposedly triple shots of whiskey, for $1.05. The drink is really a single shot, served in a glass that magnifies. That is Wes's world; no job and bars that cheat.

"You from around here?" he asks.

"Not far."

"I'm from Dayton." The beers come. Wes takes a hearty swig. "I been here long enough to settle down. I got a nice woman. She works in a hospital. In the kitchen."

"Kids?"

"I got a son. He's living pretty good. Fourteen, and never worked much. Not like me."

Wes wants to talk about truck driving. He is short and chubby and his head is a large round egg. "I try to settle down," he says. "It's hard, man. The woman makes the money, you get to feel like dirt." He raps the bar with a fat brown fist. "I picked up something helping a man load up yesterday. I'll buy these beers. Hey, Jessie." The barmaid, slim, light brown, looks at Wes and says, "Get it up, if you can." Wes finds two quarters. Jessie pours us each a beer.

He relaxes and talks about his life. "Nevah much money. I hadda quit school. I liked to keep moving. But I could drive. I got a little business going here. I got me a woman and a son. And all of a sudden I can't drive no more."

"Why not?"

"Trouble with something. It don't matter what. They busted me and another guy took the truck."

"Who's *they?*"

Wes turns and looks dead at me. "Some white mother. You always getting fucked by some white mother. This guy, Italian, said I owed him. Got a Jew lawyer. They went to some Irish judge. They got my truck."

"The white guys all the same, is that what you figure?"

"Not all. Just most."

"How did you figure that gym in the park, Wes?"

"What gym? Who's Jim? What you talking about?"

"The gymnasium Columbia is going to build in Morningside Park."

"Where them kids kicked up that fuss?"

"Yeah."

"Ain't my gym," Wes said. "Shit, ain't my park."

He is thirty-five or forty, or forty-five and he has an obsession. He wants to drive. He is a lot of black people with the vitality torn out of them, and he doesn't care about park lands, he wants to be a man again. And the white man and the white system denies him.

"Grayson Kirk says—"

"Who?" Wes says. "Hey, you gonna get me another beer?"

"Grayson Kirk. He's the president of Columbia up the hill."

"I never heard of him," Wes says. "Hey, Jessie. This guy'll pay for two more."

I put up my two quarters. "Hey," Wes asks, "this Kirk, is he a friend of yours?"

"No."

"Then why you asking me about him? You know anybody needs a man to help drive his rig? Even be a loader three days in five."

The warped life bothers me. Wes with his large brown head and his pride and failure lingers. It is unfortunate that Wes does not know about the gym and has never heard of Grayson Kirk and the other Columbia executives. But it is worse that they have never heard of him.

* * * * * *

If the Columbia problem is complex and many-faceted, then the new gymnasium, a hulking structure that will not be erected, is a model of miniaturization. The gym was not a thoroughly bad idea at the start. The university needed it. Columbia planners made modest concessions to the black poor. But the project developed into a concealed land grab, and later, when black leaders asked for further concessions, Columbia arrogance rose like a lion rampant.

In time, the new gymnasium became a disaster, an end it probably deserved. As designed, whites—Columbia people—were to enter at the top. Blacks would enter at the bottom. In the words of one administrator, "It was cheaper and easier to build the gym that way." But in the words of one young black, "The man's got to know we don't take the basement entrance anymore." Before the project died, it joined the campus left with campus blacks as nothing else before or since. That is its legacy. Without the new gym, the Columbia SDS would still be looking for a focal issue. Mark Rudd might even have graduated.

The existing gym is cramped, depressing and more than seventy years old. Harold F. McGuire, a lawyer who was chairman of the Trustees Gymnasium Committee, crowns the complaints: "People like myself, who attended the law school, have to go to one of the downtown clubs to get in a squash game."

As far back as 1955, the entire Columbia sports program was in crisis. After persistent construction, the university was running out of outdoor space for physical education classes and intramurals. Officials took their problems to Robert Moses, then parks commissioner, and Moses yielded a chunk of public land. Morningside Drive, the eastern end of the campus, runs on a cliff; this cliff and a gentle sloping area beyond it comprise Morningside Park, the neutral ground between Columbia and Harlem.

After brief negotiation, Moses let Columbia build a ball field and a fieldhouse in the park. Columbia claims to have spent $250,000 on both. In exchange for this new base for intramurals, the university would provide athletic programs for "community teenagers." Over the years, Columbia organized 2,500 Harlem boys into 115 teams. They played softball, ran track, lifted weights and scrambled through touch football. Trustee McGuire is proud of this program in a sincere, nineteenth-century way. "We can field a Morningside Park team with a Chinese boy on first, a Puerto Rican boy on second, a Negro lad at shortstop, and a white boy at third base, and they can all make the double play." To which one must add two conditions: The baserunner had better be slow and the white will have to be a "ringer." Morningside Park infielders are usually black as the old Kansas City Monarchs of the Negro National League.

According to McGuire, the idea for a new gymnasium hatched in 1958. "It had been conceived that the same sort of cooperative enterprise that had proven to be so successful outdoors in the park could be applied in connection with the construction of a gym."

At first, Columbia tried to buy a chunk of Morningside Park, following its basic policy: land equals leverage. Turned down by Moses, McGuire told Grayson Kirk that two possibilities remained. Try to buy land from private sources or try to rent park space via a long-term guaranteed lease. The third and most obvious possibility, putting up the gymnasium in the open area at the center of the campus, was not considered. *No* expansion equals *no* leverage.

Acquiring private land appealed to no one. Columbia had other uses for the off-campus blocks it owned; and putting together a large new site would be expensive. If word spread that Columbia was assembling a tract, prices would explode. (Columbia likes to acquire land quietly, in small sections.) That left the rental plan and Columbia opted for it, with great confidence, insisting upon sweeping preconditions.

The new gymnasium would have to be publicly endorsed by the mayor, the city council, the state legislature, and the governor. Kirk and the trustees wanted to be absolutely protected from the charge of usurpation.

The university would hire "an independent appraiser" to recommend a reasonable annual rental. His word would not bind; but it would influence.

The university would obtain a form of title insurance. In the event of a court decision against the project, Columbia would get her money back.

Within two years, every precondition was met. In January of 1960, Columbia and the New York Department of Parks jointly announced plans for a new "$6 million gymnasium." That March, the city council asked the state legislature to authorize the park, and on April 18, 1960, Governor Nelson Rockefeller signed a bill allotting Columbia 2.1 acres of Morningside Park. Fifteen months later, Columbia's own hired appraiser suggested that a $2,500 annual rental would be "fair." In July, 1961, the New York Board of Estimate settled for $3,000 a year, $250 a month. One-bedroom apartments in Manhattan rent for more.

In the wake of riot, Columbia people blame "agitators and politicians" for the trouble at the gym. It was the fault of John Lindsay, or Thomas Hoving, an ambitious, able man who replaced Moses. "The notion," Harold McGuire told the Cox Commission, "of attaching any sinister meaning to the location of the community facility [at the bottom of the building] is little short of childish."

McGuire's interrogator was Judge Simon Rifkind, the man who allegedly softened the ultimate report. "Did Thomas Hoving suggest," Rifkind said, "that the people on St. Nicholas Avenue should be bussed to the top of Morningside Drive, or the people on Morningside Drive should be bussed to St. Nicholas Avenue?"

"No, sir."

"He did not?"

"No, sir," McGuire said. "I did not hear any suggestion of that."

Judge Rifkind was reaching for irony. He was referring to the issue of bussing white and blacks into each other's neighborhoods, to integrate schools meaningfully. He was poking fun. Rifkind did not represent Brown in Brown versus Topeka.

Trouble at the gymnasium proceeded from the increased militance of certain blacks and from Columbia's blindness to change. Those were the general causes. A specific was John Lindsay's ardent 1965 campaign in which he looked about a city traditionally run by Democrats and proposed changes. With a fine free hand, he discussed the gymnasium during a white paper on parks.

Morningside Heights and Harlem, Lindsay suggested, should determine "largely for itself" how local park land should be used. The people near the gym site should be informed that lands were about to be appropriated for private use. After a campaign of education, they could rationally decide what they wanted done.

Generally, he observed, open areas within Manhattan were rare. These should be left open. Finally, Lindsay insisted, park property should not fall to private builders. This applied to Columbia and to all the other entrepreneuring philanthropists who wanted to transform park land into restaurants, gymnasiums and parking lots—just for the public good.

Two months after Lindsay became mayor, Parks Commissioner Hoving called a press conference. His theme rang out. Columbia was misleading the public. Giving two floors out of ten to Harlem, Columbia claimed to be donating twenty percent of its new gym. But the cliff slanted sharply and the building was constructed along natural contours. Harlem's floors were the smallest in the building.

"I think the gymnasium project is disgraceful," Hoving announced. "The public should get more than twelve percent of this particular pie."

"Is that all it's getting?" a reporter asked.

"We've measured floor space," Hoving said. "Columbia is keeping eighty-eight percent of the gym for itself."

"What are you going to do about it?"

Hoving, a tall and tidy man, smiled slightly. "I'm going to try and persuade the Columbia people to change the site."

"But couldn't the structure be redesigned?"

"I suppose it could be," Hoving said. "But understand we're not happy under *any* conditions over this appropriation of park land to private use. It's not certain at this late date that Columbia can be stopped. But if we are going to have to live with this big ugly structure, built on community land, then the community and not Columbia should get most benefit."

Hoving had seized a commendable issue. Some politicians joined with him. Others stood with Columbia. Hoving enjoyed his role as savior of the parks, but on resigning his commissionership later, he became president of the Metropolitan Museum of Art. The museum is the largest private facility on a New York park land. (However, it is open to everyone, black, tan, white, Columbia seniors and sixth-grade dropouts, on an absolutely equal basis.)

As time passed, Columbia and the city polarized. It was a year before Hoving and Grayson Kirk actually sat down to bargain together, and when they did, the exchange was disappointing. "We have two principal objections," Hoving said. "The distribution of space is unfair to the community, and the rent of three thousand dollars a year is too low. The city should get more."

"But I think you would agree," Kirk answered, "that the rental is not the main consideration that would run to the city. After all Columbia is assuming the expense for constructing the gymnasium—the community portion as well as our own."

Hoving did not agree, and left annoyed. A day later, Hugh Ferry, Democratic leader for a Harlem district, denounced the gym. David Dickens, an assemblyman, defended it. An ad hoc group began a taxpayer's suit to block construction. Then, on February 23, 1966, Columbia CORE issued a statement opposing the gym. Within twenty-four hours, Kirk, his adamancy aroused, announced, "Groundbreaking will occur in October."

It was Kirk's misfortune to misread his own power. He was not Butler, Low or even Eisenhower. And he also misread the times. That spring, opposition flowered on the campus. Both the student council and the Columbia-Barnard Democratic Club urged university conciliation with the community. Hoving made the audacious suggestion that the same gymnasium facilities be open to everyone. "All that's needed," he said, "is sensible scheduling." Kirk would not be moved.

In May, two black legislators, Basil Paterson and Percy Sutton, introduced bills to repeal the 1960 law granting Columbia the 2.1 acres. If the repeal bill passed, Kirk threatened, Columbia would sue New York State. The bill died soon, but not the issue.

By autumn, a preponderance of black politicians was aligned against Columbia. The group included local district leaders Percy Sutton and J. Raymond Jones, chief of Tammany and probably the strongest black politician in New York. Painfully, Kirk and McGuire began reconsidering. Whatever the ultimate power of men like Jones, the hot summer of 1966 re-emphasized another consideration. Blacks had begun burning white real estate.

When Charles Rangel ran for assembly from the Morningside District, he promised that he would fight to block the gym. Rangel won easily. Some read his victory as evidence that an anti-Columbia platform was increasingly popular. An aroused black community appeared dangerous now. Columbia's first conciliatory gestures followed the election by three weeks.

On December 1, 1966, McGuire stated that Columbia was considering letting local groups use the lion's share of the gymnasium "by invitation."

"Would he elaborate?"

"Well," McGuire said, "a good example might be a basketball tournament. The Morningside community basketball leagues would normally play in the community part of the gym. But when they reached the final round, it might be a good idea for them to play in the Columbia varsity gym. The varsity gym will have seating for four thousand."

An ad hoc community committee on the gym led by Rangel, Percy Sutton and others said, "Not enough." Kirk sent delegates to meet with ad hoc people and Department of Parks officials. Lindsay called a meeting in Gracie Mansion in May. Still nothing was settled. "If the city wants a better facility," a Columbia official said, "let the city pay for it."

Lindsay shook his head. "The city cannot make cash contributions to Columbia's endowment."

On June 20, 1967, Kirk felt another hot racial summer closing in. Under that ultimate pressure he agreed to add a swimming pool and locker room to the community facility. For legal reasons, the additions to the gym had to be authorized by the Board of Estimate, and Kirk asked Percy Sutton, by now Manhattan Borough President, to propose the change.

"Please be advised," Sutton wrote back, agreeing, "that while I do not believe that the addition of the swimming pool alone is a 'resolution' of the problem as a whole, I do understand it to be an improvement over the initial agreement and the maximum concessions Columbia finds itself able to make."

Columbia did not burn that summer. But in the heat, interrupted by rain squalls, the ad hoc committee gave way to a stronger group, the West Harlem Morningside Park Committee. By October, the West Harlem Morningside Park Committee was organizing a "tent-in" against the gym. Contract problems were delaying groundbreaking, and sixty people spent a night in the park. By December, State Senator Basil Paterson was sharing a platform with H. Rap Brown. "I don't agree with Brown," said Paterson, an effective moderate leader, "but I would stand with anyone against that racist gym." Then, on February 19, 1968, construction crews hired by Columbia appeared in Morningside Park. They erected a cyclone fence and set to leveling. Grayson Kirk and the trustees *would* have their gym.

The first demonstration came the next morning. About fifty protesters, drawn equally from the SDS, other student groups and the West Harlem Morningside Park Committee, appeared and shouted at the workmen to stop. They were ignored. But groups came day after day, and with warmer weather, a hotter scene was coming.

On March 24 at midday, 150 students marched to the gym site. There by prearrangement they met twenty-five people from the Morningside neighborhood. The groups merged and tramped above the now-scarred slope carrying signs:

> STOP GYM CROW
> GYM CROW MUST GO
> END COLUMBIA RACISM NOW

A police contingent observed. The union men at work ignored the pickets. "We want to be with you," one student shouted, at a squat laborer in a hard hat. "We want to work together against oppressors."

The worker looked at the student. "Hey, kid," he shouted. Then he rammed his middle finger toward the sky.

Mark Rudd was there. "All right. Let's get the hell in there," someone else shouted. The protesters found a path through the fence. A few climbed onto a bulldozer. "Wait up, wait up," a boy was shouting. "No violence." He pointed at the burly workers. "We got no argument with them."

Abruptly, in this brisk afternoon, it seemed as though no one was moving. The students paused. The workmen paused. The great earth movers halted. Then, very quickly, a detachment of police rushed at the pickets. Then policemen, formed in a tight wedge, beat several to the ground. The police wrestled about a dozen people, leaders, so they thought, pinioned them and carted them off to vans. Twelve students, not including Rudd, were arrested. So was a Harlem pastor, A. Kendall Smith.

The Reverend Smith did not resist as four policemen lifted him from the ground where he had lain down before a bulldozer. The police hustled the minister, face up, to a van and stuffed him in. Doors closed. Vans pulled away. "All right, all right," policemen bellowed.

As the rest of the demonstrators moved away, back toward the sundial and the safety of the campus, they became aware of a thick cloud all about them. Dust from the barren gym site had been kicked up in the struggle. Now it hung in the air and clung to shoes and slacks. Looking back, from an approach to the campus, one could see the dust cloud still rising above the site. Soon another, larger cloud would form.

6 THE CRUELEST MONTH

THE BOY WHO CRIED BULLSHIT

A MOST interesting description of Mark Rudd was written by Dan Bell, Doctor Daniel Bell, editor of the *The Radical Right*, Ph.D. (Columbia), L.H.D. (Grinnell), Litt. D. (Case Western Reserve), once ranking professor in the Columbia Department of Sociology, recently moved to Harvard and thirty years ago an ambitious City College undergraduate. To Bell, Mark Rudd is "hulking and slack-faced." Rudd's jaw is not merely prominent, it is "prognathic." The "blue-gray eyes are so translucent that his gaze seems hypnotic." Finally, Professor Bell points out, "Rudd's father [was] born Rudnitsky." It is a tribute to Mark Rudd's ability to shake academicians to their ganglia that one of the best of them is driven to assert that Rudd is a Jew.

The Columbia revolutionist is a curiously appealing young man, except when he is possessed by vulgarity or hostility or arrogance. He speaks earnestly and forcefully about a new order. He wants to see mankind freed from toil. How? He is not certain, and he does not take suggestions well. When someone corrects Rudd, the teeth clench and the jaw really does become prognathic. His rhetoric grows simple. "Aw, fuck off."

People at Columbia enjoy making catalogs of Rudd's weaknesses. They are ample and he is twenty-two years old. His philosophy is derivative, emotional and sometimes puerile. His speaking voice is high and often monotonous. He has no clear image of the future. He is bright and clever, rather than brilliant, not deep at all. He is irresponsible and ruthless. But against these failures of intellect, morality and technique, Mark Rudd possesses an overwhelming strength. He knows how to make his opposition cringe.

When the faculty wanted to mediate his revolution, Rudd found himself sitting across a desk from a professor who was urging "reason." Abruptly, Rudd removed his boots, and put his socks in the professor's face. On another occasion, he addressed a supposedly congenial faculty group in Philosophy Hall. It was there that he cried that mediatory talks were "bullshit." Professors were startled. Rudd keeps people off balance. He enjoys rattling them, the way good fighters do, and like a good fighter, he trusts very few.

The Columbia revolt was not Mark Rudd's doing, any more than it was the doing of Grayson Kirk or Lyndon Johnson or Ho Chi Minh. But Rudd influenced it mightily, and if one wishes to understand the events of Columbia, one must pay attention to Mark Rudd, a charismatic, not always pleasant young man. The country, as Rudd sees it —and as his father sees it as well—is surfeited with affluence. Jacob Rudd, a lieutenant colonel in the U.S. Army Reserve, owns a real estate brokerage in the north Jersey suburb of Maplewood. "My concern," concedes Jacob Rudd, "has always been making a living. Mark doesn't have to worry about that."

The absolute freedom from economic terrors provided Rudd with time to rebel. His parents speak fondly of his disinterest in material things, of his ability to be happy sleeping in the woods. It was not, however, the sleep of a hobo. Rudd, in the woods, always had a good house and warm bed awaiting his whim.

The situation is not unique. Thousands, perhaps millions of young people who have been raised in comfort, develop a need to rebel against the conditions of their upbringing. Typically, they are between the ages of seventeen and thirty. Frequently they are the children of recent immigrant groups. They are, in short, the offspring of a generation that had to drive very hard for success. As the Maplewood Syndrome seizes them, they fight against what their parents built. They attack the success and the society that lauds it. Some enact rebellion by embracing the Castro experience, or Stalinism, or by trying to embrace hostile blacks. Occasionally, the Maplewood Syndrome vanishes with maturity. But the situation does not lend itself to simplification, not the condition and certainly not the times.

In Maplewood and Bel Air, and Shaker Heights and Dobbs Ferry and Boxford and even dull, wasp Bloomfield Hills, we are rounding out three decades of a spiraling prosperity that has remade the nature of the country. The managerial-technical-professional class numbers more than ten million families. It is a class with businesses to leave to children. Or law practices. Or money in Xerox. Or investment land in East Hampton. Or cash. All one has to do to come into money is to survive.

The removal of a requisite struggle to succeed disturbs the American pattern. It would in any era. If Lincoln had been born to wealth and power, would he have ended up as a wealthy clubman, the disappointing fate of his beloved Tad? Possibly so. In this particular time, the death of struggle is catastrophic. It has taken place against the increasingly visible and increasingly desperate struggle of black America against poverty. The sensitive child of the suburbs sees this: no blacks live on his street. Some come to work but only as menials. He reads that blacks are hungry and that black children are bitten by rats. Intuitively he sympathizes with blacks and wonders why they are denied. An early symptom of the Maplewood Syndrome is a sense of the unfairness of things.

If the suburban child decides to investigate the traditional treatment of blacks in the United States, he finds, as Eugene McCarthy put it, that we practice colonialism. When the young suburbanite recognizes the colonialism, in opposition to endemic affluence, he becomes upset. He wants to say he is sorry that blacks suffer, and that *he* didn't make them suffer and that he admires them. Suffering lends the appearance of nobility. The suburbanite admires the noble blacks and tries to join them. He fails, and admires them more. ("I've never really been that comfortable with blacks," Mark Rudd concedes.)

The mind probes further. What is the source of our putative prosperity? In Marcuse's term, it is "the peaceful production of the weapons of destruction." The youth finds that military spending, in its many forms, supports factories, foundations and universities—and at the same time, spatters napalm on the children of Vietnam. The young suburbanite is ashamed of his country.

"What is this life my parents are leading anyway?" he says one night, sitting with a girl. "What is it, with the swimming pool and the extra cars and all that stuff? Who needs it? It's blood money."

If he is fortunate, the girl looks at him, warm with admiration.

"I see what money bought my parents," he says. "A better place to have their fights. A color TV that shows junk. Better Scotch so they can pretend they have a life." The young man shakes his head.

"No, sir, honey. That shit is not for me. I'm going where it's at. I want to be real." He then marches forth to live with blacks or make a revolution.

Mark was the second son born to the Rudds. His older brother, David, is a lawyer. His mother, Bertha, says that Mark was a good boy, well disciplined and mannerly. He grew up blond and plump and busy. He liked jazz and shortwave radios and the Boy Scouts. He was popular at Columbia High in Maplewood, a model suburban school. Four out of five graduates enter college. Even then, as he posted good grades in English and history and mathematics, Rudd began to believe that something was wrong in Maplewood and beyond. His grandmother owned a candy store in the Central Ward of Newark, a section going black and getting poorer. (The ward eventually exploded into riot.) It is a short drive from Maplewood to Newark, not more than half an hour, and Mark was stunned by what he saw in his grandmother's neighborhood. Children begging. Tattered clothes. Blacks without shoes. In the rotting Central Ward, a discontent seized Rudd.

Despite his fine grades and good extracurricular record in high school, he was rejected by Harvard. But Columbia was happy to get Rudd, and I suppose it tells us something of the nature of the revolutionary that he wanted to attend an Ivy League school. No free college, open to all, for Rudd. If not Harvard, then Columbia, the gem of the establishment.

On the sprawling, confusing campus, reaching to the very lip of Harlem, Rudd, the child of parents who struggled, found himself an instant Ivy Leaguer. In his indoctrination, he was bluntly told, "The mission of Columbia College is to train a small number of the most promising minds in each generation." It was not a message that he found appealing, but he did his work well enough. He grappled with Contemporary Civilization, a two-year program at Columbia, which sets out to "make the students deal, as graduate students do, with *original writings* of the major thinkers since the fifteenth century and to form and express opinions." He sweated through Humanities, another two-year sequence. Humanities proceeds from John Erskine's theory that undergraduates "advance their intellectual development" by reading and discussing one classic masterpiece a week. Today *Paradise Lost;* next week *Tristram Shandy.* Rudd's more meaningful education was taking place outside the lecture halls.

Like most other frosh, he found Columbia enormous and impersonal. Like many others, he thought, with the sureness of eighteen years, that much classroom work was useless, irrelevant. Here, it seemed to him, the blacks were being oppressed, the American nation was being transformed into a neo-fascist military state, and the professors lectured from notes about things that didn't matter, just as they'd been doing for the past dreary decades. It wasn't right, Rudd concluded, with some justification. If Columbia people refused to establish relations with Harlemites, except as duke to serfs, at least Columbia ought to recognize the present. It is perfectly fair to assert that Columbia had a hand in the creation of this rebel. Her weaknesses helped push him to the left.

While Rudd was wondering why so few blacks attended the college, why so few full professors taught freshmen and whether he would have to go to Vietnam, he attached himself to a number of upperclassmen. One, Michael Neumann, was Marcuse's stepson. Through him, Rudd learned of *One Dimensional Man*. As one philosophy professor suggests, "Marcuse's work is not only wonderful because of itself; it's also a framework in which you can find explanations for your own hangups; in fact for almost anybody's hangups." Rudd took comfort from Marcuse's argument that American society was irrational. It isn't just me, then, is what Rudd thought. He also swallowed another hypothesis: revolutions are not accidents; they are created by an act of will, the will to revolution.

Rudd joined the radical Students for a Democratic Society and as a sophomore was put in charge of organizing dormitory support for SDS. He spoke up often at meetings and developed a reputation as a skillful debater, a fair humorist and an intractable hard-liner. But in Rudd's junior year, moderates elected Ted Kaptchuk as president, and Rudd, the activist, found himself an outsider within the SDS.

Columbia SDS consisted only of one hundred or so young people and a repetitive topic at meetings was "how can we broaden our base." Kaptchuk favored discussion and explanation of "what the state of the country is and what the issues really are." Rudd favored demonstrations. Kaptchuk was a "verbalist," he charged, while the time was crying out for action. The best way to "radicalize" the student body, while believed, was to demonstrate again and again against Columbia's connection with the American war machine.

That winter, in 1968, Rudd flew to Cuba with a group of other students. Rudd's view of the Cuban government confirmed his existing beliefs. He saw the Malacon, the handsome boulevard that winds above the sea and where, in other days, fine manors served as brothels for American tourists. He saw the Miramar, a section of ornate homes, some built of marble. They once housed the rich and servants; now many had been turned into living quarters for workers. He talked to young Cuban revolutionaries. They delighted him. They had thrown out a military dictator, Batista, who was supported by strong elements in the United States. The trip strengthened Rudd's resolve to make a revolution and encouraged his belief that one could succeed. There does not seem to be any evidence to support the theory that the Columbia debacle traces from Cuba. Rudd was a hard-liner before he saw Havana. And there is absolutely no evidence to support a right-wing theory that Cuban money helped finance the rebellion. What money the Columbia rebels needed came from the sale of pamphlets and articles and from the pockets of middle-class parents. Castro (and Mao and even Brezhnev) may have cheered. They did not have to invest.

Back on campus in March, 1968, members of the SDS were impatient with the cautious stewardship of Ted Kaptchuk. Another election was coming. Rudd campaigned on a promise of action and, in that March, became president of the Columbia chapter of the SDS.

As president and leader, Rudd was motivated by two forces. The desire to remake unjust America was sincere. So was his developing ambition. During the following months, action followed action so swiftly that the Columbia left was like a runaway. There was no telling where it would go or when it would stop. Rudd did not really control the movement, but he was adroit at setting forces in motion. He sought confrontations and he found them. He did not know how the confrontations would end, nor did he seem to be concerned. What disturbed him most was someone's suggestion: "If this movement peters out, Mark, you're through."

He developed a taste for power and importance. He liked to put down professors and to dominate meetings and to see his name in headlines, although the last soon lost appeal. The press, in reporting, tended to patronize him. He resolved that shrewdly. He stopped granting interviews, and began to write himself. He was able to sell one article to a national magazine and another to a book publisher.

His leadership was imperfect. He made mistakes and antagonized potential friends, and was forever changing his mind. But it was the most vital student leadership the Columbia campus had ever seen. That is a bulky pill to administer to Columbia graduates, from the leftists of the 30's to the jocks, the muscular conservatives, of today. But it is true.

Mark Rudd at twenty-two is a successful lecturer, the chairman of one branch of the SDS and a college dropout. To regain admission to Columbia he would have to eat crow, and of course he will not. Despite difficulties, he remains a leader, *the* leader. The unity of the left at Columbia dissolved almost as it was created. The liberal left, put off by Rudd's intransigence, split with him in June 1968. The extreme left, the radicals who want to fight in the streets, to join with workmen, quickly found Rudd to be bourgeois. But to many of the radical students, Rudd is almost heroic.

"Look," one of the captains of one of the multitudinous subcommittees within the Columbia SDS has said. "It's hard to get to Mark. He's busy. He's got so many things to do. But when I do get a few minutes with him, it's worth it. He's so goddamn alive." Some women of the left find him overwhelming. A male radical celebrates this by referring to him as Mark Studd.

I talked with him a few times and listened to him on other occasions. He is busy, self-occupied, vain and careless with facts. He says that more students supported him than supported the administration. The best surveys showed that many students supported his objectives and very few, only nineteen percent, endorsed his tactics. He says that *The New York Times* is a tool of Columbia and attacks A. M. Rosenthal, "the managing editor." The first statement is excessive and the second is wrong: When Rudd spoke, Clifton Daniel was managing editor; Abe Rosenthal was his assistant.

He is a big boy, with square, rather high shoulders, and a stoop. When he listens, he cocks his head forward, nodding quickly, impatiently. He answers rapidly and thoughtlessly. One day he says that there were no issues at Columbia. "I made them all up." Another day he says, "The issues were symbolic." On a third day, "Every fucking issue was real." He means what he says, as he says it, but he cannot contain his need to be dramatic, his need to surprise, to shock, to call attention to himself. It might be difficult to take him seriously, except for what he has accomplished. And that is serious beyond question. He knows it and he means to do more. He was the right man in the right place at the right moment once. He would like to continue to play that role for the rest of his days.

*   *   *   *   *   *

In the end, it came down to unacceptable behavior. All the dreams of the communes, the high talk of revolutionary salvation, and all the slogans on the banners of spring.

Columbia Belongs to the People. We Are the People!

Stop Columbia From Taking Over Harlem.

No Help to Fascist War in Vietnam!

No Racist Gym!!

All the slogans and the poetry and the talk ended with young people shrieking obscenities and police joyfully beating the young. The faculty was revealed as superfluous. It is true that a half dozen professors were clubbed, a number of others were trampled and Rabbi A. Bruce Goldman, advisor to Jewish students, was battered to semiconsciousness. But ultimately the faculty passed resolutions, cogitated and drifted as the campus became a battleground.

The riots of April, 1968, were an explosion, but they were also a logical extension of events. It is curious that so many teachers say they were surprised.

The real issue at Columbia, or perhaps the real focus of conflict, was the gymnasium. But to the young people of the Students for a Democratic Society, the most *attractive* issue was Columbia's involvement with the Institute for Defense Analyses. A conspiracy is always most appealing when it is global. Meetings protesting Columbia's collaboration with the American government persisted through 1967 and that fall Kirk issued the ban on indoor demonstrations. In the winter, his rule was directly challenged with a calculated disturbance inside Dodge Hall.

Recruiters for the Dow Chemical Corporation, manufacturers of napalm, visited Columbia on February 28, 1968, to enlist scientific and executive trainees. They set up shop within Dodge, which fronts on Broadway at 116th Street. SDS members picketed inside Dodge, but the university response, as expressed by Proctor William Kahn, was to declare that the picketing did not constitute a demonstration. No picketer was punished. Then Mark Rudd, big, blond and militant, became president of the SDS and called a major rally for March 27. The place was the Columbia sundial, adjacent to College Walk. The subject was Columbia and the IDA.

By noon the day was sharp and blue and the wind had lost the edge of winter. It was invigorating to stand on the broad expanse near the sundial and consider the campus and the great buildings—Low, with its Pantheon dome, and Butler Library, with its inscription to Herodotus and Sophocles. To this spring scene, the radicals brought youth and the sense that time was running with them.

"No demonstrating," Rudd shouted, mocking Kirk's ruling. "If you want to yell and scream and bust up an office, that's okay. But remember, now. No demonstrating."

There was laughter. About two hundred people were gathered. On the edges of the crowd Proctor Kahn and Dean Henry Coleman stood as observers. They seemed relaxed. "They might," someone said later, "have been watching football practice."

"The administration of this university," Rudd shouted, "is a part of the industrial defense complex that supports the war in Vietnam." He was shouting into a bullhorn; a bullhorn on campus violated another of Kirk's rules.

"I say we go talk to the administration of this university," Rudd called. "I say we talk to them and tell them some things about this industrial defense complex." He paused. "But is the administration going to listen?"

A chorus of voices thundered: "No."

"Okay," Rudd said. "Let's go up to Low and ask them about it."

Rudd lurched forward and started up the steps of Low Library, pressing past the bronze statue of Alma Mater. A hundred radicals followed, including Nick Freudenberg, tall, long-haired, bespectacled, and John Jacobs, powerful and compact. As the crowd surged, a chant arose: "IDA must go."

The administration was caught by surprise. No campus policemen were stationed before Low. The one hundred radicals surged into the rotunda. "Upstairs," someone shouted. "Let's go to Kirk's office."

In the president's suite the radicals found two frightened secretaries. "President Kirk isn't here. He's downtown on university business."

"Truman, then. Where the hell is Truman?"

"He's busy."

A week earlier at Columbia, a man from selective service had been struck with a lemon meringue. "Tell him not to be afraid," one of the radicals said. "We promise no pies in the face."

One secretary retreated to Truman's office and returned. "Dr. Truman will meet any three of you, but he can't very well meet with a mob."

"Come on," Rudd shouted. He ran down a corridor toward the office of Thomas McGoey, vice-president for business. McGoey was standing near the door.

"We want you to break relations with the IDA," one of the students said.

"I know you do," McGoey said. He is a broad man, with a tough Irish face.

"We've got a petition signed by 1,400 people demanding it."

"I know that, too. But I'm not going to argue with you in the hallway."

"Come on," Rudd shouted. "There's one more of these swine around."

McGoey flushed with fury and the students rushed off to confront Warren Goodell, another vice-president. He was out to lunch. There was nobody else to see. The students milled about, then drifted back outside. A few minutes later, David Truman, assured and brisk, walked down the steps of Low, heading toward Philosophy Hall, a few hundred feet southeast.

Rudd, Freudenberg, Gold and the others hurried to the entrance to Philosophy. There they linked arms and blocked Truman's way.

"I have an appointment," Truman said.

"Adolph Eichmann had appointments, too," Rudd shouted.

Truman shook his head, but would not respond. Finally, William Kahn, speaking quietly, convinced the students to let Truman go about his business.

That afternoon, Rudd, Freudenberg, Ted Gold and several other SDS people wrote Kirk demanding that Columbia withdraw from the IDA directorate and that any professor working on IDA projects be dismissed. "Until Columbia ends all affiliation with the IDA," the letter warned, "we must disrupt the functioning of all those involved in the daily disruption of people's lives around the world." A few days later, Rudd, Freudenberg and four members of the SDS steering committee, John Jacobs, Ted Gold, Ed Hyman and Morris Grossner, received brief notices. They were to report to the dean's office. Pleased by their success so far, they refused.

Violent and portentous events were coming. It was a time to seize the day. On Sunday, March 31, Lyndon Johnson concluded an extended televised address with the surprising statement that he would not run again. Eugene McCarthy, gallant and sometimes eloquent in the New Hampshire cold, had driven the principal architect of Vietnam War from politics. That Tuesday, April 2, McCarthy won the Democratic primary in Wisconsin. A tide of liberal hope began to flow.

Then Thursday, April 4, a gunman murdered Martin Luther King. The preacher died without a word. In the days that followed, troops had to be called into Washington, D.C. Blacks looted Gary, Detroit and Saginaw. In Harlem, under the Columbia campus, policemen gathered, sixteen to a corner, and guarded the stores of 125th Street.

At Columbia, April 9 was designated as the day for a memorial to Dr. King. The service would be held in St. Paul's Chapel, a small, discreet building adjacent to Low. By 11 A.M., the chapel overflowed. Faculty was represented, and administration and students from all branches of the university. About a hundred of them were blacks.

The services began with the Reverend Dr. Moran Weston,

Columbia '30, a black Episcopalian minister, reading from King's works. An organ murmured in the background.

"I have a dream," Dr. Weston read as he repeated the famous speech. "I *have* a dream . . . "

Heads bowed.

"Let us hold hands," Dr. Weston said.

Everyone joined hands with his neighbor, except Grayson Kirk. The president was seated by himself in the rear of the chancel.

The hymn began:

> *We shall overcome*
> *We shall overcome*
> *We shall overcome*
> *Some day.*

Columbia's intellectual non-hymn-singing populace sang together, swaying and holding hands in grief. Slowly, David Truman rose and walked to the microphone. He was to eulogize the martyr. Not quite so slowly, Mark Rudd arose in an aisle seat and moved toward the microphone. Rudd cut in front of Truman and called, "Dr. Truman and President Kirk are committing a moral outrage against the memory of Dr. King." Truman looked for Chaplain John Cannon to intercede.

"Columbia's administration," Rudd said, "is morally corrupt, unjust and indulges in racist policies. How can the leaders of the university eulogize a man who died trying to unionize sanitation workers when they themselves fight the unionizing of their own black and Puerto Rican workers?"

The Reverend Cannon was not moving.

"How can these administrators praise a man who fought for human dignity when they have stolen land from the people of Harlem?

"How can they praise a man who preached nonviolent disobedience while disciplining their own students for peaceful protest?

"If we really want to honor this man's memory then we ought to stand together against this racist gym."

Rudd stepped down to the applause of forty followers. They trailed him as he departed, leaving Dr. Truman to proceed grimly with his own eulogy.

Outside the chapel afterward, members of the SDS jubilantly distributed mimeographed demands:

• Columbia was to halt construction "of the gymnasium in Morningside Park with reparations for damaged park land."

• "The university community" was to be redefined to include "local residents, neighbors and university workers."

• The Morningside community was to control totally a Ford Foundation grant to Columbia of $10 million to study urban affairs.

• Columbia was to incorporate "black arts and culture into its normal curriculum."

• The IDA connection had to be severed because the IDA was an "organization which produced weapons and controls systems for the suppression of ghetto uprisings."

With Dr. King fresh in his grave, the SDS had reawakened to the blacks. Opportunism was not the monopoly of either side.

That Friday, April 12, Truman told a reporter from the *Spectator* that he was considering taking action against the chaplain's office "for permitting this spectacle." The Reverend John D. Cannon responded smartly that St. Paul's was open to all "who wished to speak their conscience on any subject at any time."

On the day of Cannon's comment, Grayson Kirk was speaking his own conscience on another campus, four hundred miles away. For the 225th anniversary of Thomas Jefferson's birth, Kirk was to deliver the Founder's Day address at the University of Virginia. Kirk reveres Jefferson. He also recognized—more than he could concede close to home—that mysterious change was altering American society. He wanted his speech at Charlottesville to be a credo. "I labored over every paragraph," he told a friend. "I wrote and rewrote that speech in longhand." It was unfortunate that Kirk spoke his heart so far away from the crisis that was to topple him; unfortunate but understandable. One sometimes can unburden oneself only to strangers.

"Our society," Kirk told the Virginia audience, "is in a more perilous condition than at any time since the conflict between the states. Our nation is in trouble." This was a great concession from a man in his mid-sixties, economically secure and on the boards of banks and oil companies.

"Our present difficulties would ruffle even a Jefferson.

"At home disrespect for law and authority has reached such a level that violence has almost achieved respectability. Our young people reject authority, take refuge in turbulent, inchoate nihilism. I know of no time in our history when the gap between the generations has been more potentially dangerous."

Kirk is not a poetic man or very articulate, but he was facing up to the failures of his era. "The plain fact," he said, "is that we do not know how to solve the new problems. They are too complex, too immense. In New York we have almost twice as many people on relief as during the depths of the depression. We have more dependent children than the entire population of Omaha.

"No one knows how the vicious cycle of dependency, which threatens to go on generation after generation, can be broken. And yet ours is certainly the most affluent and perhaps the best educated society in history."

Kirk presented two specific suggestions. First, we should get out of Vietnam. "No other item on the national agenda can be dealt with effectively until this has been done." Vietnam, he said, had produced more bitter dissension than any issue since "the tragic War Between the States." At last Kirk stood committed with Gene McCarthy, Robert Kennedy and other heroes of the young. The Vietnamese War must stop.

His second proposal was less clear. "Our problems," he said, "are so complex that they can be dealt with efficiently only by a greater concentration of governmental authority:

> We have always said proudly that though our democracy may be a clumsy form of government, we accept this inefficiency as a reasonable price for the protection of our liberties. But today, though we cling to our liberties, we demand from government a degree of efficiency that our system was designed to make almost impossible. We should not abandon our liberties in the interest of efficiency. The price would be too great. But we cannot forever have our cake and eat it, too.
>
> We should not be afraid to remember Jefferson's counsel that each generation should be prepared to examine its political institutions and to reshape them as necessary to meet the needs of the time. We are trying to operate a complicated and sensitive society with mechanisms devised for the needs of a simpler day.

Kirk called this speech The Umpirage of Reason, a phrase he had lifted, with credit, from Jefferson's Third Annual Message to Congress. In it Jefferson spoke of bringing "collisions of interest to the umpirage of reason rather than of force."

Although the Vietnam statement was popular, Kirk's extolling of efficiency is controversial, to put it sedately. Increased government efficiency makes many think of trains running on time while thought stalled in fascist Italy, of European Jews efficiently stripped naked and murdered in well-constructed gas chambers.

Mark Rudd could hardly wait to make a rebuttal. Under Ted Kaptchuk, the SDS newspaper, *New Left News*, was direct and lacked flare. Rudd renamed the paper *Up Against the Wall*. On April 22, he printed an issue with the modest slogan: The Year of the Heroic Guerrilla. The newspaper ran eight pages. One was devoted to portraits of Che Guevara, above a caption proclaiming, "The duty of every revolutionary is to make revolution." The principal feature was Mark Rudd's "Reply to Uncle Grayson." Rudd writes with force, conviction and powerful insolence.

The contrast in styles is almost too pat: There was Kirk, white-haired, jowly, wasp, reticent, formal, speaking far off to honor Jefferson, by now a safe revolutionary. There was Rudd, fair, long-faced, radical, brazen, building a campus forum for himself with intuitive skill.

"Dear Grayson," Rudd began the answer, working for an egalitarian effect. "Though your charge of nihilism is not true, it does represent something: you call it the generation gap. I see it as a real conflict between those who run things now—you, Grayson Kirk—and those who feel oppressed by the society you rule—we, the young people."

From the outset, Rudd played the young populist. He spoke in behalf of the innocent young everywhere.

"You might want to know what is wrong with society," he continued. "We can point to Vietnam as an example of the unimaginable wars of aggression you are prepared to fight to maintain control over your empire." But what of Kirk's specific plea for withdrawal? "Now you've been beaten by the Vietnamese," Rudd insisted, "so you call for a tactical retreat.

"We can point to this university, your university, which trains us to be lawyers and engineers and managers for your IBM, your Socony Mobile, your IDA, your Con Edison. [Kirk was a member of all these boards.]

"Your cry of nihilism," Rudd proceeded, "represents your inability to understand our positive values. We do have a vision of the way things could be: how the tremendous resources of our economy could be used to eliminate want, how people in other countries could be free from your [American] domination, how a university could produce knowledge for progress, and not waste consumption and destruction, how men could be free to keep what they produce, to enjoy peaceful lives, to create. These are positive values—but since they mean the destruction of your order, you call them nihilism. In the movement we are beginning to call this vision socialism."

The dream of hope, dreamed by young men even before Marcuse, before Marx, before Plato, before Micah.

"The situation is potentially dangerous," Rudd wrote. "For if we win, we will take control of your world, your corporations, your university and mold a world in which we can live as human beings. We will have to destroy at times, even violently, in order to end your system, but that is a far cry from nihilism."

The conclusion of this remarkable document rings with heroic and ridiculous defiance. "There is only one thing left to say. It may sound nihilistic to you, since it is the opening shot in a war of liberation. I'll use the words of LeRoi Jones, whom I'm sure you don't like a whole lot. 'Up against the wall, motherfucker, this is a stickup.' "

Motherfucker is a word born in the black community, where according to a New York police official the incest rate, though slight, "is higher than in the city at large." Major league baseball players, whose language is severe, say that black athletes brought the term into bench-jockeying. Others report having first heard *motherfucker* on the lips of black troops during World War II. The black origin makes the word immediately attractive to New Leftists, but its repetitive use by middle-class radical whites indicates something more.

In the bland neighborhoods where they grew up, incest was unknown and sexual mores tended to be conventional. If father had a mistress, he remained silent. If mother had once fallen, never mind. Growing up in this seeming blandness, discovering sex and guilt, a boy came to conclude that there was only one motherfucker on earth. That is, only one man fucked *his* mother. The man was Dad.

When Rudd and his middle-class colleagues shout "motherfucker," they employ a cryptic word, fraught with obscenity, meaning "father." Thus they tend to make father himself an obscenity. What the radical, disappointed in the world, may really want to shout at Grayson Kirk (who shaped it) is "You, you FATHER, you." By calling Kirk "motherfucker," Rudd was doing just that.

It is not necessary for the radical to have disliked his own father per se. The upper-middle-class father is a symbol of authority, of a system, and to the young radicals, the system and all the symbols of the system are obscene. The radical shrieking "motherfucker" cries out for attention, for help and misbehaves all at once.

He may not have had so much fun since he was a baby.

On April 22, the day after Rudd's letter was distributed on campus, he and four other SDS leaders were called to the office of Alexander Platt, associate dean for student affairs at Columbia College. (A sixth SDS member had left school.) Platt told them they were accused of having participated in an "indoor demonstration on March 27, in violation of the rule against indoor demonstrations of any kind." That was the day of the ramble through Low Library.

The five students waited silently.

"Now, what you are to do is plead guilty or innocent," Platt said.

No one spoke.

"If you plead guilty, you can then explain your side."

"We're not going to plead," one of the boys said.

"If you don't deny your role," Platt said, "and don't explain it, you'll force my hand."

"We don't have to deny or explain anything to anyone."

"Well, in that case," Platt said, "I'll have to put all of you on disciplinary probation for the rest of the semester. Any further disruptions of university life will cause me to ask for your suspension or outright dismissal. Is that clear?"

According to one observer, the five students left Platt's office "in a huff." Another describes them as "defiant, but perplexed." To a third, they were "calmly confident things were running their way."

That night, the SDS held a solemn emergency meeting in an empty classroom at Fayerweather, a building given over to graduate studies, which backs on to Amsterdam Avenue. No more than seventy-five students attended. Platt's action, Rudd began, was undemocratic. "We think," he said, "that this is a political repression. Kirk is making a conscious attempt to bust us. If we permit them to do this," Rudd said, "then SDS might die by the end of the year, and this is what the administration wants."

Rudd rambled on. The meeting drifted toward ennui.

Paul Rockwell, the sandy-haired, compact graduate student, rose. "We have a tactical problem," he announced, "in that we're trying to save our ass."

The sense of the meeting was despair. In this bleak session, a slight black-haired sophomore radical named Steve Komm began to read a "Proposal for a Spring Offensive Against Columbia Racism."

Steve Komm does not appear to be a belligerent young man. One of his arms is slightly deformed. He looks very intense, very intellectual, very serious, but hardly what once was called a club fighter. Still, at eleven o'clock at night in a half-empty classroom, Komm bravely read off a set of militant proposals.

Komm's opening suggestion was predictable. The SDS should stage a noon rally at the sundial. After that the demonstrators should march into Low, breaking Kirk's rule again, and confront Kirk with a demand for open hearings on the "IDA Six." Then Komm proceeded to long-range plans.

"Contingency A," he read. "Fist fights, police violence, similar excitement. Steering committee plans larger demonstration, perhaps with campus antiracism coalition [the blacks]. We all pull out quotations from Martin Luther King. If it goes right, we escalate. We have even bigger demonstrations, effectively shutting down afternoon classes until they give in. Five hundred or more people sit in Kirk's and Platt's offices until the demands are granted. Next we get outside help, a sympathy strike."

Komm was the most serious person in the room. Others were grinning. Later, Komm said, "there could be open struggles, perhaps with city cops."

A cheer began, partly sarcastic.

"We get community support," Steve Komm predicted. "Then the black students and the liberals begin to come in. A week later, we have the occupation and blockade of Low Library."

"What?"

"We occupy and blockade Low Library by May 7," Komm persisted, "and continue pressure until the university capitulates."

There was a long and raucous laugh, but within thirty-two hours, the radicals would have taken over Low.

7 KIDNAPPED

THE TEMPORARY DEAN

HIS hair is cropped short, the way a marine officer's might be, and his features are rugged, but not gross. He is trim, past forty, and still youthful. He could be a retired halfback, who goes to the gym regularly, although on consideration he seems light. He is casual and informal and typically, although his name is Henry, people speak of him as Harry Coleman. "Harry," say men with more degrees than he, "may not be a deep thinker. But he's hard-working, loyal and sensible. He was fine as temporary dean."

What is the dean of one's imagination? Swift, fierce and angry, or Inge, spinning out enormous sentences to argue that progress is cyclic, or is the dean one envisions simply an overwhelming disciplinarian? Henry Simmons Coleman is none of these. He is a warm, apparently untroubled man, a champion of geniality. He is a fourth for Saturday golf, an undemanding doubles partner in tennis. He was a curious and accidental target for student violence.

His office is bare when I walk in. By now he is no longer acting dean of Columbia College, but only dean of freshmen, and the new smaller office has not been furnished. He doesn't mind. He relaxes and smiles, talks easily and fully in response to questions.

He was born in New York in 1926—he was just forty-two when he fell victim to the riots. He went to the Hill School at Pottstown, Pennsylvania. After that he meant to go to Princeton; but in the navy during World War II, he was assigned to study at Columbia. He earned his B.A., went to sea and came back to Columbia for postgraduate engineering. He signed on as assistant dean in 1949 and went back to the navy during Korea. "I rowed in the varsity shell," he says. "I don't have to tell you that the Columbia crew wasn't the greatest in the world. But I won my 'C.' "

He is a comfortable middle-class man, with two daughters and a son, and a pleasant home in predominantly white, predominantly affluent New Canaan, Connecticut. His establishment credentials are in order. "For some time I was dean of admissions," he says. "Before that I worked with alumni groups to help recruit good students. There is a kind of oddity here. I was the dean of admissions who admitted Rudd."

He grins. The telephone rings. "Oh, surely I remember you—hello." Coleman looks at me and holds up one finger. "Yes," he says. "I appreciate that. We're doing everything we can. It's good of you to be concerned. Yes. Surely."

Three minutes later he hangs up and starts to explain. "They all want to know—that was an alumnus—can't we just prevent people like Rudd from coming here. Harvard rejected Mark, you know. As if it was as simple as that."

"Did you accept Tony Papert?"

"Oh, sure," Coleman says. "He was a very bright kid. And quite polite. He comes from Great Neck, and he'd started out at Princeton. He was unhappy there, but he made a brilliant record. When he saw me and wanted to transfer here, I recognized that this was an unhappy kid. I think being Jewish had something to do with it; Princeton was a long way from what he was used to in every sense. We were glad to take him in. We thought he'd do better closer to home."

"And Rudd?"

"As far as anyone could tell, Mark was fine. I think he was a Scout leader in high school."

The phone rings again and Coleman winces. He handles the call quickly.

"Well, what's an answer?" I say. "If you screened differently, could you keep out a boy like Rudd, if that's what you want, keeping him out?"

Dean Coleman grins. "I wouldn't propose him as the soundest Columbia man ever. But, look," he says, and the broad open face becomes earnest. "You know what the problem is with these kids?"

I shrug.

"Part of it is between them and Columbia and part is even as they say between them and society. But it isn't only that. If you have a home where there is a strong father, general respect and a good relationship between the father and son, then you aren't going to produce the sort of boy who protests outside reasonable channels. The home with solid father-son relations simply is not going to give us people who believe in disruption as a way of life."

"You mean usually."

"Of course, there'll be exceptions. But mostly boys with a strong sense of their own value and their own identity, which they get in a large measure from their parents, will be constructive. Look, I don't mean they won't dissent. I think the time has been right for dissent. We need some. But the sort of dissent I have in mind is not, uh—"

"Kidnapping deans?"

"Exactly."

"Very well," I say. "Suppose I accept your position. It's at home, not at Columbia, where these riots began. Now, can't you revise your admission procedures to find out who is riot-prone? Then if you feel a boy should be kept out, for the greatest good of the greatest number, keep him out."

Coleman nods. He has thought of this or something like it on his own. "The only way to be reasonably sure of the kind of kid you're getting is to investigate the family. Find out what the relationships are within the home. Is the father a strong man and willful? How does he get along with his son? What does he want the boy to be? Is the mother stable? Has she provided the boy with the support he needs? And you may find you want to go further than that. How do the mother and father get along? Do they fight? Are there clear and well-defined relationships in the home? Does the boy, as he comes out of the home, feel secure, feel that the home will always be there for him?" Coleman pauses and runs his fingers on his desk and starts to examine a pipe. "I'd be very much against anything like that," he says, "any investigation like that."

"Why?"

"Invasion of privacy. I don't think a university has any business poking into things like that. It isn't a university's business, the relationship between the parents of a boy who has merely applied. That goes much too far, don't you agree?"

He is a one-degree man in an academic community and I doubt very much if he can quote either Pliny by rote. He is a middle-class man and he has suburban trappings and he likes to talk sports and he once rowed in the crew; but an important thing is that he thinks for himself.

"You wouldn't run an investigation even at the risk of having another Mark Rudd at Columbia?"

"That's right."

"I read somewhere that your kidnapping was really a kind of lark. Could you describe it briefly?"

"Very frightening," says the dean who admitted Mark Rudd, and who still believes in privacy.

The questions they raise and the men of academe themselves are rarely as simple as they seem.

* * * * * *

On the morning that their revolution began, the leaders of the SDS seemed to be in trouble. Their college careers were all but ended. The future of their organization was uncertain. In a sense, Mark Rudd was up against a wall.

Their response was fierce and somewhat undirected. Late at night and early in the morning of April 23, they worked on plans. They would meet at the sundial. They would enlist black support. They would invade Low Library. And then what? They weren't sure. They would have to see.

When representatives of the Students Afro-American Society agreed to join them that morning, the whites felt less depressed. A new unity with the black power establishment could build a formidable bloc. The SAS, begun as a discussion group during 1964–65, had been organized to create in Columbia College's Negro students a "stronger sense of identity." There were fewer than 50 blacks in the College at the time. Presently more were admitted—27 in the 1967 freshman class —and the SAS assumed a new strength and unforeseen militance and independence. Although SAS had worked with white groups once or twice, by 1968 the blacks were insisting on the right to walk by themselves. In one black's sentence: "How can we trust a middle-class kid from the suburbs, who's playing radical?" But now, on April 23, the blacks were willing to work with, if not to trust, Rudd, Freudenberg and the others.

Combined, the blacks and the radicals were 400 strong; 400 on a campus of 17,500. But they were a vanguard, an arrow of anger, behind which in that troubled spring hundreds and eventually thousands of moderates would follow.

Reacting to the growing radical activism, campus conservatives banded together as the Students for a Free Campus. On the morning of April 23, the conservatives distributed a mimeographed leaflet, calling for a counteraction.

"Tired?" the flyer began. "Tired of a university that gives virtual immunity to SDS agitators while you are subject to immediate suspension if you toss a paper airplane out a window?

"Can democracy survive at Columbia University?

"Will Mark Rudd be our next dean?

"Be [at the sundial] and be prepared."

There was a clear danger of violence, "a desperate situation," David Truman said long afterward. "The only thing worse than police on campus beating students," he added, "would be students beating other students."

The morning of the twenty-third was cool and clear and windy. It should have been a day for flying kites. On campus students stood about in knots, talking intensely. Some tried to be humorous. Most were charged and nervous.

"Do you think the faculty gives a damn?" said a tall, thin, blond boy in an open-throated shirt.

"I don't know how they pick those guys." The boy next to him was almost as tall, but dark-haired. "They're going to give this course in Afro-American history next fall, so who do they get to teach it? A white."

After a discussion with Truman, Harry Coleman had asked several dozen college faculty members to attend the sundial rally. Their presence might forestall violence. Along College Walk, the broad stone pathway that bisects the campus, instructors were chatting with students.

"I don't condone the gym," one teacher said, "and I don't condone violence, either."

"What do you condone then, sir?"

"Moderation. Caution. Reason."

The student winced, and spun away.

As the morning warmed toward noon, the conservatives issued a second flyer.

The headline cried: *Cool it for Victory.*

"We will have as many students as possible on the Low Plaza steps," the conservatives warned. "We are going to be on TV and in the national press and we are going to give them a real show. SDS will have to wade through our picket line to break the rules, to trample our rights; and America will watch them. So cool it. We are going to win by making the SDS look like dirt." This was the counsel of a number of administrators, including Coleman, in the days to come. No violence. Above all, no violence. The academic community is on trial. A final word from the SDS was quoted in that morning's *Spectator.*

The two questions at issue are: Shall the university continue to support materially the U.S. government's imperialist policies? Shall the university repress political activity against it? Join us in demanding:

   1. An end to Columbia's ties with the IDA.
   2. That no one will be punished for opposing Columbia's unjust policies.
   3. That all accused [the Rudd group on probation for the earlier demonstration inside Low Library] be granted an open hearing before students and faculty, with due process.

Somehow, through weariness perhaps or simple haste or self-involvement, the white radicals forgot the critical issue, the issue that had forged their unity with the blacks. In their last pre-battle bulletin, the radicals forgot to mention the gym.

Nick Freudenberg, tall, bespectacled and topped with a halo of hair, spoke first. It was four minutes after noon. The crowd numbered five hundred, including forty faculty members and, in great majority, the uncommitted curious. In front of Freudenberg, on the long series of steps leading toward Low, pickets from all factions carried signs. "Open Hearings for the IDA Six." "End University Racism." "Send Rudd Back to Cuba." "Kirk is Illegitimate." "SDS Must Go." Behind, on the long mall toward the library named for Nicholas Murray Butler, the lawn was brilliant green and a brightness of tulips bloomed.

"Columbia University," Freudenberg shouted, "is a part of the war machine, because it is affiliated with IDA. Grayson Kirk and David Truman are war criminals." So it began, and a cool wind stirred the flowers.

Cicero Wilson, intense, thick-necked and black, was next. He took the bullhorn from Freudenberg and began with a cry: "This is Harlem Heights, not Columbia Heights." The crowd applauded. "What would you do if somebody came and took your property? Took your property as they're doing over there at Morningside with this gym? You'd use every means possible to get your property back, and this is what the black people are engaged in right now."

Cicero Wilson and the gym excited the crowd's sympathies, but Wilson was preaching a strange radicalism. He was invoking property rights.

Mark Rudd walked behind the sundial with Dean Alexander Platt. The dean had a letter from Vice-President Truman. Rudd read it slowly, shook his head and showed it to his friend Lewis Cole. They talked for a while and then Rudd smiled.

Out front Wilson was shouting, "When they're speaking about racists, if you want to know what they're talking about, go look in a mirror. You people better realize that you condone Grayson Kirk with his rough-riding over the black community. But do you realize when you come back there may not *be* a Columbia University? If insurrection occurs this summer, do you think that this white citadel will be bypassed?" Wilson drew an ovation.

Rudd followed and talked quietly. He made the customary attack on the Columbia administration. There were neither cheers nor heckling. Rudd droned on and began to lose the crowd.

"All right," Rudd shouted commandingly. "I have a letter here from that son-of-a-bitch Dave Truman." The crowd abruptly silenced. "Listen and you will understand this man's mind." Rudd read, interspersing comments of his own:

Dear Mr. Rudd:

You are aware of the university rule against demonstrations within buildings. Since it is the announced intention of the SDS to conduct a demonstration inside Low Library today and since there would be a hazard both to people [*that's important*] and to property [*maybe that's not so important*] Low Library has been closed, except to individuals who have scheduled business there.

If your group wishes to present a petition, I shall be glad to meet with you in McMillin Theater immediately.

Sincerely yours,
David B. Truman
Vice-President and Provost

The entire SDS and SAS membership could be seated in McMillin Theater, which has a capacity of 1,100. Truman felt that if he sat on the stage, with perhaps a dozen selected faculty members seated behind him, a rational discussion might develop. But here, as we would later see at Chicago and San Francisco, the politics of liberalism was overmatched against the realpolitik of confrontation. There was not going to be any sensible dialogue, much less an interchange of ideas between the young radicals and Dr. Truman. The radicals did not want dialogue. Dialogue could blunt their resolve. But this late in the season of riot, Truman still did not understand his adversary. Rudd's radicalism, erratic and uncertain, was not an ideal but a passion in an existentialist sense. Sartre distinguishes opinions, which he respects, from passions, which cannot be argued. By now Rudd's passion, which he called radicalism, was to rebuild Columbia, and to rebuild society and to lash out at authority, and himself to lead.

"Truman gives us this alternative to present a petition or to meet," Rudd shouted, "because he is a very liberal man. After we've gone to the son-of-a-bitch a million times and he hasn't responded to us, now he asks us to meet with him. Our force has brought him down. But this letter creates a problem."

He then proceeded to list choices for the crowd. He was sorting possibilities in his mind, not certain which was best. "We could make a demonstration inside McMillin, with chanting. We could have the students decide about the discipline stuff against us. We could have Truman talk to us about IDA. But if we go to McMillin we will just talk and go through a lot of bullshit."

He rambled for four minutes. Although radicals call this listing of choices "participatory democracy," it is not really democratic at all. The speaker controls the choices. Rudd did not list, "We can hear out Dr. Truman." Instead he said, "We could have Truman talk to us about IDA." He did not list disbanding. He was stacking the deck, in full view of one thousand witnesses and loudly calling for fair play. He was also moving too slowly. He talked until the fires of revolution dimmed.

Tom Hurwitz, a radical junior at Columbia College, finally climbed to the pedestal. Hurwitz wore a red bandanna round his forehead. "Did we come here to talk," he shouted, "or did we come to go to Low?" He shoved his right fist toward the sky and started forward.

At the foot of the final steep flight of steps that led up to Low Library, a hundred counter-demonstrators waited. As Hurwitz began his charge, most of the hundred spread across the steps as a barrier.

It was a raggle-taggle kind of charge. First Hurwitz led. Then Rudd was able, with his good legs and high resolve, to retake the lead. Within and around the crowd reporters ran and photographers trotted, spun, snapped and trotted again. A tall professor of Spanish shook his head. "In Europe," he said, "I've seen what happens when students take over a university. We can't let that happen here."

Erwin Glikes, a short, balking young assistant dean of students, ran alongside Rudd, crying, "Stop this march, Mark. Call it off." Once or twice he tugged at Rudd's sleeve. Orest Ranum, an associate history professor, tried to hold back the crowd calling, "Come on, now. Come on."

The crowd, ignoring faculty, mounted the steps of Low, closing with the barricade of conservative students. There the pace slowed. No one was running to a fight. Briefly the forces rubbed against each other. There were shoves but no punches. The demonstrators shouted "IDA must go." The counter-demonstrators shouted "SDS must go." "We don't want bloodshed here," Rudd called. "Let's try the security entrance."

He moved to a doorway in the southeast corner of Low that is always kept open and is used by campus police. Some students describe these guards as "rent-a-cops."

Three security men saw Rudd's crowd coming. They slammed the door. Twenty students managed to push it open. The students relaxed, and the the door shut again. This time the rent-a-cops locked it. Low was secure.

"Now what do we do?" Mark Rudd was climbing on top of an inverted wastebasket. "Tell 'em," someone said, "we could have gotten in, but someone might have gotten hurt." Rudd did and began again to list choices.

"We can go back to the sundial. Or we could go to the gym site. We want to think about what we do next, because we've got the bastards on the run and we don't want to make any mistakes."

"Gym site," someone yelled. "Gym site." The cry erupted from a dozen places in the crowd. Young radicals rushed toward a campus exit on Amsterdam Avenue and 117th Street. The crowd was flowing away, disintegrating, and Rudd was standing on the trash basket. Cicero Wilson led the vanguard. White SDS boys were following a black. They trailed him toward Morningside Drive, past the brick residence of Dr. Grayson Kirk with its steel window shutters, on to the disputed acres of Morningside Park where workmen were roughing out the foundation for the gymnasium.

Back at Low, the counter-demonstrators were amused and relieved by what had happened. Rudd, off the basket, was talking with a friend.

"Mark's lost command," someone said, cheerfully.

"No," corrected Rodger Huehner, editor of a student newspaper. "He never really had command."

"Let's start chanting," Rudd said to Ted Gold.

"Okay," Gold said.

The two SDS leaders began: "IDA must go, *I—D—A must go.*"

The counter-demonstrators laughed. Rudd's head was low. He walked rapidly away.

"Rudd *will* go," a counter-demonstrator shouted. People laughed at the angry radical.

When Rudd was halfway across Low Plaza, a dark-haired student told him, "The action's at the gym site." Rudd broke into a run and rejoined the demonstrators he meant to lead while they were filing toward Morningside Park. In the early afternoon sunlight, the gym site shocked those who remembered it in other springs. On a slope of handsome parkland, where elegant shade trees had grown beside polished granite outcroppings, the site showed as an open wound. The grass was gone. The bare earth, sloping toward Harlem, looked sandy; stone chips from demolished boulders were scattered about. The disorder of the land matched the disorder of the day.

The cyclone fence protected this barrenness. Inside twenty policemen waited. They were locals, from the 26th Precinct, less likely to overreact than cops from somewhere else.

The students burst into the park along a dirt path near 114th Street and headed for a gate. The police tried to close the gate, but the students swung it open. Then, ignoring the police, they tore at the fence. A group of 50 did the actual work. Another 150 students proceeded farther down the hill to watch. The radicals ripped the wire mesh out of the ground and then, with ten or twelve hands working at the same point, pulled a fence pole from the earth. Bodies leaned, and a stretch of fence was down. Proceeding quickly, the activists leveled the fence for a length of thirty feet.

The policemen stared intently. Looking at some of these men, who were there to protect property, one could see jaw muscles working furiously. A lieutenant called, "Let's move in." The policemen rushed without raising clubs and began dragging demonstrators away from the fence. Someone lifted a patrolman's cap and sailed it downhill toward the watching crowd. There students flung the cap, shouting, "Hey." The police continued to pull bodies from the fence.

Fred Wilson, Columbia '70, wrestled with a patrolman. "You're under arrest," the policeman shouted. Student and policeman struggled. A circle of students gathered around them. "Let him go, let him go," the students chanted. The policeman slipped and fell into the rocky dirt, but kept his grip on Fred Wilson. One or two students began kicking at the cop. Wilson broke free but did not move away. Another detachment of patrolmen, clubs out, charged down the hill. They reached the fallen officer and collared Wilson. The student demonstrators grew subdued, as though suddenly aware that they had pressed too far.

Someone said, "Get them to cool it, Mark." Rudd nodded and ran up to the lieutenant. "Call them off," he said, "and I'll try to get things quiet." The lieutenant agreed and the police backed off. Wilson was with them, arrested. He would be charged with felonious assault and two other counts.

Rudd climbed a pile of dirt and for a third time that day listed choices. "We can go back to the sundial," he said.

"There are three hundred people at the sundial now," a student shouted. "Let's go to Low. That's where the power is."

"I say no to that," Rudd said. "I say we ought to call a student strike for the day after tomorrow. They arrested that guy and they either free him tomorrow or we go out on strike."

A new chant grew: "Free Fred, Free Fred, Free Fred."

"The strike won't work," Robbie Roth shouted at Mark Rudd. "We don't have time to organize it. Let's go to the sundial. There's a big crowd there. We can still salvage it, man."

The demonstrators began to leave. A dusty pall hung over the site. The students trudged up the dirt path. Most looked tired. Faces showed bruises. All the boys were covered with fine dust, the dust of battle. They were retreating and they had lost one of their privates, but the radicals had made a point with which Columbia administrators must now reckon. For the first time, this raggle-taggle band had placed its bodies on the line to fight police for what its people believed. In the coming days, the physical courage of students would be one factor precipitating tragedy.

Young people, like primitives, enjoy chanting. Students chant rhythmic cheers at football games and sing nonsense songs and make up words and phrases. Rhythm appeals to them and beyond that there is a security in knowing that you are chanting exactly what the person six rows away is chanting and that you both know how the chant began and how it will end. Tired and worn, the radicals marched back to the sundial, not with a single chant but two.

"Free Fred, Free Fred," one group was shouting.

"Gym Crow Must Co," chanted the majority.

The boys spilled loudly into Amsterdam Avenue, a busy two-way street that forms the eastern edge of the main campus. They ignored traffic. Horns blew. Drivers leaned out of the windows. "What the hell are you doing?" "Watch the goddamn lights."

Back on the campus, Rudd climbed the sundial pedestal again. More than 300 students waited to hear him. For a fourth time he tried participatory democracy. "I've sent runners to several points," he shouted. "They'll scout for the best alternatives."

"Jesus Christ," someone said. "Alternatives again."

Rudd's speech was halting. "We're learning to criticize and learning from our mistakes," he said. He rambled about the student strike and other possibilities. Then Cicero Wilson replaced him on the sundial. "SDS can stand on the side and support us," Wilson said, "but the black students and the Harlem community, they'll be the ones in the vanguard."

Challenged, Rudd shouted, "What are your proposals?"

"We're not proposing anything," Wilson said. "You people are going over there protesting the gym. Well, I'll tell you something. You're not too much better than Columbia. You're trying to decide what black people should be doing."

It might have ended then. Rudd functions well in chaos, but now the chaos and his own uncertainty might have brought his movement down. He had gone from the sundial to storm a locked building; and when that failed, he made a speech to a disappearing crowd; and after that, he watched and goaded while others wrestled with policemen; and now he was back at the sundial again, bickering with a black.

In this darkness of Rudd's career, a black student from the School of International Affairs rescued him. Mild-looking William Sales, who wears eyeglasses, did not list alternatives. He made a crisp, coherent speech.

"I thought up until this stage of the game," Bill Sales began, "white people weren't ready, but I saw something today that suggests that this is not true." The crowd was instantly attentive. "Maybe you are ready. Maybe. Because when the deal hit the fan you were there. You were with me. And this is all we want. If you're talking about revolution, if you're talking about identifying with the Vietnamese struggle, you don't need to go to Rockefeller Center, dig? There's one oppressor— in the White House, in Low Library, in Albany, New York. You strike a blow at the gym, you strike a blow for the Vietnamese people. You strike a blow at Low Library, you strike a blow for the freedom fighters in Angola, Mozambique, Portuguese Guinea, Zimbawe, South Africa.

"You did pretty well today," Sales said. "Hope it's not an isolated incident. It was beautiful. Almost soulful. All we need is some sophistication. The only way you win in a technological society is by your superior/organization and your superior commitment. And that's what we need. Next time we go down there [to the gym site], TPF [Tactical Patrol Force of the New York Police] will be waiting. An incoherent mob will not be able to deal with them. So we have to be more sophisticated. Need I say more? I don't want to get arrested for sedition."

At this point, then, black really was better. Bill Sales's words brought everyone together. When Sales was through, Rudd regained the sundial, confident again, and began asking rhetorical questions. "They arrested one of our guys," he shouted. "Are we going to allow them to take one of us?"

"No," came an answer from twenty or thirty boys.

"Are we going to waste time waiting for them to release him?"

"No." Fifty now.

"They got one of ours. Now are we going to take one of theirs?"

"Yes."

Low was locked tight. "Let's go to Hamilton," Rudd shouted. The narrow path from College Walk to the entrance of Hamilton Hall is bordered on the left by the building and on the right by a high, luxuriant hedge. With Rudd, Sales, and Nick Freudenberg marching in the front, a crowd of more than a hundred walked down the path, being careful not to trample the hedges. They were going to Hamilton Hall to face the dean.

Harry Coleman was having lunch at the faculty club, about three blocks away. It was ten minutes before he returned. The time was 1:40. The massed crowd started chanting, "We want Coleman." "Hello, Mark," Coleman said. "What's going on here?" A path opened and he walked inside the building.

Rudd answered by listing demands. No IDA. No gym. No discipline against the IDA six. "Another demand," Rudd said, "is that our brother who got busted today—some sort of assault charge—that he be released."

"Mark," Coleman said, "I have no control over the majority of demands you have made, and I have no intention of meeting them under circumstances like this." The crowd milled, shouting. Coleman was wearing a light brown suit. Rudd wore a plaid shirt and blue jeans. "As far as disciplinary actions, where I do have control," Coleman said, "I'm certainly not going to advocate policy change right now. I have no intention of calling the president or the vice-president under these circumstances."

"Well, Dean Coleman," Rudd said loudly, "I guess we're going to keep you here." The path closed behind him. Coleman was standing with William Kahn, the proctor, and Dan Carlinsky, the director of public relations for the College.

Coleman entered his office with Carlinsky and Kahn and closed and locked the door. A crowd of demonstrators pressed after him. When the old hardwood doors closed, boys stood before them, arms behind their backs, barring the way. There was no exit now, nor would there be a turning away. The dean and his cohorts were on their home ground; still, in a sense, they had been kidnapped.

8 A DAY'S OCCUPATION

THE ENGLISH GIRL WHO SLEPT
AMONG THE BLACKS

SHE wears large round earrings and a short skirt, and she walks smartly to the table as she comes for lunch. It is the middle of a hard day's teaching at New York Medical College, and she means to enjoy the break. She is a groomed and poised young woman rather than pretty. "Yes," says June Finer, M.D., "I will take a drink, thank you." Then to the waiter, in a polite, commanding British way, "A Tanqueray martini, very dry, please."

She turns and smiles. She is in her early thirties, a physician and an assistant professor of medicine, and she has faced onrushing cops in Chicago and in Washington and at Columbia. But she retains, as some English women do, an air of youth, incense of innocence. "Nothing," she says, forcefully, "that happened in Chicago during the convention was any worse than what went on at Columbia. The only difference is that the convention was more intensely covered. Chicago got more national publicity."

"I understand what happened at Columbia made you cry."

"No," she says. "I was very upset, but I didn't cry." It is obviously a point of pride. "There was a time when the police wouldn't let me get to my patients, get to people whom they had injured and who needed treatment. That made me very upset, you know, the helplessness of it. I lost control a little bit. But I didn't cry."

"Were you hurt?"

"I was knocked over in one police rush, and my knees were skinned, but not badly."

"Were you wearing a medical outfit?"

"You mean a white jacket? Yes, and I was carrying a black bag. We wondered sometimes if the white jacket didn't make a target for the police." She smiles. "I treat policemen as well as students, you know. I treated one policeman at Columbia who had been bitten."

"Where?"

"In the belly. In a way it was amusing, those tiny teeth marks in that enormous belly."

We order lunch. Dr. Finer will have chef's salad. We are meeting in a small, rather faded hotel dining room just off Fifth Avenue, close to the hospital where she teaches. Some forgotten waltz issues from hidden speakers. The waiters are in their sixties. The white tablecloths are long, almost touching the floor, like women's skirts during the time, after World War II, of the so-called New Look.

But there is a gentility here, a sense of propriety and station, and it is hard to imagine, while speakers play the music of Wayne King, policemen knocking down this young lady physician. It is harder still to imagine this young lady, with the large earrings and the British intonation, braving the violence of riot.

"Dick Hausknecht of the Medical Committee for Human Rights called me at five o'clock in the morning," she says. "You can describe Dick as a concerned health professional. He's one of the doctors who involves himself in civil rights and other important causes. He'd been invited to Hamilton by the blacks to set up an aid station. Dick teaches at Mount Sinai. He's an obstetrician."

June smiles. Her hair is severely upswept. "Dick's one of the few O.B. men who has political sense, political compassion."

She finishes part of her salad and is through eating. "You find," she says, "more politically sensible American doctors are in psychiatry than in any other field. You know Tom Harper? He's a psychiatrist. The police actually clubbed him inside Low."

"I know."

"Dick Hausknecht called me very early on the morning of April 24. It was a Wednesday. He said they needed help in Hamilton. So I went."

"I didn't think there were any whites in Hamilton."

"That isn't true. I went there and we got along and they trusted me. There were minor injuries, squashed fingers, sprained ankles, scalds, splinters. A few days later we began to get colds and coughs and gastric disturbances. They had brought blankets and I sent out for some medicines. Aspirin. Maalox. I was setting up the simplest kind of infirmary and we blocked off a room.

"I stayed in Hamilton constantly. There were quite a few people there, even in the beginning, and then people came in from outside."

"From Harlem?"

"I suppose."

"I mean were these new people also black?"

"They certainly were." The waiter brings coffee, but June Finer says she would not care to have a brandy. "I want to get *some* work done this afternoon."

"Where did you sleep?"

"In one of the upstairs rooms in Hamilton."

"Were you concerned?"

"Why should I have been? They liked me and respected me and I they." She looks distant and begins to drink the coffee.

"They were beautifully organized, you know, beautifully purposeful. They got food from the community, and gradually my infirmary supplies increased. I had alcohol, bandages, antiseptics, but no prescription drugs, no injectables, no syringes. I wasn't setting up a field hospital, but an aid station.

"There was a hospital right around the corner, but the university medical service could not be counted on even to provide first aid. There's an attitude there that's comfortable for doctors. When the trouble is unusually severe, don't get involved."

Dr. Finer comes from a British medical family. Her father was a physician and she always assumed she would be one too. Not for the money. Relatively few British doctors are handsomely paid. It was just something that June wanted to do, and when she was old enough, she studied at Middlesex Hospital, an affiliate of the University of London. Later, America piqued her curiosity. She emigrated, studied further and opened practice as an internist at Chicago. She is not a mercenary woman, not economically competitive, and the avarice of the American medical profession distressed her. She abandoned practice for the public health service and after that, she started teaching. Still June Finer has not forgotten that the primary work of the doctor is healing, binding up wounds, regardless of anything else, including fee.

"There are a number of us in medicine here who feel that," she says. "Not enough but a number." The waiter fills the coffee cups again. "We felt rather alone against the establishment, the AMA and the big hospitals and the impersonality and the rest. It was the civil rights movement that got us together. In the summers when things were really bad in Mississippi, we set up the Medical Committee for Human

Rights and sent doctors to look after the people who were trying to register black voters. They weren't local doctors."

Other committees developed out of the first, most pledged to help minority groups, and members of unpopular causes get decent medical care. June felt at home practicing without fee among the blacks of Hamilton. She was happy working there. She found the people "organized and realistic." They understood that the police might use tear gas or mace. They wanted to be prepared as best they could.

"We have a certain amount of medical experience with mace," she says over coffee. "The recommendation is to shield the face with wet rags and to wash affected areas as soon as possible. For tear gas, water helps.

"Everyone was meeting constantly on other matters, of course. But there was time, and we got together in some classrooms and went over details."

The ancient waiter hovers. Dr. Finer ignores him. "There were not as many women as men," she remarks, "and the leaders worked out an ingenious plan. When the police came, the group would march out in a column, three abreast. The first third would be all male. The police, if they wanted to fight, would have to fight them first. The second third consisted of men on the outside, on each flank, and women in the middle. Then the back rows again were solidly male. These students were protecting their women." She smiles. She is a disciplined woman and she dislikes disorder. "After a few days in Hamilton, I went to Fayerweather for a while. Almost everyone there was white and liberal.

"You can't imagine greater contrast. The blacks in Hamilton knew reality, mace, tear gas, defense. In Fayerweather it was endless seminars, political debate, talk, all talk."

There is no doubt which group Dr. June Finer of London, Chicago and New York, physician to minorities, prefers. Then she is off, a brave unlikely radical, thanking the waiter in aristocratic tones.

*   *   *   *   *   *

No one had a monopoly on courage, or even righteousness, at the desperate hour when Richard Hausknecht's call roused June Finer. Harry Coleman was on the telephone, too. The dean had endured sixteen hours of kidnapping with calm and reason but now he was becoming alarmed. He dialed David Truman at Truman's apartment on Riverside Drive, awakening the vice-president.

"It's getting dangerous," Coleman said.

"What's the matter?"

"We have a report that some people here have guns."

"Where are they?"

"Outside. Our doors are still locked and we don't know exactly what's going on. Apparently the black students have been joined by outsiders from Harlem. And the report is that these outsiders have brought guns."

"I'll call the police at once," Truman said.

"You don't have to go that far," Harry Coleman said. "The bars on the windows of my office are at ground level. Get a tow truck to rip them off."

Mark Rudd was gone from Hamilton by now, along with all the whites. June Finer had not yet arrived. The shaky union between white radicals and black power advocates was dead. And so were prospects for peace at Columbia.

As soon as the demonstrators imprisoned Coleman, the movement acquired new importance. The many serious events of the day proceeded inexorably. In retrospect they possess a sense of dramatic inevitability: first the physical fight with a policeman, then the arrest of Fred Wilson, now the imprisonment of Dean Coleman. But the incidents had not been planned. They were true happenings. The rebels drifted to escalation.

After Dean Coleman disappeared, a half dozen muscular young men detached themselves from the conservative counter-demonstrators and stationed themselves in front of his wooden doors. They were going to protect the dean. Rudd ignored them. He was striding the lobby of Hamilton, an ornate hall heavy with marble pillars, and writing names on a little pad. The protesters were gathered at the lobby center. One corridor was clear on each side so that other students were free to enter or leave classrooms. The protesters wanted no violence. "I felt this was a simple sit-in," says Josie Duke. Rudd shouted for attention and proposed a steering committee. Among the names were Bill Sales and Ray Brown (but not Cicero Wilson) from the SAS and Freudenberg, Gold and Rudd himself from the SDS. In a discussion that followed, Cicero Wilson's name had to be added.

Sales threw a challenge at the whites. "I want to see what you grays can do," he shouted. "Can you white people tie up Columbia? Can you beat the administrators?

"That's what it's about," Sales said. "All right. We're going to stay right where we are. We're going to feed you. If it gets cold tonight, we're going to keep you warm. We're going to get this place together, man."

The steering committee went upstairs to draft a statement of position. When they returned an hour later, they had adopted six basic points that would remain as long as the protest movement.

One tactic in the politics of confrontation is to mingle the feasible with the unfeasible. Feasible demands give a movement the appearance of rationality. Liberals may be seduced into believing that there can be dialogue between contending parties. But the radicals want not dialogue, but confrontation and victory. Extreme demands make certain that confrontation will continue. (That Columbia has since largely met the six demands confuses some radicals. As one observes, "I guess we should have gone for twelve.")

Point one, the precondition, was amnesty for the original "IDA Six," the group on probation, and a general amnesty to everyone in the present demonstration. Unless this point was granted, the radicals said they would not discuss their other demands. These were:

• An immediate, permanent halt to construction of the Morningside Park Gymnasium.

• An end to university affiliation with the Institute for Defense Analyses and the resignation of President Kirk and Trustee William A. M. Burden from the IDA executive committee.

• Abandonment of Kirk's ban on indoor demonstrations.

• Resolution of all future "judicial decisions"—questions of student discipline—by a committee of students and faculty.

• University agreement "to use its good offices" to have police charges against demonstrators dropped.

The new steering committee loped downstairs shortly before 3 P.M. Rudd read the demands aloud. People cheered each point. "We propose," Rudd shouted, "that we stay right here, until these demands are met."

More cheers.

"Look," Rudd said, "we really can't tell who's with us by the yelling and clapping, although that's fine. People who plan to stay here until these demands are met, raise your *left* hands." Scores and scores of left hands shot up. The lobby outside the imprisoned dean was festive.

Behind the wooden doors and the strong silent guards, Dean Coleman, Proctor Kahn and Dan Carlinsky were discussing what to do. The phone kept ringing and the men kept assuring callers that they were safe inside. At 3:30 Coleman emerged. He wanted to make a point for the record.

"Am I to understand that I am not to leave this building?" he asked in a strong voice.

"Yes, you are," said Stu Gedal of Columbia College and the SDS. Gedal wheeled and called to the crowd, "Is he to understand that he is not to leave the building?"

"Yes," the crowd shouted, above a few counter-demonstrators shouting, "No."

"All right," Dean Coleman called. "Are those students who aren't going to let me leave willing to sign a statement to that effect?"

Another shout. "No!"

Coleman returned to his office and made telephone calls to David Truman and Dean Alexander Platt. The three-way conversations produced a university concession. Truman offered to hear out *all* the demonstrating students in Wollman Auditorium. After caucusing, the students agreed to send their steering committee, if the university first granted a general amnesty. No one, not Truman, Platt or Coleman, thought this was satisfactory. Coleman made arrangements for the women of his office staff to depart safely. He returned to his office, behind the wooden doors and the football players, at about 4:35 P.M. He would not be able to pass beyond the threshold until the following afternoon.

At 5 o'clock representatives of the steering committee established a command post in Room 311 of Ferris Booth Hall. The Student Activities Building stands, tall, modernesque institutional architecture, near the southwestern corner of the main campus. The radicals occupied the offices of the Columbia Citizenship Council, a student group that was sympathetic to the demonstrators and that has conducted extensive research on the university's relations with the surrounding community. From two spare modern rooms, some students telephoned friends and other SDS units around New York City, at New York University and at the City College and at Hunter. Others prepared and mimeographed a document, the first issued by the Columbia Strike Committee. It stated the six demands and entered a childlike plea for support:

Join us! In Hamilton Hall now. We're staying until our demands are met.
Already there or coming are: Columbia Band, Soul Syndicate [a black rock group], extensive news media, Prof. Shenton, Prof. Collins, Prof. H.

Brown, Prof. Larson, Prof. Zevin, Prof. Danto and more! Plus group participation by hundreds of students. You wouldn't want to miss it!!

SDS & SAS

Within an hour, the conservative Students for a Free Campus issued
their paper and *their* four demands. Both sides were about even in
prolixity. Here is a digest of the conservative flyer:

Had enough of SDS insolence and contempt for your rights? Let's close
the Authority Gap.
SDS seeks minority rule in the guise of Student Power. They do not
shrink from the use of force, such as imprisoning Dean Coleman. The
Students for a Free Campus calls on the university authorities to:
1. Stop yielding to SDS blackmail.
2. End the demonstration in Hamilton Hall.
3. Punish the demonstration's instigators effectively.
4. Enforce all the rules all the time.
We can save the university from SDS violence and the increasing number
of outsiders in Hamilton. We *can* win.

The Columbia administration ignored the urgings of both sides.

Twilight came noisily into Hamilton Hall. The Soul Syndicate
blared hard rock music against the marble pillars. Although the
promised Columbia band did not appear, Professor Danto, Arthur C.
Danto—B.A. Wayne, Ph.D. Columbia—did. The students and the
Soul Syndicate quieted to hear a philosophy professor who was
crowned with the endorsement of Mark Rudd. "The fundamental
thing called for is discussion," Danto began. "You've made your point
by imprisoning Dean Coleman. Now that's enough of that, it seems
to me."

"Coleman can leave," someone said. Danto made his way to Coleman's office and reported what he had heard.

"We have no desire to remain," Coleman said. "We're ready to
leave right now."

"Fine," said Arthur Danto.

Then Danto stepped out to clear a path for Coleman. None opened.
Danto left and the dean remained imprisoned.

Professor Collins, George R. Collins, B.A. and M.F.A. Princeton,
an art historian, opposed the Morningside Gymnasium on the grounds
of ugliness. He spoke on aesthetics, but none of the radicals in Hamilton very much cared.

Most of the dozen university people who had crowded into the
lobby opposed both the radicals and the radicals' objectives. John

Wellington, the admissions dean, and Alexander Platt suggested that the students go home. But the Reverend William Starr, a tall, bald Protestant chaplain with a "horror for middle-class values, especially when I find them in myself," announced to the demonstrators, "I give you all sanctuary." No one was certain what that meant.

The conservatives wanted Law and Order and All the Rules Obeyed. The administrators conceded that some changes were due, but would not make tangible concessions. And the faculty bumbled. With a few exceptions, the teachers remained remote and passive. What could Fritz Stern, the historian, or Robert Bush, the psychologist, or Wallace Sayre, Eaton Professor of Public Administration, do, when they were confronted with the reality of change? The Columbia faculty could meet. It could resolve and debate, like the 1933 Reichstag. But the faculty could neither act nor influence others. The uprising tore from faculty its academic standing, its office, rank, and automatic power. Stripped of these, the Columbia faculty was only prolix and confused. It is doubtful if anyone who participated in the Columbia chaos could ever take quite seriously the absolutes that academics offer with (absolute) certainty in class.

As night came to Hamilton, the scene inside taxed credulity. Student radicals and their girls—more girls seemed to be coming in all the time—camped around the lobby. Volunteers bore quantities of food. Fruit, bread, canned meat and bologna predominated, but some of the protesters had ingenuity enough to arrange for Chinese dinners from the Moon Palace Restaurant on Broadway. They sat along the west wall of the lobby eating egg rolls, spare ribs and shrimp chow mein from paper plates.

Dungarees were the order of the time. The radicals liked dungarees and sports shirts made of denim or cotton plaid, which they wore open at the throat. Ties were unusual. Girls wore blouses and sweaters with short skirts. A few wore slacks. Several of the girls were grim, a genus of utilitarian female revolutionary. Others looked quite attractive.

Most of the revolutionaries, unlike Rudd, were dark-haired; many boys had let their hair grow. "I suppose," a student said long afterward, "the first thing you noticed was all that hair."

Someone had hung posters of Lenin and Che on the marble pillars. The dean's mahogany doors were framed by large portraits of Stokely Carmichael speaking and Malcolm X surveying all angrily from death. Red was everywhere. Red balloons floated. Red crepe hung. The hall was red. The Soul Syndicate with its effusive music came and went.

Students lounged on the floor, reading comic books, stroking guitars, studying, jawing.

"What do you know. We really did it. Man, we took Hamilton Hall."

"Yeah, but if we're so great, how come we don't win in football?"

"Do you think the cops will come?"

"Who gives a shit?"

"Hey, you see that guy over there. Where's he taking that girl?"

"Upstairs."

"Upstairs?"

"Yeah, people are getting laid all over the sixth floor."

"You're kidding."

"Go up and look."

"Hey, no joking now. But wait. What the hell will we do if the cops come?"

Grayson Kirk had been tied up, canvassing grants. For a college president, the business of fund raising can be stayed for no cause, and David Truman did not interrupt Kirk until late in the afternoon. Then Truman explained that Dean Coleman would probably have to spend the night in Hamilton.

Kirk reacted with anger. "I think we should call the police at once and stop the protest."

"Well, there's some feeling here," Truman said, "that we have a kind of dangerous mix in Hamilton with the SDS and the SAS on one side and the other students opposing them, and we don't want to throw a spark in there."

"What might happen?" Kirk said.

"A hell of a battle," Truman said.

Kirk considered and told Truman, "Well, you do what you think is wisest."

Inside his office, Dean Coleman and his colleagues were taking their imprisonment with good spirits. Since windows at the rear of Hamilton face College Walk, the men were within easy reach of their sympathizers. Coleman opened the windows and colleagues and students passed essentials through the bars: towels, razors, a toothbrush, hero sandwiches, cans of beer, a bottle of Canadian whiskey, two fifths of Scotch.

For ten hours, the men had complete confidence. They were well fed. They could telephone outside.They had a table radio tuned to WKCR, King's Crown Radio, an AM station that transmits a wattage just powerful enough to reach the immediate Columbia area. WKCR was broadcasting a complete account of the action. Coleman, Kahn and Carlinsky ate, had a drink or two, listened to the radio and heard announcements called over bullhorns beyond the doors. "There seemed to be a steering committee announcement," Coleman says, "every hour."

Coleman kept in touch with Truman. All the men called home. Coleman told his wife in Connecticut to get a good night's sleep and to kiss the children for him. There was nothing to worry about. He was locked in.

The first alarming turn occurred at 11:30 when black students in the lobby seized the janitor.

"What do you want?" the janitor said.

"Your keys, man."

"I can't give you my keys."

"*All* the keys, man."

The janitor complied. Coleman heard the voices from within. Students who wanted keys might not be content with imprisoning the dean. They might want to do him violence. Coleman, Carlinsky and Kahn pushed desks in front of the doors. Still, the barricade was no guarantee of safety.

The festive lobby mood was disappearing. Numbers of students, belatedly distressed at being party to the kidnapping, or frightened, or simply uncomfortable, got up and went home. Others climbed to the sixth and seventh floors for sleep, or perhaps to go as far, in the semipublic liberated corridors, as their liberated women would allow. "I wanted to make out and I did make out," one student boasts, "just to show the goddamn passive faculty what nonpassivity was. My girl and I call what we did in Hamilton a symbolic fuck."

In the lobby, blacks and whites moved apart. The coalition of the afternoon was cracking. For their part, the blacks distrusted the whites and thought the exercises in participatory democracy were childish. The whites, at least Rudd and his coterie, were unable to win over the blacks and unwilling to follow black leadership.

A number of Cicero Wilson's Harlem acquaintances began arriving after six o'clock. Some brought food and blankets. Others, silent and expressionless, brought a sense of black power. The first group came from neighborhood organizations and from SNCC and CORE. Others are described as "members of the Harlem Mau Maus." By their favorite posture—back straight, feet apart, arms crossed before them—they appear to have been influenced by the Fruit of Islam, the solemn,

muscular guard that vigilantly protects the Honorable Elijah Muham-
mad, messenger of God and leader of the Muslims. To one normally
contained white student, "those men were terrifying ebony machines."

The first split between black and white developed at about ten
o'clock. The SDS strategy, as far as it had been conceived, was simply
to sit. In succeeding days, the sit-in would dramatize the conflict.
Students would talk of nothing else. They would take sides. Since
some radical issues were sound and particularly appealing to young
people, many students would stand with the SDS. Others would oppose them. The great middle, moderate liberals and moderate conservatives, would disappear. The campus would polarize into left and right.
The SDS leaders hoped and believed that the polarization would
radicalize thousands of students. The enduring slogan of the white
radicals was "Join Us."

The blacks were looking for something else. The most militant of
them wanted victory, not recruits, and victory was the physical capture and the symbolic fortification of Hamilton Hall. The men from
Harlem were people who had been raised in rats' alleys, offered no
hope or, worse, false hope as they grew. Above them Columbia, the
elite fortress, towered on the hill, and when they came to Morningside
Heights, they marched as warriors. These blacks, along with their
seeming brothers, the middle-class young blacks who attended the
university, had imprisoned the College dean and had captured a Columbia building. What does the warrior do with conquered territory?
He fortifies it. The blacks, caucusing among themselves at ten, decided
that Hamilton would have to be barricaded.

Rudd responded unhappily. He didn't want to "turn off" the mass
of students, and that would happen if they were kept from Wednesday
classes by a barricade. He didn't want to "alienate all the faculty." A
few other white students spoke in support of Rudd. The blacks
caucused again and told Rudd and a few others that their brothers
from Harlem had brought guns. A rumor started that the blacks had
hand grenades. At least a dozen whites defected.

In this volatile atmosphere, a phalanx of black men, marching in
step, approached the Columbia football players standing in front of
Coleman's doors. "You are relieved of duty here," one black said
quietly. "We're replacing you."

"You're not replacing anybody."

"You want to argue with a gun, man?"

The whites gave way. Black muscle men replaced them in front of the dean's door and stood, arms lightly folded, ready to strike out with the side of either hand in the punishing strokes of karate. The white athletes walked out of the building. Several continued outside and around Hamilton to the dean's barred windows on College Walk. A boy called, "They've got guns in there."

"How many?" Harry Coleman asked.

"I think twelve rifles and some pistols."

It was then that Coleman telephoned David Truman.

Outside in the lobby itself, the blacks were proceeding to make Hamilton monochromic. Bill Sales, the graduate student, who had spoken toward unity earlier, made another statement over a bullhorn. "We ask all white students to leave the building," Sales said.

There were some protests. "Look, everybody," Rudd shouted. "Gather around me so we can leave as a unit." One white radical said, "But what about the dean?"

Nobody answered.

Black power carried the dawn. All the whites came stumbling out of Hamilton, Rudd and the other leaders who had first come to the lobby, young men who had joined in lightly and eaten shrimp chow mein from the Moon Palace and even the lovers, if there ever really were any, who had huddled defiantly, passionately in blankets on the sixth floor.

THIS OTHER EDEN
THE PHYSICIST WHO WENT IN
AND OUT OF THE MOVEMENT

SETH Shulman was twenty-five when Columbia erupted, and preoccupied, as he had been for some time, with elementary particles—the cosmic rays of many young men's fancies. Seth is slim, with dark hair, a neat black beard and a dry sense of humor. "I remember," Seth says, "at one point in the commune there was a lot of talk about what we had on our side. Right. Morality. Decency. And someone said, *Yeah. All they have on their side is the law.*"

He is a physicist, a physician's son, a scholar, compassionate; in short, precisely the kind of middle-class young man that the leaders of the SDS hope to "radicalize." For a time, Seth was swept along by the radical cause and passionate idealism. But only for a time.

Seth sits in a small seminar room on the eleventh floor of Pupin Hall, the center of Columbia's physics department. I. I. Rabi, university professor emeritus, who won a 1938 Nobel Prize, maintains an office on the eighth floor of Pupin. The office of Tsung-Dao Lee, Enrico Fermi professor of physics and winner of the 1957 prize, is a few doors away. Professor Polykarp Kusch, who won the prize in 1955, occupied office 911, until he became an assistant to Cordier. This was the densest concentration of laureates on Morningside Heights.

What Seth wants to discuss is his work. We sit at a table under a blackboard where someone has chalked a maze of physical equations. "Someone is always chalking things to unnerve English majors," I say.

Shulman laughs. "What I'm doing is interesting," he says, "at least to me. If you want, I can show you my lab." I follow him up a flight of stairs, into a hall and to the door marked, "Danger: High Voltage." Inside, an air conditioner hums. "For the computer," Seth says. "We have to keep the transistors cool." During the next half hour or so, he lectures, with demonstrations, on the cosmic ray particles he is trying to find. The particles travel through walls, windows, humans at almost the speed of light, but always at the same speed. Seth is working with three detectors—plastic sheets which produce light whenever a charged particle passes through. The sheets are wrapped in aluminum foil to exclude extraneous light and they are spaced so that the speed of the particles can be calculated. Seth has rigged electronic equipment to tell a computer how frequently the particular particle appears. In a year or so, when Shulman finishes his project, knowledge of elementary particles will have been increased by a trace and he will be Seth Shulman, Ph.D.

We go back to the seminar and he talks about growing up. His father, an allergist, lives in Boston and summers in Boxford. Seth has been sheltered and more than comfortable. He went to Andover, Harvard, studied in France and then, attracted by the laureates, he enrolled in Columbia's Graduate Faculties. He is popular, seemingly easygoing, and has a girl. He is a supertypical nice boy. His doctoral research, nonclassified, is helped by government grants.

"Obviously," Seth says in the seminar, "it's nonsense to oppose *all* government grants." Out the window, far below, stand the old brick buildings of Teachers College. "There is a question about a university helping war research in Vietnam, and there's a question about the way Columbia treats the people in the neighborhood, but there's also a question of oversimplifying."

Seth was going to his laboratory one April morning when he heard that two buildings had been occupied by radicals. He talked with friends, David Osher, a graduate student in social history, and Garry Wasserman, a doctoral candidate in international relations. They agreed that there was some sense in what the radicals and the blacks were saying. "This was *so* important," Seth says, "I knew I had to give up lab work for a while." That is not something Seth would do lightly. "I mean," he says, and the words come slowly, "that here was something where it seemed important to take a stand. Really important."

It is difficult for him to say just what he means. He believes in precision. So many roentgens going from one particular field to another at the specific rate of so many thousand miles per second mean that so many specific particles marked omega have passed through. The information is fed to a computer, which refines and analyzes. Seth likes precision. The radical cause seemed precise and just and, early one morning, he marched in a vanguard of graduate students who occupied Fayerweather Hall. A few conservatives, now calling themselves the majority coalition, came to the door after a while and shouted, "Come on, you goddamn Reds. Come out and fight." But Seth was not a Red, and he was not looking for a fist fight. He was taking a stand at a moment of conscience against an autocratic, cruel and, in some ways, pro-military institution. He says, and still the words come hard, "It was a pretty big step for me."

Fayerweather was never sealed. Until the police onslaught, there was free traffic in and out. But for most of the next five days, Seth Shulman lived (and ate and slept) in Fayerweather Hall, while the particles passing through his laboratory on the eleventh floor of Pupin went uncounted. This was the radicalization the SDS was counting on.

"Boring," Seth says, "is what it was. There were some interesting things, and there was a wedding that was beautiful, but most of the time it was boring, boring talk."

The talks droned, sometimes led by instructors. Columbia was not really a university, but a copying machine, a giant Xerox, turning out people who were imitations of people who were already out in American society. One didn't learn critical economics challenging the system. You learned how to make the system, which was unfair, function smoothly. Seth remembers the Fayerweather meetings as full of trifles.

"I would like to say, and I want to get it on the record, that I personally resent being part of an institution that only turns out copies . . ."

"I don't know if *copies* is the right word."

"Adaptations?"

"No. That's not it, either."

"What the hell's the word?"

"Who the hell cares?"

"Please. Let's come to order."

"An adaptive copy?"

As the days passed, Seth Shulman decided that the forums were not only burdened with triviality, but weighted with prejudice. A number of heroes such as Che Guevara were Christlike, beyond reproach. "It was the night that the cops were coming," Seth says. "We all kind of knew this was it. And there was a lot of talk about Che and starting another Cuba here. I'm not a Communist. I don't particularly admire Che. I don't want to live in Cuba. I remember thinking that if I was going to be busted, it ought to be over something I believed."

The radicalization process reversed more rapidly than it had begun. Seth, a moderate, comfortable in his laboratory, walked out of one of the final Fayerweather exercises in participatory democracy. He stepped into a cool and ominous night.

Then, lest there be any doubt in anyone else's mind or in his own that he was acting out of conscience, not fear, Seth walked a few dozen yards to Avery Hall, the architecture building. There Seth stood with others who were putting their bodies between the police and the people inside. He did not believe in Che, but neither did he believe in police violence. During the bust, when police overran the peacemakers, Seth Shulman was battered by nightsticks. He still bore bruises on his back two days later when he returned to the lab.

*   *   *   *   *   *

More than two hundred white students had been flushed out of Hamilton at 5:30 and Rudd, stubble-faced now and weary, suggested that the setback was a victory. "No one has to know why we left," he said. "We can say it was to open a second front." It was chilly outside Hamilton. Mist veiled the lights on the campus lampposts. To this day, no one remembers who first initiated the next step in the escalation. Some of the rebels went home, but most remained. Then a group of about one hundred "just kind of drifted" over to Low Library where, eighteen hours earlier in daylight, locked doors had blunted their resolve.

They approached the southeast entrance, which leads to the security office, but these doors, usually open at all hours, had been locked. Two sets of wide glass doors protect the entrance. A campus policeman sat quietly beyond them.

The students were indecisive. Technically, they had trespassed, obstructed police and kidnapped a dean. But the next step, breaking and entering, actually shattering glass, made them uneasy. "After all we'd been through," Josie Duke says, "some of the kids were still hung on fucking property rights. When one of the guys grabbed a plank and cracked the glass, a lot of the kids flinched."

The broken glass startled the policeman. He looked up and blinked. The students opened the outer doors and then one—his identity is still guarded—used the plank again and broke the windows of the inner door. Glass shards cut the guard's hand.

Boys in the vanguard, including Rudd and Tony Papert, hurried past. Other campus policemen in the building froze. They had no idea how to contend with a rushing mob, purposeful if messy, in the hour before the dawn.

The leaders charged up flights of marble stairs to the rotunda and to the floor above. There they followed a corridor and, breaking glass for the third time, entered the private office of Grayson Kirk.

The president and David Truman shared a large suite on the second floor. As one enters, passing the secretaries' pen, Kirk's office was to the left and Truman's was to the right. There was only one bathroom, a consideration that would assume significance.

Of the hundred who left Hamilton, only about thirty actually entered Kirk's office. They found a square, high-ceilinged room, and when someone flicked on lights they saw built-in bookcases, pale green walls, a row of gray filing cabinets, a large heavy desk, a portable television, a Xerox machine, a box of White Owl "President" cigars and Rembrandt's *Portrait of a Dutch Admiral,* which has been appraised at $450,000.

Tentatively, the rebels poked about. Someone tapped Kirk's typewriter. Mark Rudd reached for a cigar. Someone else flicked the television on and off. A boy opened a cabinet and held up a bottle of Harvey's Bristol Cream Sherry. "Hey," he called, "see what I found here."

"Hey, where are the files?"

"Maybe there's a file on us."

"There better be."

The radicals began looking for documents to "liberate." They found a memorandum in which Kirk proposed rigging a defense of the gymnasium project as a news story for *The New York Times.* They found letters in which he avoided meeting Marie Runyon, chairman of the Morningside Tenants Committee, local residents who oppose Columbia's expansionism. At length, the haul was disappointing. No secret documents were discovered. There were no messages hinting espionage. Rudd later insisted that the group did come upon a box of condoms.

Within Low, the students themselves were uncertain. After poking about Kirk's office, they gathered in the anteroom, where Rudd and Tony Papert led the discussion. Papert wanted neither violence nor retreat. Rudd said, "Let's go back to Kirk's office and barricade ourselves in." The group herded into the square green-walled room, moved a few desks and was barely settling in, when allies outside shouted, "The cops. There's gonna be a bust. The cops are coming."

"Well, what we ought to do now," Rudd said, "is call a general student strike. Clear out and call the strike for tomorrow."

"Clearing out is retreating," Papert said. "We have to stay. If we stay more and more students will come over to us."

Some stayed. A few, including Rudd, did not. They fled through open windows, climbing over a ledge and down iron grillwork to safety. When the police marched into Kirk's office, only twenty-seven students remained. They were sitting in a circle on the floor. "We didn't know what was going to happen," Papert says, "whether they'd arrest us, or slug us or what. I don't remember if we were singing then. Maybe we were continuing our discussion. We just felt we didn't want to run anymore. We'd run enough."

Campus cops in gray entered with the blue-uniformed city police. Four campus guards removed the Rembrandt. Two others carried out the television set. The city police looked on, auditing an extremely nervous exercise in participatory democracy. A few asked individual students, "What are you doing here?"

The city police assert that they had no authorization to make arrests for the offense called criminal trespass. They were to act only "to avert serious violence." Truman contradicts this and says he did want arrests "if they had to be made." But apparently his hope was that the appearance of police would frighten the radicals out of Low. He had set up machinery for this contingency. Students leaving through the southeast doors, the only ones open, would be asked to surrender their identification cards. Criminal charges would not be pressed, but discipline would be enforced within the Columbia community.

A hundred yards from Low Library, in Hamilton, Dean Coleman was still imprisoned in a building that had been occupied by blacks, many not Columbia people and some with guns. Truman was concerned for Coleman's safety. Kirk was worried about an invasion from Harlem. The morning grew with negotiation, discussion, indecision. The words of various Columbia and police spokesmen came to this:

COLUMBIA: We have considered, and painful as it is, we want you forceably to remove the students from Low.

POLICE: On what charge?

COLUMBIA: Criminal trespass.

POLICE: But you don't have one trespass situation on your campus, you have two.

COLUMBIA: But we don't want any arrests at Hamilton. Just at Low.

POLICE: You are willing to file a complaint charging criminal trespass on your campus?

COLUMBIA: Yes.

POLICE: But you want us to ignore the criminal trespass at Hamilton?

COLUMBIA: We're worried about Dean Coleman. Besides we don't want to infuriate Harlem.

POLICE: We can't work that way. Either we remove *all* criminal trespassers from the campus, or *none.*

COLUMBIA: Let's talk some more.

POLICE: You are really asking us to arrest whites, but not blacks. We can't operate that way.

COLUMBIA: But aren't there times when you arrest only blacks and not whites?

POLICE: Let's talk some more.

It was easy afterward to point to this particular chilly morning, April 24, 1968, and say that resolute action could have averted blood in the small hours of April 30. But Truman was caught in a liberal dilemma. He believed in dialogue, negotiation and the special quality of university ground. To this, Kirk added an exaggerated view of black power. The result was an inability to act, which cost both men their jobs.

The faculty walked to work as the early mist turned to rain. A raw wind blew out of the northwest. Approaching from Broadway down College Walk, one passed a small crowd gathered about Low. Walking closer, one saw students, bearded and ragged after a sleepless night, leaning out the windows of the executive suite. A few sat placidly on the second-floor ledge. Someone had placed a sign in the south window of Kirk's office. In red capital letters, it pleaded, "Join Us." Many did. It was easy to clamber up the bars protecting the ground-floor windows of the summer session office and reach the crowded ledge. There, helping hands and arms waited. Papert's band grew steadily larger; Rudd would rejoin them before noon.

Farther east, at Hamilton, there was no easy access. The blacks had piled desks and filing cabinets against the front doors, effectively closing the building. Draped over the edge of a third-floor balcony, a black lettered sign solicited no recruits. Instead, it proclaimed Malcolm X University. Columbia College had been transformed.

Blacks leaned out of windows on the third floor. A crowd was gathering in the courtyard under them. Wednesday was a normal class day and College classes begin as early as 8:35. Students, walking to Hamilton through the rain, were finding out that no classes could be held, that the blacks had taken their college and kidnapped their dean. They were variously amused and irritated. The loudest were enraged.

"Why don't you go home?"

"Malcolm X can go to hell!"

"He's already gone."

"Why don't you goddamn guys obey the law?"

Like good occupation troops, the blacks maintained discipline and did not acknowledge the taunts.

The majority of Columbia instructors who were scheduled to teach that morning worked in other divisions: Graduate Faculties, General Studies, the professional schools. Most conducted classes as usual. Professors at the college, locked out of classroom and office, assembled in the lobby of Philosophy Hall, which is slightly north of College Walk.

There, Assistant Dean Colahan outlined the events of the night. Daniel Bell, the sociologist, said that he thought it might be helpful for individual faculty members to visit the occupied buildings and talk with the students. Richard L. Greeman, assistant professor of French, had already been in both. "Control of Hamilton," he said, "is not in the hands of students. Militants from outside have taken over. They have weapons and they have gasoline." What about Harry Coleman, then? That was what everyone wanted to know. A general faculty meeting was called for 3 P.M.

The blacks in Hamilton, the mysterious outsiders and the students led by Cicero Wilson, knew that they had caught the university off stride. Coleman was the key to their position. He was also the key to their safety.

Wilson, with his thick neck and bristling hostility, is easily drawn as a monolithic angry black man. But like Bill Sales and Ray Brown, he is much more. Wilson is a black who has cracked the Ivy League. By now, he was nervous, not worried about his Ivy career as much as he worried about the New York cops. Blacks learn early about the white police. They hear that if the police want to make a man cry, they take him into the back room of the stationhouse on 135th. Then they beat him on the kidneys with canoe paddles wrapped in wadding. After a while, he cries. There are no bruises later. If he acts tough again, they hold his head in a toilet and flush and flush. After a while, he goes limp. In Hamilton, the blacks were remembering these stories. Coleman and the other white hostages were insurance against police brutality. It made no sense to let the people go.

Roy Innis, the deputy chief of CORE, arrived at 10 A.M. to praise the young blacks. Standing in front of Hamilton, Innis announced,

"I'm proud of these kids. They've got the dean in what you might call *an extended dialogue.*"

People from SNCC, the United Black Front and three Harlem community groups appeared carrying food and bedclothing. The Hamilton group was preparing for a siege and the news was everywhere. Radio stations and television channels were full of it. The morning *Times* account was incomplete—the black-white split had occurred after its normal deadline—but the afternoon *Post* led with the Columbia story. The front page of the tabloid, which comes out at II A.M., carried a picture of Hamilton under this headline: "Columbia Students Hold Dean Captive."

By midmorning, politicians crowded the campus: Basil Paterson, the black state senator who had opposed the gym, and William Booth, the New York City commissioner of human rights, a Negro who was to leave his job under pressure from Jewish groups. At Columbia's request, John Lindsay dispatched Barry Gottehrer, an intense, dark-haired young man who had been progressively a book reviewer, a sports writer, a columnist and the mayor's expert on defusing racial bombs. Gottehrer mounted his dark charger, arrived and pronounced this bomb alive. "I see some faces in there," he said, "that I recognize. Pretty revolutionary people, who carry guns."

After eighteen hours of imprisonment, Coleman, Carlinsky and Kahn were tired, but well fed. Through the bars on College Walk students passed breakfast: orange juice, scrambled eggs with bacon, toast and sweet rolls, coffee. In their barricaded office within the barricaded building, the men ate glumly. Coleman called home and told his wife that all was well. Privately he was wondering when rescue would arrive. The first policeman to enter Hamilton, a Negro deputy assistant chief inspector named Eldridge Waithe, came with State Senator Basil Paterson, who wanted to discuss negotiations.

Wilson, Sales and Brown, as the steering committee, received the mediators in the lobby and announced preconditions for the release of Coleman: There were to be no arrests of anybody in Hamilton; there was to be no university discipline against any black. It was a few minutes after noon, and still raining. Basil Paterson, who had been struggling futilely against the gymnasium for two years, walked over to Low Library. He found Grayson Kirk in the office of Adam DeNisco on the ground floor. DeNisco is security chief. Paterson repeated the students' conditions.

"The first," Kirk said, "might be acceptable. It doesn't seem imperative that we bring criminal charges against these people."

David Truman agreed.

"But the second is out of the question," Kirk said. "We have to discipline our own dissidents. That's essential."

"I think it's essential that we start negotiations," Paterson said.

"What's at stake," Kirk said, "is not merely Columbia. If these students succeed in disrupting the disciplinary procedure—if discipline and not the violator is suspended—then discipline at every university in America will be weakened. We are on trial here. Other universities will look to us for strength. We intend to demonstrate that at Columbia discipline is not negotiable."

Paterson considered. "Would you promise no expulsions?"

"We are not going to be forced into making promises."

Paterson shook his head. "I know Harlem, Dr. Kirk. Settle this by nightfall." He wheeled and left, his suggestion again to be ignored.

At 2 P.M. Wednesday, two whites, Immanuel Wallerstein, an associate professor of sociology, and Samuel I. Coleman, an associate in the philosophy department, entered Hamilton as representatives of the faculty. Professor Wallerstein teaches Social Change: The Colonial Situation, in which he lectures on the "decline of traditional authorities." He devotes special attention to Africa. Mr. Coleman teaches Ideology and Society, examining "equality, freedom and human nature as related to utopias."

"We can only talk about our preconditions," Bill Sales said, as Cicero Wilson stared solemnly. "No prosecution and no discipline. Until we have those guaranteed, we will not talk further." The academicians left, settling nothing.

At three o'clock, Booth, Paterson and Barry Gottehrer were admitted. The two black politicians spoke to the steering committee about consequences. "You are not only facing the charge of criminal trespass," Paterson said, "but they can charge you with kidnapping as well."

"We haven't kidnapped anybody," Sales said.

"The dean," Gottehrer said, "is locked in."

"But the door," Sales said, "is locked from the inside.' We didn't lock it."

"How can they charge us with kidnapping," Ray Brown asked, "when we didn't lock him in?"

"You had better inform the dean that he is free to go," Paterson said.

The three city officials felt they had made their point, and left. At 3:28 P.M. Sales, Brown and Wilson knocked on the door. Coleman moved with caution. He had no idea who was knocking. The students identified themselves. "We hope," Sales said, "you'd like to leave the building."

Opening the door, Coleman was relieved to see that he was facing unarmed Columbia students, not rifles in the hands of strangers. "We certainly would like to leave," he said.

"Good," Sales said. "We want you to leave."

Coleman stepped back into his office. He picked up his briefcase, put on his raincoat and, with Carlinsky and Kahn, started outside. He was surprised to see the lobby so crowded. The three men proceeded silently to the barricaded doors.

"Make them crawl under a table," someone shouted.

"No," Coleman said. "We won't do that."

"Move the table," Bill Sales ordered. At 3:30 P.M., Coleman, Carlinsky and Kahn, blinking at the sunlight, walked out of Hamilton Hall. "We were treated fine," Coleman told reporters, "and we've been released without any conditions."

Coleman concluded the interview and walked to a faculty meeting at Havemeyer Hall, where he received "the only standing ovation of my life."

Late in the day, the administration ordered all buildings cleared by 6 P.M. The idea was to prevent other occupations. In Avery Hall, northeast of Low, a small, undistinguished building that houses the School of Architecture, students ignored the order. They were used to working late and saw no reason to follow what one describes as "academic whim."

The architecture students were unhappy with Columbia. They were studying an aesthetic craft in a university with "a hodge-podge series of buildings unique in their lack of artistic distinction." That was embarrassing. Columbia's overall approach to urban survival was infuriating. "We decided to sit in," one architecture student says, "just kind of naturally. I mean here we were, maybe sixty of us, trying to learn how to save the urbs and we find that the place that's supposed to be teaching us doesn't give a damn about anything in New York except carving out its private preserve."

The architects' decision excited the radicals. For the rest of the evening, other students were seen entering Avery, within fifty yards of the northeast tip of Low. Classrooms on the upper stories of Avery became bedrooms. At the same time, some architecture students decided to plan a model urban university. They began by designing a new gymnasium to be built within an existing campus.

At 2 A.M. Thursday, April 25, a vanguard of fifty students, many entrusted with building keys, let themselves into Fayerweather. Fayerweather backs onto Amsterdam Avenue. It is similar in size to Avery and stands about thirty yards farther east. Four Columbia buildings were occupied now, and the strongest protest was the shouting of conservative students.

At 1 A.M., on Friday, April 26, a group from Low and a group from Fayerweather converged on Mathematics Hall, a large building on the west side of the campus, near 118th Street. The boys from Low approached quietly. The boys from Fayerweather charged, covering the equivalent of a long block with great speed. The action was planned at central strike headquarters as a quasi-military pincer movement. The plans were unnecessary. Math, undefended, fell without a fight.

The building score now stood: Columbia, 47; students, 5.

10 SONS OF HOPE AND GLORY
THE PROFESSOR WHO EMBRACED
TWO WORLDS, AND WAS SLUGGED

DICK Greeman, Richard L. Greeman, M.A., Ph.D., former assistant professor at Columbia College, has helped poor people organize against slum landlords, including Columbia University. He has tutored ghetto children, unionized dishwashers in the Columbia cafeteria, and although he has battled Columbia, he is deeply sorry he has had to leave her. "I studied at Yale," he says, "but in a way Columbia is my college. It's the place I'm used to."

Greeman is a trim man of thirty, with dark hair, an intense manner and a pointed black beard. When we meet he is in his office, Room 112, Hamilton, a modest basement room. He rises to greet me, smiles, says, "Just a second," and finishes reading a letter. On his desk are copies of two novels by Victor Serge, a contemporary French socialist. Greeman has translated the English versions.

"You heard about my encounter with the police?" he asks, laying aside the letter.

"Bruce Goldman was telling me about it."

"It was pretty rough for him, too," Greeman says. "The police worked him over. The difference is that I was not surprised. The rabbi was."

"I wouldn't place all the blame on the police."

Greeman nods. "Of course. They're functionaries. But I know how they act, how they always act when they're let loose in a radical situation. They get violent." One plainclothesman split Greeman's scalp with a club.

"Even without that incident, and without all the events of spring," Greeman says, "I'd probably still have had to leave Columbia. Someone like me is difficult for senior people here to take. I don't simply write monographs; I'm active. Well, next year I teach at Wesleyan, which seems a much freer place. My wife and I like everything we've seen about Wesleyan except one." He grins. "It's not in New York."

In the stratified, formal and elitist society that is Columbia, Greeman never became a member of The Faculty. Technically, The Faculty is the group of 840 men and a few women who have achieved lifetime tenure. These people are fixed in their positions and assured of pension. Barring secret vices, incontinent lavishness or multiple divorce, they are financially secure for life. When Marcuse talks about free enterprise as "the freedom to starve," he is not referring to The Faculty of Columbia College.

Faculty members who are full professors earn upwards of $18,000 a year. The top figure in humanities is about $25,000. In the sciences it goes considerably higher. A number of science professors double their teaching income by consulting to government and private industry. "For some of these people," Greeman suggests, "the Columbia salary amounts to a tip." Nor are they overworked.

Faculty professors teach as little as one or two or three hours a week. Some call four lecture hours a brutal overload. Their basic work year runs eight months, from mid-September to mid-May. Someone sums up the faculty situation in a witty phrase: The leisure of the theory class.

Faculty members conduct about thirty percent of Columbia College classes. People like Dick Greeman do most of the instructing. In 1968–69, Greeman taught Introduction to French Literature, a survey class conducted in French, and a section of humanities, the two-year review of great works of philosophy and art that is a Columbia man's passport to culture. For these efforts, Columbia paid Greeman $8,750. Meanwhile, his wife, a B.A. teaching in a grade school, was earning $8,300.

"The system," Greeman says in his basement office, "is heavily weighted against teaching. From the time you're hired, you have eight years to make tenure, to be appointed to the faculty. Papers and books count most. If you are ambitious in the academic world, teaching time can seem damn close to wasted time.

"I like to teach. I was a Woodrow Wilson fellow in 1961—and later finished my Ph.D. under a Faculty Fellowship. I went to the Sorbonne —and started teaching as soon as I could.

"Every college has its own individual character. At Wesleyan, I understand there are fewer grades, no course requirements and the students grade the teacher. Here the senior faculty is pretty conservative, but not cliché wasp conservative. There are a lot of Jews. Someone who left here to teach at Yale remarked that at his first faculty meeting in New Haven things looked different. Then he realized. No Jewish faces."

Greeman conceives of a good teacher as a scholar, reading good books with young scholars. He despises taking attendance ("police work"), letter grades and pushing students through a required course, say Humanities. Greeman himself came to French naturally with family encouragement. His father drove an ambulance in France during World War I; Edward "Ted" Greeman's outfit included Hemingway and E. E. Cummings. He came to love the French language and literature, particularly Hugo and Balzac, and wanted to teach. But, for reasons that have been forgotten, he went into the importing business. When Richard showed early proficiency in languages, his father was delighted.

In the basement office, Dick Greeman describes Columbia darkly. "The undergraduate carries the financial load," he says. "The undergraduate is overcharged."

"The administrators say they lose money on every student."

"Do the arithmetic," Greeman says, and he proceeds to on a single sheet of white paper. Calculating the tuition, conservatively, at $2,000 a student, he produces Columbia College income and fees at $5.4 million. (Two thousand, multiplied by 2,700 students.)

Most of the college faculty is also on Graduate Faculties. Greeman contends that the college teaching staff at any one time actually numbers about 150 and that few of the 150 are tenure faculty. He calculates salaries for the teaching staff of 150 at an average of $10,000 a man. The total is $1.5 million.

"Look at that difference," Greeman says. "It's $3.9 million. Now that's not clear profit, of course. There are laboratory expenses. One hundred thousand dollars is generous there. The building is paid for and tax free. It needs to be heated and maintained. Let's allow fifty thousand dollars a year for heat and maintenance. How is your math?"

"Terrible."

"Then I'll calculate for you," Greeman says. "Columbia College is making a profit of about $3.7 million a year."

To the rulers of Columbia, these figures, and minds like Greeman's, are popular as leprosy. It is true that Columbia loses money on many graduate students, who need expensive equipment and meet in small seminars, but the idea that the College and perhaps most private colleges in America are institutional paupers would seem to be fiction.

"What's been happening since World War II," Greeman says, "is astonishing. Before the war, the liberal university, like Columbia, was the final rite for young people moving into the ruling elite. Most of the students were from elite families; a small percentage from lower classes were allowed to move up. Now the university has assumed other functions. Clark Kerr's idea of a knowledge pool is sound. The university is set up to create products. Drugs like tetracycline and the toothpaste fluorides have come out of university laboratories. Then the university trains raw material for the industrial society. It produces technicians in the sciences: engineers, doctors, architects, and in the humanities, too. Humanities programs produce business executives and public relations men."

"And teachers."

"Yes, teachers to perpetuate the system. It would all be very smooth, but for one complication. Students read great books. The university requires it. Great books are dynamite. They set young people in motion, and young people in motion cannot always be controlled." Now he smiles. "They go and sit in buildings."

Greeman was close to his students. His voice is rich and full, and his lectures can be exciting. Bonds developed, and the radicals felt they could trust him. As the occupation of buildings proceeded, Greeman found himself more concerned about students than about anything else.

At 2 A.M. ON Friday morning, Mathematics had been occupied. Inside Low, Grayson Kirk and David Truman, having taken over ground-floor office space as a command post, were telling faculty members they would have to call the police. There were some protests, angry debate.

Dick Greeman was one of twenty-five teachers standing outside Low. "We were hoping to avert violence," he says. The evening comes back to him in the basement office, and he begins to pace back and forth.

"We wore white armbands to signify our faculty status. I was standing in front of the southeast entrance. Uniformed police could pass, but we wanted everyone else entering Low to identify themselves. A tight group of burly men came up. They wore sweaters and raincoats."

The burly men moved quickly. "We are members of the Columbia faculty," said Dick Greeman. "Please identify yourselves."

"We're going through," one of the outsiders said.

Greeman and several others shouted over and over: "We are faculty members. Who are you? Identify yourselves."

A pushing match developed. None of the outsiders showed identification. None wore a badge. When the professors stood their ground, the men became more violent. Finally, someone grabbed Greeman and spun him around. Another man drew a nightstick from the left sleeve of a lumberjack and crashed it into Greeman's skull. Greeman staggered and fell. His scalp gushed blood. The men were plainclothes New York City patrolmen.

Inside Low, David Truman and Grayson Kirk had decided to call the police to clear the campus. Sidney Morgenbesser, the philosophy professor, had been arguing passionately. "If you call the police," he told Truman, "it will be at the expense of faculty blood."

Truman was telling Morgenbesser not to be so dramatic when another professor charged in shouting, with Greeman's blood on his hands.

Truman went white. Presently the police were sent away. "And I," Greeman says, "had the dubious privilege of being the first victim of excessive police force. Later on, I had four stitches, and a long time after that I filed a formal complaint with the police department. It doesn't surprise me that I haven't heard from them."

"You knew what you were doing?" I ask.

"The most dangerous policeman," Greeman lectures, "is the one who isn't wearing a uniform or badge. He's not accountable for his actions because he's not identifiable. The group of us at the entrance to Low wanted to make sure that no one without identification got into the building, got at the kids. We thought that was worth the risk."

Upstairs, on the main floor of Hamilton, where Carl Hovde sits in a carpeted office, it strikes me how odd that the first faculty blood flowed from a man who would never be appointed to The Faculty. And not only odd, but unfortunate; the unfortunate thing is that Columbia could not find a permanent place for Richard L. Greeman. One does not have to like his politics any more than one likes the Humphreyesque liberalism of David Truman to understand that when a university finds a man like Greeman unacceptable, then dialogue dies, homogeneity advances and students are truly deprived.

*   *   *   *   *   *

For seven days, amid rain, apprehension and disorder, the community of Columbia split into two dominant groups. There was the faculty, prosperous, arrogant, verbose, gifted and, when it mattered most, ineffectual. There was the rebellious student body, scruffy, disparate, nervous, horny, vulgar, but above all things, resolute. When the disaster was over, when the police had come and gone and the old norms were being restored, the students had been masters of reality, the real leaders on Morningside Heights. Some expressed their scorn for instructors by wearing buttons mentioning the Columbia professor who fathered pragmatism. The buttons read: "Dewey Is Dead."

There are, to be sure, almost as many ways of regarding the Columbia spring as there were observers. The faculty was never unanimous, and for a time it fragmented into large sub-groups. Among students there was an anti-rebel bloc and a still larger collection of voyeurs. But as the single week of occupation built, two great questions developed. Would the students remain in the buildings, and work out life styles, and define what they believed and stood for? (To some degree they did.) Could the faculty with its potpourri of degrees, and with its expertise in all the disciplines from anthropology to urban studies, move a laggard administration and make peace in its own house, The House of Intellect, in Barzun's term? The faculty could not. The faculty had been content to grow plump at Columbia over all the decades of this century. The plump do not become men of action within a week.

The thought nags that this is a demanding judgment, but perhaps a demanding judgment is the only just judgment for a college faculty; for them, perhaps, Pound's hard Sophoclean light. If a man teaches in freshman English, *I a stranger and afraid in a world I never made*, perhaps he should be able to look behind a freshman's beard, listen through the vulgarities and sympathize. If he teaches urban economy, he should raise his voice against the economic aggressions of Columbia. If he functions with a curriculum that claims to "reaffirm and re-express the aims and the powers of civilization," he should insist upon civilized respect for the needs of all groups, including the needs of students. If he wishes to stand with the statement of Irwin Edman that "it is the mission of Columbia to make the complexities of the age intelligible," then he will offer time to students out of the classroom as well as in, and he will face unpleasant complexities as well as easy problems.

It is easier for a professor to sign a petition against Soviet imperialism than to attack Columbia's effort to colonize northern Manhattan;

easier and less useful. It is not socially awkward for a professor to speak out against capital punishment; it may be awkward to oppose military grants for physicists who are colleagues. Generally, the Columbia tenure faculty is too well fed to want to face or even see the hardest issues. They are previously committed to their own prosperity, to their leisure, to their status, and to the rightness of the system that has given them success.

With few exceptions, the faculty did not protest seizures of power by the administration. They accepted the Columbia system, which, although it treated most of them well, was inequitable. In April, 1968, when a difficult, immediate issue lay before them, the Columbia faculty became confused. Professors made little power plays. They debated and they deplored. They did not act. Watching the interplay then between teacher and student, one remembered *The Admirable Crichton*, the play by James M. Barrie. In *Crichton*, upper-class English people are shipwrecked along with their servants. On the desert island, the old rigid positions become irrelevant. The question is survival; the group does indeed survive through brilliant leadership. The leader is not a lord, but Crichton, a butler.

The faculty lords, reacting slowly, like a sleeper facing the cold, met at Lionel Trilling's place on Claremont Avenue. It was Tuesday night. Harry Coleman was barricaded inside Hamilton. Trilling is a white-haired man with fawn eyes, a slight figure who towers in American letters. Claremont Avenue runs between Broadway and Riverside Drive for five blocks. The group gathering at Trilling's apartment, Number 35, was comprised mostly of senior faculty, heavily involved with the college. Daniel Bell was there. He is an expert in theories of contemporary social action. Arthur Danto, who teaches a three-credit course in the philosophic theory of action, attended. So did Herbert Deane, a professor of government, and Eugene Galanter, the smooth psychologist. The discussion was calm and reasoned. A central point was articulated by Trilling. The radicals were threatening to turn Columbia into "some scruffy Latin American university."

Someone spoke about the right to protest, and its abuse. One professor mentioned police action. The men agreed that abuse of rights and summoning police were undesirable. Dan Bell, short, portly and bright, then decided to prepare a set of proposals.

With Coleman still held prisoner, the College faculty met at a few minutes after three o'clock Wednesday in a roomy lecture hall at Havemeyer, an old building fronting on Broadway north of 118th

Street. Chemistry classes are held in Havemeyer.

Grayson Kirk chaired the meeting. At the beginning he recognized Daniel Bell.

Speaking loudly and clearly, Bell read a set of resolutions.

"1. A university exists as a community dedicated to rational discourse and the use of communication as a means of furthering that discourse . . .

"2. This faculty endorses the right to protest, but we deplore the use of coercion and the seizing of Dean Coleman. We condemn the invasion of the president's office and the rifling of his files."

Professor Bell, a skilled debater, was setting up a pseudo participatory democracy of his own. Rudd controls meetings by limiting choices. Bell operates by establishing premises.

Is Columbia really "a community dedicated to rational discourse"? Only in a limited way. There was no "rational discourse" about building the gymnasium. An executive decision was made. There is no "rational discourse" about the Columbia faculty's performing war work. Much of the relationship and much of the work is "classified"; deliberately kept secret. If Dan Bell told people resident in Morningside Heights that Columbia was "a community dedicated to rational discourse," he would be hooted down. To them, Columbia is a corporation dedicated to aggrandizement at the expense of its neighbors. Bell's first proposition defined the university in a most flattering and incomplete way. It went unchallenged.

The second statement proceeded from the first. Students might protest, although not in the particularly effective way they were then employing. "What Danny Bell was saying," one radical student points out, "is would we please protest in ways proven not to work."

Bell's third proposal was direct. "We believe," he read to the 150 faculty members, "that any differences have to be settled peacefully, and we trust that police action will not be used to clear Hamilton Hall."

Finally, Bell continued, "We call upon the administration to set up a tripartite body to discuss disciplinary matters, the issue of the gymnasium and any other matters which are of legitimate concern." The three parts would be faculty, student and administration.

Two speakers followed. David Truman summarized events. Immanuel Wallerstein described his moments inside Hamilton. Wallerstein was speaking when Harry Coleman walked in through swinging doors at the front of the room. The faculty rose and gave the dean an ovation. Then they resumed deliberating.

Bell's first two proposals were accepted in toto. The third was broad-ened to suggest that the police "not be used to clear Hamilton Hall *or any other university building.*"

At point four, controversy began. Marvin Harris, a professor of anthropology who teaches the abstracting of cultural events into behavioral theory, arose and spoke with great passion. The faculty, Harris said, was being challenged; it had to respond. Harris suggested one amendment consisting of three points. There would be a moratorium on all discipline until the convening of open hearings "involving due process." Construction of the gym would stop until faculty and students helped decide if the building was "in the best interest of the university community." All contacts with the IDA would be suspended, pending a similar discussion.

Faculty leaders consider Harris a radical, and his proposals, which seem temperate as a Yalta spring, were angrily attacked. The moratorium, which might have turned out to be a step toward amnesty, was defeated 99 to 66. The IDA clause was badly beaten too. The gymnasium provision was tabled. Harris could not get anything past faculty conservatives. But the gym was so obvious a gaff that the faculty did adopt a more complicated proposal. Robert Belknap, an associate professor of Russian, wanted work suspended. He proposed that the project be reviewed "with community spokesmen," and "a group to be designated by the mayor." Belknap did not specify the Columbia representation, which meant faculty might be excluded and students certainly would be. The Belknap proposal carried along with the four points prepared by Dan Bell. At 6:15 the meeting ended. In three hours the faculty had failed to contend with amnesty, the issue that to the rebelling students, black and white, transcended everything else.

The immediate danger on campus was violence from within. Out-side both Low Library and Hamilton Hall, crowds of conservative students were gathering. Early on this Wednesday, Low was the focus.

"Kirk must go," chanted the SDS people from their windows in the president's office.

"SDS must go," shouted the conservatives.

Newspaper and radio people crowded toward the building. One reporter was interviewing Tony Papert through a window.

"What are you doing and why?" the interviewer began.

Papert, who keeps his hair cut, wears neckties and speaks softly, articulated the radical position. "We are here to protest Columbia's racism and imperialism." Leaning out, he was an inviting target. The conservatives, many of them athletes, had brought eggs. As Papert expounded, they began to throw.

Tony is a disciplined young man; he continued answering questions. Eggs landed above him and below; they spattered, discoloring the gray walls of Low. Two radicals appeared at another window, carrying publicity pictures of Kirk, lifted from the files. They held the photos out a window, face to the sky. Egg yolks dripped on the spotless pictures. Soon half a dozen photos were smeared with yolk. Some of the crowd laughed and shouted. An egg hit one of the radicals in the chest. Conservatives in the crowd cheered.

There was no humor in the scene developing outside Hamilton toward noon. Black and white sympathizers formed a thin protective line around the base, but the grassy area, the Van Am Quadrangle, was crowded with white students who were furious. "The conservative kids," one journalist recalls, "felt that here these arrogant blacks had seized property. And the liberals were goddamn sore, too. These future lawyers felt pretty good when they extended a new benefit to blacks. But now they couldn't give anything. They could only ask. The liberals were as sore as the conservatives. And the blacks inside looked ready to fight."

Rudd appeared near Hamilton at 4 P.M. The faculty was still meeting. He climbed the steps and began to talk. "I've just come from Low, and I want to tell you that I've had some of Grayson's sherry and some of his cigars and they were very bad." The blacks behind Rudd laughed. The whites in front jeered. Rudd restated the six demands and left.

His appearance deepened lines of anger. Soon after he left, egg throwing began at Hamilton Hall, too. A few people in front of the building were hit. The radicals and conservatives moved toward one another. Then Alex Platt, the dark-haired, youthful associate dean for student affairs, stepped to the marble pedestal under the statue of Alexander Hamilton, who attended Columbia briefly two hundred years ago.

"In order to prevent bloodshed," Platt shouted, "will anybody not supporting the demonstrators move down the steps. Those in support of the demonstration [the occupation of the building], please stay in front of Hamilton Hall." The crowd parted with much milling. The radicals backed to the building wall. The conservatives retreated to the mall. The steps between were clear, a no-man's-land. "I can't describe what it was like to walk between the lines of students," Dr. Ralph

Halford says. "The hostility, the hate, the pent-up violence between these groups." Halford is a slight man, who speaks softly. "I don't think I'd ever seen anything like it before."

A day later, Thursday, with Avery and Fayerweather both occupied, Lionel Trilling, Carl Hovde and Eugene Galanter called on Grayson Kirk in his temporary office on the ground floor of Low. They asked if the tripartite disciplinary tribunal could be set up immediately. The answer was that it could not. Although both black and white rebels were rejecting the commission, the three professors were keenly disappointed. A concession here would have been a step toward mediation. But Kirk would not be budged.

Outside Fayerweather, that Thursday morning about seventy-five conservatives, proudly wearing neckties, chanted: "Throw them out; we want in; we want in." From inside Fayerweather someone shouted, "You dumb jocks." The taunts built. At II:30 A.M. a small group tried to rush Fayerweather. They failed. One of the occupying students walked outside and shouted into a bullhorn: "Our reason for closing Fayerweather is to call attention to the unconscionable violence in Vietnam, to the police state in Harlem and to the intolerable oppression by the United States in Latin America." This was a relatively mild statement; it did not implicate Columbia or refer to the SDS demands. Still the conservatives responded with boos.

At I:30 P.M., 450 conservative students, including more than 200 members of Columbia's athletic teams, gathered on the basketball court of the old Gymnasium, situated behind the School of Business in Uris Hall. What the conservatives wanted, one explained, "was action against these insurrectionists."

"Why student action?"

"Nobody else around here has the guts."

"Will you just go and drag them out?"

"Maybe. Or maybe we'll blockade the bastards and starve them."

Jim Quattrocchi, a junior and a varsity wrestler, got up to address the conservatives. "We're sick and tired of SDS pushing this university around with lies and stormtrooper tactics," he said. "If they want to reduce America to a barbaric society, it's the survival of the fittest and we are the fittest." The old gym rang with applause. Someone might have sunk a twenty-foot jump shot in the dying moments of a tie game with Princeton. But this was no game.

John P. Rohan, Columbia '53, is associate professor of physical education. He is also the basketball coach, and a very fine one. Light-haired Jack Rohan is popular and sensible. "I am a little ashamed," he shouted at the 450 students, "that you fellows are acting like heavies in a Grade B movie. I know you're impatient," he said. "So am I. But the major issue here is not impatience. It's law and order." The coach's voice rose. "What are you guys? You want to be responsible people. Well, responsible people have to have faith in law and order. If you are willing to take part in mob violence, then I can only say I take pity on you—on you and on the university.

"The issue is, do you want to become a part of an anarchy? If you do, you'll just be following the SDS. You'll become a part of this disrespect for majority rights that SDS has initiated."

"But, Coach," someone called, "what about the gym?"

"I've always had a lot of pride in Columbia," Rohan said. "That's not the great gym Columbia deserves, anyway."

Like Casey, Rohan stilled the roaring tumult. The students quieted and started telling themselves that something had to be done, but that violence was no answer. Dean Harry Coleman followed Rohan and announced, "I have no intention of letting down 2,500 students in the college because of the tactics of the other 200." Then he said that he expected President Kirk "to take definitive action, possibly by this evening." The wrestlers and tackles and guards cheered. Then they left the gymnasium docilely as flower children.

There is no question that the jocks could have cleaned out some, and possibly all, of the buildings. Hamilton is questionable because of the possibility of arms inside. Josie Duke talks of the strength of some radicals. "We have our jocks, too," is how she puts it. Miss Duke is a tough young lady, but also starry-eyed. That Thursday a combined force of college wrestlers, weight-lifters and football players would have overwhelmed the young leftists and the comparatively few muscle men among them. Why then were angry conservatives dissuaded simply by Rohan's good speech and Coleman's vague and ultimately misguided promise?

The answer brings us to the sort of mentality that makes a man conservative. He likes law, authority, fixed landmarks. He believes they are good, often simply because they are there. "I mean, I'm not saying Columbia is perfect," a conservative observes, "but it's been good to me and it's been around a long time. Who the hell do these pukes think they are to tear it down?" Most conservatives grew up in settled situations. Some lost fathers early or had fathers they disliked. It is not a matter of simple formula. But the majority grew up in homes where certain values and standards were preached, if not necessarily practiced. These included Honor thy Father and Mother, God Is

Good, Thou Shalt Not Socialize, and God Bless Our Home. By college age one has usually decided whether to accept such values. Conservatives do accept them. Their approach is expressed tersely in an Ivy League motto that Heywood Broun called the greatest anticlimax in the English language: For God, for country and for Yale.

I don't think it is important to the tides of Columbia to consider further the conservative doctrine's merits. What is important is how conservatives act in times of trouble. They like to be idealized good soldiers. They like to think one does what one has to. They believe one stays loyal to the system by which one has lived. One follows the leader.

The conservatives at Columbia thus were as responsive to authority figures as the radicals were insolent. It is psychologically difficult for Rudd to confront adult authorities without defying them. (If he did, he would lose his identity as a rebel.) It is psychologically difficult for Jim Quattrocchi to defy properly constituted adult authority, such as Coach Jack Rohan. If he did, he would lose his identity. He would not be a conservative, but a rebel. By his own standards, he would be a mere anarchist.

To preserve themselves, the conservative students had to follow the leadership of Rohan, Coleman and every other authority, from Kirk and Truman to third assistant deans. As long as faculty performed in channels of order, any professor could command the conservatives. From this point, from the time of Rohan's excellent speech, the conservatives of Columbia had a minor role to play. They provided humor, as we shall see, and swelled a few scenes. But essentially, they were a chorus to the drama. "A chorus," one radical says hotly, "of oafs." Young radicals concede nobody anything.

After the gymnasium meeting, Kirk and Truman held a press conference. "There will be no amnesty," Kirk said. It was still Thursday afternoon.

"What about police?"

"We have exercised great restraint because we want to avoid physical confrontation. We shall continue to do so."

"Would work on the gymnasium be stopped?"

"Contracts," Kirk said, "oblige us to continue construction."

The intransigence troubled faculty members, but they seemed unable to proceed beyond the idea that the tripartite committee, which neither Kirk nor the rebels wanted, held a solution. The man who finally interjected reality into faculty councils was a dark-haired, bespectacled, ambitious professor of public law and government named Alan F. Westin. A forty-two-year-old New Yorker, Westin had taken a B.A. at Florida, after which he set his Ivy credentials in better order. He enrolled in Harvard Law School, graduating in 1951. He took a Ph.D. from Harvard fourteen years later. Westin is intense and forceful. Some suggest that his actions were prompted by a sudden drive for the presidency. "He looked around," one colleague suggests, "and said to himself, hey, who's running this place? When he found out nobody was, he figured, *why not me?*"

Westin says that he was disturbed by the "hard line" of the press conference. He was a friend of David Truman's and afterward asked if Truman would address a faculty group in the lounge of Philosophy Hall. Truman agreed, and spoke with perhaps 100 professors and instructors for twenty-five minutes. Columbia could not stop the gym, he said, because breaking contracts would cost $6 million. No change in disciplinary process could be permitted under pressure. "Otherwise the disciplinary process becomes meaningless."

Somebody called, "Well, what can the faculty do to help?"

Truman shook his head. "I can think of nothing," he said. Then he left quickly, because, "I have to go to an important meeting at Low."

"What the hell?" someone shouted.

"What's going on?"

Anger burst all about the lounge. The faculty had just been told directly that it was superfluous. Then Alan Westin rose and talked along classic lines. It was not that he loved Truman less, Westin said, but that he loved Columbia more.

"As much as I like Dave Truman as a friend," Westin began, "and as much as I respect him as a scholar, I think that the faculty of this university must play a separate role, an independent role." His audience was receptive. Westin said he "had heard" Dean Coleman was hinting at police action. "What I suggest," Westin said, "is that we, as professors, form an ad hoc committee to mediate between the students and the administration before nightfall."

Some professors were not interested. Trilling, Hovde and Galanter were trying to decide on names for the tripartite commission to discuss discipline and the gym. Some were opposed. But Walter P. Metzger, a City College graduate and a historian who has specialized in American civilization, supported Westin. "We have business to do here," Metzger said. "I am going to ask Professor Westin if he will come forth and take charge." The Ad-Hoc committee was born. The time was four o'clock, Thursday, April 25. It was fifty hours after the occupancy of Hamilton.

As an informal group, the Ad-Hoc unit was less encumbered by caste. They could welcome junior faculty men like Dick Greeman, who lacked tenure. Younger men, such as Robert Fogelson, and men who claimed to stand left of center, such as Sidney Morgenbesser, had more power here. These were the swingers, such as they were. The new group was less likely than the old to debate whether to conduct future debates.

Fogelson, an assistant professor of history, had made studies of urban riots. He honestly believed that Columbia was in danger of becoming engulfed. "It's time now," he said, "for professors to interpose their bodies between contending forces. That's dangerous, but we have to take a chance.

"Further," Fogelson continued, "we have to be willing to strike." Strike? One could see the men recoil. Faculty at Columbia strike, even as sanitation workers and schoolteachers? "It's close to our ultimate weapon," Fogelson said, "but the situation is so terribly dangerous that we have to be ready to take extreme action. A strike may be the only way we can get both sides to settle."

The faculty lounge of Philosophy Hall, with its wood paneling and high ceiling, was getting more crowded. Young instructors, ineligible for faculty meetings, heard of the ad hoc committee and quickly filed in. The young faculty was more sympathetic to the radicals.

An older professor arrived, breathless, and called out, "President Kirk is agreeing to the tripartite commission. And he's going to ask the trustees to stop the gym."

Sidney Morgenbesser, natty and sharp-nosed, stood. "Then, perhaps," Morgenbesser said, "what we should do is not get involved in a whole new set of proposals. We could simply endorse the [tenure] faculty resolutions."

He was shouted down. The Ad-Hoc committee then passed a four-part resolution. It asked for a stop in gym construction, and for the delegation of disciplinary powers to the tripartite committee. Points three and four were new.

"We request the students to evacuate all buildings now . . . Should they be willing, we will not meet classes until the crisis is resolved [by halting gym work and by establishing the tripartite body].

"Unless the crisis is settled, we will stand before the occupied buildings to prevent their forcible entry by police and others." These proposals were sent to student leaders, to administrators and to trustees.

About three hundred professors signed the Ad-Hoc statement. The students turned it down at once. As far as I can learn, the trustees never dignified it with a reply.

Haste was important to the young professors, who were trying very hard to be pragmatic. They honestly were afraid of death by fire. And not someday, but then, Thursday night.

Someone in Harlem printed a flyer on green paper. An angry black carries a banner in his right fist, which is raised. Three men hold guns that are firing: "Bratabratabra." The superscription warns that "The People Will Run Columbia," or the people will burn it down. The threat is then spelled out:

> LET IT BE CLEAR! Kirk and his goons have refused to respond to us, so we must respond to them. COLUMBIA BELONGS TO THE PEOPLE & WE ARE THE PEOPLE!
>
> Residents of Harlem will no longer tolerate a racist paradise in the center of their community; a fascist encampment of landlords & trainers of bourgeois oppressors who grow fat on their squalor.
>
> Students will no longer tolerate the university as the authority which governs & suppresses their life; training them to be racist masters or to research poison gases & plagues for imperialist wars.
>
> The students are fighting those who oppress them the same way the people of Harlem are fighting their oppressors. Together they will control the university or destroy it. The ashes of Columbia will be tomorrow's lesson.

This document was made more ominous by the announcement of a rally Thursday night at 116th Street and Broadway, in front of the main entrance to the campus. Negroes would lead. It had been called by the United Black Front.

At dusk about two hundred Harlem blacks made a forced march up Morningside Heights. They gathered at 110th Street and Eighth Avenue, the southwesternmost corner of Harlem, climbed the steep incline to Morningside Drive and wound their way around the campus until they stood before the main gates on Broadway. Word of the rally had brought hundreds of people out, from the neighborhood, and from all over the city, mostly young people and mostly anti-Columbia. The rally had also drawn, to the gate of Columbia, the assembled jocks, on the advice of Harry Coleman. "It's your campus," the dean said, "and if you want to keep outsiders off it, I think that's fair."

Across the street from Columbia, Helen Reid Hall, the main residence for Barnard, rises eight stories high. As the blacks gathered, the windows of Reid filled. The girls meant to use their balcony views of current history.

Police milled on the edges of the crowd. The conservatives formed a solid white wall at the Columbia entrance. The first black speaker was large, wide and jovial. He mounted the roof of a sedan for a podium and began to talk about the gym. "I can't speak too long," said the giant black man, "because this car roof won't *hold* me for too long." Next the Reverend Kendall Smith, who had been arrested at the gym site, attacked racism. He supported everybody in the buildings, he said, and so did Harlem. Then Charles 37 X Kenyatta climbed the car. Muslims are required to drop their last name, their so-called slave name. As Malcolm, they replace it with "X." Joe Johnson, becoming a Muslim, becomes Joe X. The second Joe Johnson becomes Joe 2 X. And so on. Kenyatta was the thirty-seventh man named Charles to join the Muslim temple in Harlem. The African last name came as an afterthought, and for all its sound of violence, its suggestion of wild Mau Mau deeds, its bearer proved to be a curiously docile militant.

He paid lip service to the anti-Columbia offensive, but the crowd around him was tired of talk. They were standing on the sidewalk very close to the Columbia jocks, who were needling.

"Go home," someone shouted. "Get the hell back where you belong."

"We gonna get you, honkie motherfucker."

"Beat it, nigger."

Scuffle.

"Let's burn 'em down."

"Yeah, burn 'em down."

"We'll burn you, nigger."

Scuffle.

"Awright," Charles shouted. "Awright. Now come here round this car so you can hear what I say about this racist place."

No one wanted to gather around Charles. The action was fifty feet off, at the great iron gates where the two lines were scuffling. "Awright," Charles shouted, "we got to go into that campus." The leader followed the movement that had gotten ahead of him.

The large jovial black, not so jovial now, was a central figure. He was pushing with all his might against the conservatives. Others, blacks and white radicals, were helping, but the large black became the point of a wedge. The bodies swayed. The girls in the Barnard dormitory stared and shouted. Slowly, the blacks began to gain. The line of jocks moved back, one step and then another. The blacks pushed through the gate. The battlefield was the campus now.

Two buildings wedged combatants. Dodge, to the north, houses the publicity department. A dozen reporters watched from the windows. Journalism Hall stands sixty feet to the south. The blacks and radicals surged and pushed up the narrow corridor. The jocks fell farther and farther back. Suddenly, they were behind the rear walls of the buildings. The campus was open now to the blacks of Harlem. The jocks had failed.

High above, one newspaperman turned to another. "That's Columbia for you," he said. "Never could hold on fourth and one."

Fist fights broke out as the groups spilled into open areas. Dean Harry Coleman had a bullhorn. "All right now, cool it," he was shouting. "Come on. Cool it." The young conservatives did what they were told. The fist fights stopped. What the blacks wanted, Charles 37 X shouted, was to show solidarity for the young men in Hamilton. They wanted to march down College Walk from Broadway to Amsterdam Avenue. "Freedom march at Columbia," somebody said. Coleman, plus a number of city and police officials, personally escorted the blacks. The group crossed the campus. Some lingered outside Hamilton. Most drifted down the hill to Harlem. Again the black threat was greatest in white minds.

Broadway was full of people. Chanting began. "Up against the wall, motherfucker." A group stood in a circle and cheered, as though at a football game. "Kirk is a Jerk. Stop the gym. Amnesty NOW, amnesty NOW, amnesty NOW." Always the loudest cheer was "Up against the wall." The noise ran very late into the night.

It was too much for one of the Barnard girls. She looked down at one of the radical groups, being led by stumpy, impassioned Paul Rockwell. "It's great," she called down from her window in Helen Reid Hall. "It's just great the way you're giving it to those motherfuckers."

Rockwell looked up. "Join us," he called.

"I can't," the Barnard girl shouted. "I'll get a lateness."

At 1:30 A.M. David Truman walked wearily into the lounge of Philosophy Hall. The sharp face was gray. The skin was puffy under the eyes. The mouth was downturned. He stood at the rear of the lounge and the teachers turned to face him. About two hundred, a mix of Ad-Hoc men and tenure people, were still there. They had been deliberating. "Truman looked," someone pointed out later, "as if he had to announce a faculty salary cut."

"Gentlemen," Truman said. "I want to make an announcement that I expect most of you will not like." He was speaking strongly, but evenly. "Another building [Mathematics] has just been taken over by striking students. The situation has reached a point where we have no alternative except to call in police."

He did not pause. "In ten minutes, the president will call Mayor Lindsay to request such action. Thank you for your concern and efforts. I'm terribly sorry." He turned and was gone.

The faculty reacted late and hotly. For a few seconds silence shrouded the hall. Then someone cried, "Shame!" Others shouted, "No, no." The Reverend William Starr, of the Protestant chaplain's staff, cried, "Liar." Serge Lang, a professor of mathematics, called, "Vote of censure." Eric Bentley, the drama professor, announced, "I resign."

At least three professors—Westin and Alexander Dallin, the Adlai Stevenson professor of international relations, and Sidney Morgenbesser—pursued Truman. Brushing past security men, they caught up with him near the gound-floor command post at Low. Already a platoon of plainclothesmen was entering the campus from Amsterdam Avenue. The police marched in a column of twos. They were broad, rugged-looking men. Some carried nightsticks in their jacket sleeves.

At the moment the columns reached Low, Sidney Morgenbesser was urging Kirk to reconsider. The president and the vice-president were adamant until Dick Greeman's scalp was cut. It was 1 A.M. Friday. Blood softened them and they relented, although long afterward Truman would refer to the wound as "Greeman's bloody nose."

A mini-crisis followed outside. One faculty member asked a guard if he could enter Low to use a men's room. The guard returned shortly and said no. The teacher offered to let a guard accompany him to the men's room. This discussion took place in shouts through a closed glass door. Eventually, after hurried consultations, two guards returned and allowed the man to enter; and a crowd remained by the door, shuffling its feet, whispering in the dark.

Kirk, sitting in his borrowed office beside ranking professors and administrators, was unhappy about the Ad-Hoc committee, but the smell of blood and violence had finally reached him. "You are asking for time to effect a solution," he said to Westin.

"That is correct."

"Well, then, you will have to assume certain responsibilities. There is an increasing threat of violence on this campus."

"We are prepared to contend with that," Westin said, "with faculty patrols. We have passed a resolution. We will back it up with our bodies."

Kirk looked at Truman, then nodded. Discussions continued for a long time.

At 4:30 A.M. Truman emerged from Low. Through a bullhorn he announced: "No action will be taken against the occupants of the buildings tonight. The university will be closed the next day [Friday]. Until the crisis is resolved, access to the campus will be limited to those with identification. Finally, at the request of the mayor, we have suspended construction of the gymnasium." Slowly, the crowd dispersed. About forty minutes later, the plainclothesmen left, although a small detachment of uniformed police remained.

Mediation efforts continued. On Friday night, the Ad-Hoc group met, talking past midnight and approaching, as nearly as it ever would, the issue of amnesty. A number of young professors and Tomec Smith, of the student council, described amnesty as a necessity.

Close to one in the morning, Robert Zevin, a lecturer in economics, telephoned Mark Rudd in Ferris Booth and said that a direct appeal might yield a pro-amnesty vote. Rudd had been talking privately with Alan Westin. "You might want to get back to your meeting," he said. "Something interesting may be about to happen."

Westin returned to Philosophy. Rudd followed afterward. When Rudd walked to the front of the room, Westin was saying that his talks with students were making progress. He later said he thought Westin was about to finesse amnesty.

"We've had exploratory talks," Rudd told the professors. He was unkempt. He had not shaved for two days. "Very exploratory. More in the line of *bullshit.*"

On that vulgarity, the meeting turned. Rudd continued. "Total amnesty is the only answer. You faculty guys ought to be fighting with us. There are no neutrals." But no one cared to hear any more. Rudd's passion to shock had shattered the peace. The meeting grew disorderly. The professors were offended or upset or angry. There would be no amnesty vote. There would be no amnesty. Westin gaveled the meeting to a close.

From that Saturday morning onward faculty members stood in front of every occupied building twenty-four hours a day. Others stood at the main gates, on Broadway and on Amsterdam Avenue. Full professors, experts in exotica, checked the identity cards of everyone who passed. The press was admitted. Police were admitted. Columbia students and staff were admitted, but no one else. (Except, of course, scores of others who had borrowed I.D. cards.) Faculty members derived a sense of importance from performing what they believed to be useful work.

On Sunday, the Morningside faculties, the senior teaching staff of most of the colleges on the Heights, adopted vaguely worded resolutions that called for a quick end to the crisis, offered no viable proposals and passed 466-40. This new body excluded younger teachers and professors from liberal Barnard. Later the Ad-Hoc committee adopted a four-part proposal. The Ad-Hoc people warned that they would obstruct police action unless Kirk accepted the tripartite commission and gave the community a veto on the gym. If Kirk accepted these conditions and the students rejected them, then the Ad-Hoc committee promised to stand aside for police action. Kirk and the students *both* rejected this proposal. When the police came, in the hours before the dawn of Tuesday, they ran over faculty and students with complete impartiality.

11 THE GARDEN OF MARX

DOTSON Rader, six foot three, B.A. Columbia College, twenty-four years old, was holding his erection, wondering if it would be with him permanently. Dotson, who majored in comparative literature, was standing before a urinal in the downstairs men's room of Mathematics Hall, a completely liberated building. Even the bathrooms of Mathematics were liberated. Sexual segregation was part of the obscene and capitalist past. While Dotson attempted to urinate, two Barnard girls washed at a nearby sink. It was early morning and the girls were giggling.

They were fully clothed and trying to concentrate on cleaning their own hands and neck. But the sight of tall Dotson Rader leaning over a urinal was too much. The girls continued to giggle. Dotson stared at the wall. Someone had scrawled "Fuck Grayson Kirk." Dotson was feeling neither militant nor sexual. He wanted a bath, a shave and a Bloody Mary in that order.

"I stood, it seemed, for hours," he explained afterward, "erection in hand, leaning tightly against the cold wall, wishing the girls would leave. All week, and I had never learned the revolutionary art of sharing bathrooms with women. I stood planted to the tile, ignoring the girls' giggling. What if they *never* leave, I thought. I'll be stuck here like a madman in *Marat/Sade*, permanently erect, while they wash and wash and wash. . . ."

They finally left, and the erection passed and Dotson tried to write and thought of Bloody Marys. He had come here out of friendship,

175

not out of politics. His politics were that he wanted to write. But in the end, when the police came, they drew no distinctions. They beat the giggling girls and the radical activists and Dotson Rader. The cops drove the revolutionaries out of the troubled utopia of Mathematics, throwing them down flights of stairs, kicking them and beating them on the kidneys.

The police stayed in Mathematics for some time. They found a treasure chest of liquor that Dotson Rader had concealed and drank it all. Then some of the policemen, tipsy now, ignored the bathrooms that they had unliberated. They urinated on the floor. What the hell. They could always say the Commie kids had done it. The Commie kids were little pissers anyway.

* * * * * *

The society that developed in each occupied building acquired an individual character. Low was hard-line SDS, practical, purposeful, compact. Math had a core that was even harder—the building was taken with a raid hyperbolically described as "Viet Cong style"—but there were giggling freshmen, too, and much more room. Fayer-weather was sprawling, moderate and wordy. Avery was moderate and manual. Hamilton was resolute, orderly and, except for Dr. June Finer, entirely black.

This disparity ended at a focal point, a command post. Several hours after the police allowed the Low commune to survive, Rudd and a number of other SDS leaders met on the third floor of Ferris Booth Hall. Sleepless, overstimulated, they talked and argued. At one point Rudd resigned. Eventually they stopped quarreling and occupied the offices for the duration. Here Rudd, Lewis Cole and the other strike leaders spent most of the following week.

The strike coordinating committee, Strike Central, was not entirely an SDS group. Other student organizations were represented, along with delegates from each occupied building except Hamilton, and two from Ferris Booth. Although Strike Central wavered at times, it never relented on the six demands.

For several days, Columbia administrators left all the telephones connected, but when these were cut off, Strike Central, using walkie-talkies, became the communications headquarters. When students in Fayerweather debated dropping the amnesty precondition, this defec-tion was localized. Word did not spread from building to building: "Fayerweather's backing down." The word stopped at Strike Central.

Then Fayerweather stiffened and that was that. It is fundamental to modern revolutionary movements to control communications.

When Josie Duke climbed back into Low Library on the afternoon of Wednesday, April 24, Tony Papert had been conducting a meeting. After scrambling out of Low early that morning as city police were arriving, Josie went to a class at Barnard and read a forty-five-minute paper on the 1948 Berlin blockade. She commended Stalin for his resoluteness. A forty-minute discussion followed. Catherine Kelleher, Josie's government instructor, graded the paper A minus. Now Josie was climbing back into Low where Tony Papert was discussing avenues of action. A semicircle of boys and girls sat before him in Grayson Kirk's office with walls of green.

"We are living, you understand, in a prerevolutionary society," Papert said. "That is America today. Not many people are aware of that, but it's true."

A dark-haired girl said, "Many people are aware of it."

"Well, not enough," Papert said. "What happens in the prerevolutionary society is a kind of undirected protest. People are unhappy. The society isn't working. If it were, it wouldn't be in prerevolutionary state. People do not make mass revolutions against equitable societies."

Josie slipped quietly into the semicircle and sat. She looked up and saw an off-color rectangle on the wall where *Portrait of a Dutch Admiral* had hung. The idea of Papert preaching radicalism in Kirk's office excited Josie. Secretly, privately, she was a little ashamed of having left the building. "Scaredness had something to do with it," she conceded later. But now she was not frightened any longer.

"One characteristic of the prerevolutionary society," Papert said, "is the exhaustion of legal means for change. I think I'd better explain that in detail." Papert was studying to be a teacher. His lectures were not shocking like Rudd's speeches. Rather they seemed informed. He could simplify abstractions and clarify and define. "Listening to him," one of the girls of Low said afterward, "was like listening to the teacher you never had at Barnard."

"In the prerevolutionary state," Papert said, "people gradually exhaust the so-called legitimate means of protest. These means may be effective, but most likely they are not. A state does not classify means to bring about its destruction as either legal or legitimate.

"People who feel there is something wrong with the state petition. We petitioned here at Columbia. And what did we find?"

"I was part of a group petitioning Warren Goodell [the vice-president for administration]. Can I tell about it?" Josie Duke asked. She was wearing dungarees and a pea jacket and looked fifteen. Papert nodded.

"Well, you know, David Truman says he's against the war in Vietnam," Josie said.

"Who says so?"

"All right," Papert said. "Let her continue."

"And Kirk takes a kind of an antiwar stand."

"Yeah."

"So we told Goodell," Josie said, "if Kirk is against the war and Truman is against the war, what is this invisible hand that keeps the university working for the war through the IDA?"

"What did he say?" A boy with spectacles and bushy hair asked the question.

"He told us that he didn't know because he didn't make all of the business decisions for the university."

"So much for the right of petition," Tony Papert announced.

Dozens of radicals were climbing the lattice of bars to join the occupiers. Tony Papert's discussion group in Grayson Kirk's office grew.

"A prerevolutionary period is when people's normal methods of struggle, of winning improvements, lose effectiveness," Papert said. "Student governments, and student social groups, can't get the students that they need any longer. Political machines and local poverty groups are no longer sufficient for the blacks. Given spiraling inflation and mounting taxes, trade unions can no longer be depended on to win significant gains for their members.

"A new form of organization is necessary. A *class* form, that goes beyond local or parochial groups. Our strike shows this in embryo. We are students, ghetto residents, university employees, fighting together for what we all need. We are putting our common interests first—our six points—and our special interests second. We are on the way to becoming a class.

"The professors can't understand what's going on because the strike is a new form of social organization, at least to them. Our strike, and our representative strike committee, is the real leadership of the university now. It's a soviet in embryo, a French strike committee in embryo. When what is happening at Columbia happens on a national scale, the movement will have a chance to become the government, just as we are the administration. A movement involving majorities of students, black people and blue-collar workers.

"We are playing a dress rehearsal for revolution. I hope everyone learns his part."

He is not big. His features are somewhat broad, but regular. The dark brown hair is cut at a normal length. His face is not memorable. Tony Papert looks like a pleasant college boy.

"Another legal means," Tony, the studious radical, said, "which can be part of the elective process is to try to enlist mass support. We've seen that through recent American history. Socialist Party candidates and Communist Party candidates and Progressive Party candidates, all running as legal, legitimate candidates in the American system. But they do not get mass support. The masses remain apathetic.

"All right. There are no more legal means and the society is out of control, threatening to destroy everything. Then you must say, as we have said, and as we say by our presence here:

"No. Legal means are not effective.

"Legitimate is only a word of rhetoric. We will change society by *any* means. We will make a just society by *revolution.* "

Again the quick smile. "In case anybody asks you why you are breaking the law, that's the answer."

The smile was gone. "Concentration camps," Papert said, "have disabused people of Christianity. Now is the time to teach them Marx."

Tony Papert is quiet and mild mannered. Great Neck, where he grew up, is upper middle-class, liberal, Jewish, and, like any prosperous suburb, generally respectful of laws. Tony's father was in the fur business, but Tony grew up with a sense of humanistic radicalism. That is one of the great American Jewish traditions. Western European Jewish immigrants, German and Alsatian Jews, were centrists, but Eastern European Jews, raised in muddy ghettos under a chain of malevolent Czars, turned not to a new Judaism, but to the theories of an apostate Jew. Karl Marx's communism was a passport into the modern world. East European Jews came here and enriched the American political scene with socialism, communism, anarchy, a dozen variations of the left. "It distresses me," says Alex Stoia of the Columbia administrative staff, "to find Jews denying that the radical heritage exists. They should be proud of it." Tony Papert grew up knowing who Engels was and that Jacques Monard assassinated Trotsky, and that the theory of surplus values was being questioned, and that unless the tools of production were owned by the men who used them, there was little hope for justice in America or in the world.

Tony believes that the student movement is fleeting. It is too closely tied to emotion and to accident, to Lyndon Johnson and to Richard Nixon and to blundering in Vietnam. What can save America, Tony believes, is a federation of students and workers. He does not think that this can be easily achieved, but he thinks there is a chance. He says that if someone goes to the subway and sanitation workers and explains economics, they might listen and respond.

"That's a terrible job, collecting garbage," Tony says. "Nobody should have to do it as a lifework. It should be rotated. It would be better if everyone had to collect garbage for a two-year stretch. That and all the other dehumanizing work that persists despite our technology.

"Take the subway workers," Tony says. "Now if you talk economic theory, you won't get anywhere. But put it in real terms. They want more money. So what city officials tell them is the only way to give them a raise is to raise the subway fare from twenty cents to a quarter or more. Rob the poor to pay the poor. It's irrational.

"But there are municipal transit bonds," Tony says, "paying millions and millions of dollars a year in interest. That's where the subway workers' raise should come from. If you eliminated that interest, that kind of capitalist financing, you could have the men make more and have no subway fare at all.

"Somebody has to reach them. Somebody has to tell them these things."

"But maybe not you," I say.

"Maybe not me," the leader of the Low commune agrees.

The Low Library revolutionaries had practical problems from the beginning. They had to eat and sleep and believe in themselves. Food, floor space and bathroom facilities were all in short supply. Additionally, they wanted to prepare against the inevitable police attack. Papert supervised the establishment of committees on food and housekeeping. A defense committee became a power on its own. By Friday night the commune, about 130 people in all, was a tight little utopia.

Papert felt that Kirk's office should be kept as living and meeting space. That meant most of the people would sleep in Truman's office and in the secretaries' anteroom. Some students brought in blankets; many had none. Boys and girls lay side by side in one another's arms, but a hint of orgiastic nights would be misleading. There was no privacy. Not everyone left Low as chaste as he had entered, but not everyone was gratified, either. "I wanted to do a lot," a girl recounts, "particularly in the beginning, but not in the middle of a crowd. There was no place."

The food committee worked efficiently in Grayson Kirk's tidy kitchenette. The refrigerator was small, and the best kind of food was non-perishable. Milk commanded most of the refrigerator space. Boys and girls brought bread and processed cheese and peanut butter and jelly; bolognas and cans of coffee and grapefruits, oranges and bananas and apples and cookies.

There was only one bathroom in the suite and it was always in use. Under the constant tension, constant excitement, diarrhea became a part of the liberated life.

Friday, the Low defense committee prepared plans. Its members included Joe Tashiro, wiry and strong, and John Jacobs—J.J.—who had dropped out of Columbia College earlier in the year. Late that day, the commune and particularly the defense committee was encouraged by the arrival of a bald-headed fiftyish physician. Thomas S. Harper, clinical assistant professor of psychiatry at Cornell Medical College, explained possible defenses against tear gas and mace. By his years and by dignity, Harper provided comfort and new seriousness to the Low commune. Here was a man of real substance joining. His talk calmed nervous people, and the medications he dispensed helped with diarrhea.

The first basic defense plan was simple. All furniture would be removed from the offices of Kirk and Truman and piled against the large double doors at the front of the anteroom. Drag out the heavy darkwood desks. Carry out chairs. Bring coffee tables, typing tables and fat upholstered chairs. Make a barricade with a Louis XIV decor.

The doors to the anteroom open on the wide corridor where secretaries work and lead straight to a plaster wall.

"Look," one communard said, as the barricade took form. "Let's work out this stuff along lines of force. A straight line of furniture from door to wall. Then, when the cops push against the doors to open them, they end up pushing down this inside wall."

"Hey, great, man."

"What's he, a physics major?"

"Shit, just do what he says."

The barricade was carefully constructed. J.J. and the others studied the lines of force. There was a real chance that if the police had pushed the double doors in, the far wall might have collapsed.

But the police never had to push in the double doors.
They opened out.

Liquor and marijuana—grass—were banned from the start. As Tony
Papert expressed the logic: "Quarters were tight. We didn't want
anybody going wild, and we wanted to have all our senses when the
cops came." A visitor to Low on that Saturday, a crisp and pleasant
day, was greeted with the smell of oranges. Devouring oranges was the
evident vice.

The rooms were transformed but not damaged. Blankets were scattered in the anteroom. Truman's rectangular office was shuttered and
dark; people were sleeping there. People caught sleep when they
could. In Kirk's office, Tony Papert was leading a group through a
discussion on the ideal university. "To sum it up," he was saying, "we
see that the renaissance university was a success. It proved to be a
training ground for social change. And the modern university is a
failure. It produces people committed to social stagnation."

"Tony?" A girl with brown hair combed back asked for the floor.
Papert nodded. "Could Columbia as it exists be made a success, or do
we have to burn it down?"

Someone laughed. Papert was serious. "We could make certain
changes. The library, Butler Library, a tax-exempt building on tax-
exempt ground, should be opened to all people, not just the Columbia
elite. Invite kids from Harlem in. Invite bus drivers. Open up the
place."

"Let's get on to defense," said J.J.

"But," Papert said, "a university controlled by imperialists is not
going to allow these changes. So the practical answer is that we'll have
to take it over."

"Let's talk about the fucking pigs," J.J. said. He comes from a
prosperous suburban home, and although he is not very large, J.J. is
compact and strong, built like a welterweight fighter. "I want to take
these window poles," J.J. said, pointing, "and when the fucking pigs
come, I'm going to poke 'em off the ledge."

Police talk made every meeting come alive. "Suppose they shoot in
canisters of tear gas?" someone said.

"I'll belt 'em with window poles," J.J. said.

"Maybe we ought to board the windows," Josie Duke said.

"That's a good idea." A half dozen boys and girls began taking down
Kirk's bookshelves. Someone went out for a hammer and nails. Josie
was hammering shelves in place when somebody said that with win-

dows boarded, the place would become fetid. "Besides, if a canister does get through, there'd be no way of getting the tear gas out. We'd be in trouble." The window-boarding was never finished.

Later, Tom Hayden, in an earlier time the moderate leader of SDS, had a most inventive thought. Low Library houses Columbia's collection of oriental vases. Columbia will not reveal the value of its Sackler Collection, because, one university spokesman says, "We want people to enjoy it as sheer art." "We take these pieces," Hayden said, "and put 'em out on the ledges. First time a cop takes a step toward us, we shove off a Ming vase. Wham. Columbia blows ten thousand dollars. They shoot tear gas. Three vases. Thirty thousand. They don't go 'way, I knock off all the jade with Jayjay's window pole there."

Hayden's plan was voted down.

By Saturday, armbands appeared on campus. The faculty had begun the trend with white. Now red signified sympathy to demonstrators. Green signified pro-amnesty. Blue meant no sympathy. The best indication of general campus feeling is that it was mixed. According to a survey conducted by Allen Barton of the Bureau of Applied Social Research, fifty-eight percent of the students favored the "main goals" of the radicals; only nineteen percent favored their tactics.

Late Sunday afternoon, one hundred conservatives formed an outer cordon around the faculty cordon surrounding Low. Wearing jackets and ties, the boys stood shoulder to shoulder, with their backs to the faculty and to the building. Their purpose was blockade. The conservatives were going to starve the radicals out of Low. The faculty, wedged between conservatives and the building, took no action. For themselves, the teachers had safe passage through the conservative line.

When the first group bringing food was stopped, the radicals improvised an airlift. They would throw food up to their allies on the second floor. Soon boys and girls crowded the ledges to catch parcels.

Tin cans were easiest to throw. A can of tuna fish weighs enough so that it can be thrown with reasonable accuracy. But without a glove cans make hard catching. There were a few yelps from commune members on the receiving end. Citrus fruits were easy to throw and easy to catch. But some tosses were wild. Grapefruit and oranges spattered against the gray walls of Low, occasionally dripping onto faculty.

Bread was the ideal missile. It had the bulk and just enough weight

for an accurate football toss. It floated in a gentle arc. And if the throw
went wild, nobody was spattered.

The conservatives leaped to knock down food. A tall black-haired
boy smashed down a grapefruit in midflight. Onlookers cheered.
"Throw higher," someone shouted. "Block 'em. Knock 'em down."

Presently the conservatives lifted others to their shoulders and
brought up garbage can covers as shields. The throwing and the blocking of throws with shields became intense. Each successful throw, a
grapefruit lofted to a rebel on the ledge, drew cheers. A poor throw,
a wild can of tuna, a blocked bread, drew cheers from the other side.
In the growing darkness the cheering went on for a long time. But
eventually everyone tired of it and began to drift away. Arc lights
played on Dodge and Kent, and as the spectators wandered off from
Low down College Walk, their silhouettes grew sharper in the distance.

Monday morning came with a terrible roar. The majority coalition,
still standing in a cordon around Low, was leaping through calisthen-
ics. Coatless in the chill, the boys were arranged in a double row.
"Hey-yup," they roared in unison. "Hey-yup." Feet in. Feet out. Clasp
hands above the head. Feet in. Feet out. "Hey-yup-yup." It was a half
an hour drill: run-in-place, pushups, kneebends. Columbia was still
closed this Monday, but the campus was loud.

The day warmed and the sealed campus was pleasant, if one could
forget that it was sealed. At Low there was more sunning on the
ledges. The blacks in Hamilton put out their garbage. Students and
faculty wandered the campus wearing armbands.

Early Monday afternoon, a squad of thirty rebels came bursting out
of Mathematics. They were coming to break the conservative lines;
they meant to open Low by force.

A well-muscled boy with close-cropped light brown hair was in the
lead, along with several well-built blacks. Not all the blacks were in
Hamilton. At least a few non-separatist blacks helped occupy every
building.

The well-muscled boy was wearing a bright red softball shirt. The
team name, written in script across the front, was *Cardinal Realty,
Ferndale,* a resort town in the Catskill Mountains. On its back the shirt
showed seven, Mickey Mantle's number.

Some of the radicals had put on narrow leather headbands like
Indians. They trotted to Low and circled clockwise, chanting to themselves. Some wore sandals. Others went barefoot. Their feet made a
swishing sound as they moved.

The outermost ring of Low consisted of hedges. Inside the hedges stood the conservatives. Inside them, utterly immobilized, stood faculty. The radicals circled, and the conservatives linked arms and redeployed to stand off the coming charge. Behind the outer line of conservatives, other groups moved back and forth. They were the reserves. They would plug holes, wherever the line gave. The conservatives were ready to fight with jackets on.

J.J. was leading the rebels; the sound of their feet rose and fell and rose as they circled. When they passed outside Kirk's office, demonstrators leaned out and held fingers aloft in a V. "Now, now," the demonstrators shouted. Still the militants circled, getting ready.

One of the conservatives, slight and wearing eyeglasses, suddenly broke into tears. He sucked his lower lip and cried with fright. "Hold your place," said a large boy to his right. The smaller boy continued to weep.

Suddenly, from a point on the west side of Low, the leftists stormed the line. The jocks there—where the boy was sobbing—looked most vulnerable.

The conservative line buckled, heaved out and held. "Hold the line," some chanted. "Hold that line." The rebels regrouped and charged again. One of the blacks broke through. He was scrambling toward Low when two conservative reserves tackled him. Denim jackets flying, the leftists charged again and again. The conservative line was pushed back, but not pierced. Newspapermen and television cameramen crowded close to the west wall of Low. The students were shoving each other and cursing.

"Fucking fink."

"Commie bastard."

"Nigger lover."

One of the conservatives took a slash on a cheek. One leftist was knocked over and stepped on. A few fist fights began. The faculty watched, doing nothing.

The violence was getting out of hand. Then a few dozen students from Union Theological Seminary marched between the combatants, calling, "Break it up. All right. Break it up." In five minutes the shoving was over. The rebels retreated to Math. The conservatives had held. The blockade of Low Library continued.

Inside, in Kirk's office, a pretty girl with long brown hair was trying to hide her disappointment. She had a lovely oval face, the face of a nun. "When the police come," she said to a crew-cut boy in a green shirt and old white slacks, "you know what."

It wasn't a question. "No, what?"

"We should take off all our clothes and walk out of here naked. The police wouldn't know what to do."

The boy grinned and looked at her very hard. Then he touched her arm.

"Scared."

"Uh-huh."

"If the police don't come, then we've won. And if the police do come then we've won, too." He squeezed her arm. "We can't lose."

"I know," said the girl with the oval face, and buried her head in his arms.

Fear rose in the buildings day by day. The defense committees met and talked; some worked out elaborate plans. In Avery, the architects decided on an interesting response. When word came that the police were coming, the students would assume stations according to their militancy. The people who wanted to walk out rather than face the police would take the first floor. The people who wanted to resist passively would take the second floor. People who wanted to fight would be higher. That way, perhaps only the most militant could be hurt.

Seth Shulman remembers boys in Fayerweather talking about turning fire hoses on the police and others at the same time talking about dropping the precondition of amnesty. But people were happy there. Eleanor Raskin, a married student at the School of Law, cheerfully moved into Fayerweather. Eleanor is an attractive, dark-haired girl who comes from Brooklyn, went to Barnard, disliked it and moved to England. She finished college at the University of Manchester, where she also worked as a folk singer. "Barnard was not a human place," Eleanor says. "In England when I was singing I got to know workers. It was real." Eleanor's favorite folk song, which she sings in an appealing reedy voice, is called "My Hand Is on the Plough." Eleanor lived in Fayerweather, ate and slept there, except some evenings when she sneaked out of a window and went to her apartment in an old building on Riverside Drive to take a bath. Eleanor led folk singing in Fayerweather. "The sense of living there," she says, "was a sense of joy. I sensed what it could be like if this country were free."

People talked in Fayerweather and argued and joked and even went through a ceremony of marriage. Andrea Burrow, a dark-haired girl with a well-fed suburban look, and Richard Egan, a slim boy with a British campaigner's moustache, were united in a Sunday night ceremony. The Reverend William Starr performed the service, without benefit of license.

Andrea wore a white turtleneck sweater, jeans and white sneakers. Richard wore matching jeans, a white Nehru jacket and black boots. Andrea glowed as she walked down the stairway in Fayerweather Hall. But her mother was upset. She felt Andrea should have worn a dress.

The Reverend Starr was solemn. "Do you, Richard . . . do you, Andrea?"

"I do."

"Then," Starr intoned, "I pronounce you Andrea and Richard Fayerweather, children of the new age."

The lobby was lit by scores of candles. Someone struck a large pan, making the sound of a gong. Andrea and Richard kissed. A column formed, everyone holding a candle aloft, and in the darkness Andrea and Richard were escorted to the sundial. "It was beautiful," Seth Shulman says.

Then Andrea and Richard walked to Mathematics Hall and climbed to the top floor. Others kept a respectful distance from them that night.

"Oh," says Eleanor Raskin, "those were exciting days." She cannot really put them into words. She reaches into her pocketbook and finds a poem someone wrote. It is not a good poem perhaps or even, by some standards, a poem at all. But it is what Eleanor has to show for the joy and hope she felt for life while she lived in Fayerweather and the numb lines may be touching in view of what was to happen after they were penned.

> In Marx's park,
> You can run.
> People get married.
> Into this garden
> No cops can come.

12 WALPURGISNACHT

THE MIDDLE-CLASS GIRL
WHO CRIED MOTHERFUCKER

THEY are instantly a nice couple, soft, sensitive, in love and full of hope. She glances at him while she speaks, reassuring herself that he is there. And he waits for her to finish, pausing after she is silent to be certain that she has finished her thought. Neither means ever to offend.

Their names are important, but best changed here. What happened to them under police assault was frightful and her own actions were somewhat embarrassing. Call them Victor and Celia. These are two young, aesthetic people who are excited at the prospect of a lifetime spent with books. Nothing else in their lives is as important. They come from Connecticut, but now they are sitting in The West End, that liberal-radical haunt on Broadway, and they are at home. He is slim, with gentle, patient eyes and quiet speech. She is more intense, darker, attractive. Her good looks grow on you and take hold.

"A pretty light drink that radicals settle for," I say. We are sitting at a too-small table, across cocktails.

"Oh, it's not so bad," he says.

"I'm not much of a drinker," she says.

Celia works as a secretary in one of the humanities departments at Columbia. Victor is taking his Ph.D. He has been working toward the doctorate for six years. Afterward, he will teach.

"Are you radicals," I ask, "or liberals?"

"We're not very political people," Celia says.

"Well, you're against the war in Vietnam."

"Of course," Celia says.

Victor waits. Then he explains, "We're not *active* members of a formal political group."

"Then how did you get involved with the police?"

Again Victor waits. "Everybody became involved," Celia says. "You wouldn't have believed what happened. You couldn't believe it."

"I've seen police in action."

Now Victor volunteers. "Well, then you know."

They are middle-class people who met in college and who married soon afterward, and she does not mind working as a secretary to help. He is her man, and she will do what she has to for him. Later there will be children, of course, and trips to Tanglewood and Europe, and a house, or one of those gracious large apartments on Riverside Drive. He will write books and she will be hostess. But now they are working their way upward. They accept the system, although they know it is flawed. Talking to them you understand how it was before the bust. They are young people but already settled, already secure. Security comes early in academe; it is the narcotic of the professor's trade.

"Some of Victor's friends were young faculty people," Celia says. "They were connected with the Ad-Hoc faculty committee. We set up a telephone relay system. That is, in case the police were coming, we'd all have certain people to call, to get them on campus."

"What could you do?" I say.

"You know about interposing bodies," Celia says. "The idea was to have as many faculty bodies as possible to interpose."

She looks at Victor, who nods. "There was a sense of stability, too," he says. "The idea was that faculty people and even people like us, who are not quite faculty but are older than undergraduates, would be a calming influence by our presence."

"And you could bear witness," I say.

Victor and Celia live twenty minutes south of the campus, in three rooms of a reconverted brownstone. They had been busy all through the week of troubles. On the night of April 29, they did a turn of watch on the campus and got home at about midnight. There were rumors of a bust, but there had been many before. They went to bed exhausted. Victor and Celia had been asleep for perhaps an hour when the telephone rang. It was someone from the Ad-Hoc committee relay system. "There is every indication," the voice said to Victor, "that the police are about to clear the buildings. Please come to the campus, if you're willing." Civility in academe. *Please come, but only if.*

The phone had jarred them both awake. Victor put on slacks, a shirt and a jacket. Celia drew on a pair of black tights, pausing to straighten the seams. She slipped into a miniskirt and blouse and pulled a dark kerchief over her head. The evening was mild. They taxied to the campus, and at the Broadway gate a professor, whom they recognized, and several policemen, whom they did not, asked for their identification cards. Inside, they started toward the flights of steps and the green statue of Alma Mater before Low Library. A man dressed in a lumberjacket shouted, "Hold it. Hold it. You can't go up there."

"Are you a policeman?" Celia said.

"Yes. I'm a policeman. And you can't go up there."

The man was not wearing a badge. Celia was not used to being addressed so rudely. She bit her lip.

"Where can we go?" Victor asked.

"Stand over there," the policeman ordered. He pointed across College Walk toward South Field.

Victor took Celia's arm and gently led her. "Don't let him bother you," he said.

"He talked as if he owned the place," Celia said.

South Field is bordered by privet, and in the dim light of the campus, Victor led Celia through the hedges until they were standing in the open field. On steps above, they could see lines of police moving, silent. Hundreds of others, Columbia people, had been herded into South Field with them. Victor and Celia stood helpless in the open field, beginning to feel claustrophobic under the dark night sky. Then someone came through the hedges shouting, "They've locked the gates. The campus gates are locked. They've sealed the campus."

In The West End bar, among the liberals and the radicals, Celia is telling most of the story, but always looking toward Victor, making sure he is there. It is as if recalling the April night makes terror close, and she needs comfort. I ask if she wants another drink.

"No," says Celia, with soft, black, puppy eyes. "I want to get everything just right, just the way it was."

Low Library was illuminated. They could see that from South Field. A great bank of police lights played on the massive Romanesque facade. Although the sight was striking, the lights were there simply to facilitate arrests, and to prevent escape. Sound carried the first hint of violence. Victor and Celia heard sounds rolling from Low Library. Men and women were screaming, in pain and in terror.

"Do something," Celia said.

"We can't," Victor said. "We can't go anywhere. You see those uniformed police." Victor pointed to a line on top of the steps. "They're TPFs, the Tactical Patrol Force. There's no way we can get through."

The screaming rolled down, as if from a madhouse. "You're being used," someone shouted at the TPF patrolmen. "Can't you understand you're being used?" The TPFs faced the crowd in South Field but you could not make out their faces. It was too dark. All you could see were bulky forms, with helmets and with nightsticks.

In front of Low, police began dragging students down the stone steps. One policeman would hold each leg, and then the men backed downstairs rapidly in tandem. At intervals on South Field, you could hear heads slamming rhythmically against the stone. One student was screaming, "I'll walk. I'll walk." Then, as the pain and terror magnified, he lost speech, and made a high shrill horrifying sound.

The crowd on South Field began chanting, "Strike, strike, strike." A policeman bellowed, "All right, now back up toward that building over there." He indicated Butler Hall. The crowd was only vocally aggressive. People spun and backed quickly. Celia turned her ankle in the spongy grass. It stung and would hurt more. The crowd was shouting, "Kirk must go! Truman must go!"

No one admits just who gave the order, but suddenly, the Tactical Patrol Police charged the retreating crowd. "Link arms," someone screamed. "Link arms and they can't move us."

The police held clubs high. The crowd turned and ran. The police beat the retreating people on their calves and thighs and buttocks, and poked anyone who turned with the point of a club thrust hard toward the groin.

Celia was running as fast as she could. Her ankle ached. She wanted to tell Victor she had hurt her ankle. They were running toward the southwest corner of the campus. They had been standing where the police told them to stand. They had not been asked to leave. They had not been warned. And now they were running toward a corner of the campus. But the campus had been locked tight. Celia stopped for an instant. She still heard the shrieking from Low. It was just wrong.

"Motherfuckers," she screamed at the TPFs. "Motherfucker fascist pigs."

"You know," Victor says in The West End bar, "I've never seen her like that. Never. Ever."

Policemen chased her. She was terrified now. They would beat her, Celia thought. The soft, puppy eyes were wild. The injured ankle made her limp. Running awkwardly, Celia fell over a small fence that protected flowers. Her tights snared. Celia felt she could not move. A policeman began bending her legs backward, against the hip joint, as if to force her heels against the back of her neck. He had a square hard face; his lips were drawn across set teeth.

"Let go of me," Celia screamed. "Let go, you motherfucker." The policeman's eyes were small and very bright.

Victor was trying to help her, but a plainclothesman beat a nightstick at Victor's back. Victor turned. "I'm trying to help my wife."

The word was shocking. This woman, draped brazenly across the fence, was a wife. The policeman took his hands off her legs. Then he and Victor helped her up. Celia was crying with fright.

Five feet from where she stood, students crouched in a circle shouting, "It's our university, it's our university."

"Bastard kids," roared the policeman. He whipped out handcuffs and charged. He held one cuff and swung the other at faces. A boy yelped and collapsed holding his nose.

It was still dark. Celia was screaming and shrieking. Victor fixed on an objective, a building beyond the battle.

He led her firmly and they made good progress, but a few yards away from the entrance, Victor saw a boy who had been brutalized. Blood ran from a scalp cut. So much blood ran down his eyes that he could not see. The boy was very young, probably a freshman. He was wailing over and over, "Somebody help me."

A uniformed policeman watched clinically. "You have to get him to a doctor," Victor said.

"*You* get him to a doctor," the cop said.

Victor took the dark kerchief that was still on Celia's head. She was crying less loudly now. He wiped the boy's bloody eyes and pressed the kerchief against the wound. Then, taking his weeping wife with one arm and the weeping freshman with the other, Victor led them to a door into New Hall, a men's residence.

They had not gone very far through the glass doors, the graduate student, the bloody freshman and the weeping wife, when a Columbia security man ran toward them from within. Victor offered a small smile of welcome.

"Hey," the guard said. "You can't come in here."

"Why not?"

"No women in the men's dormitories after ten o'clock."

They are holding hands at the table. The remembered experience has brought them very close together. "It was ten days before I could go back to the campus," Celia says, "but I'm pretty well over this now."

"I got her to bed and asleep and I went back," Victor says. "I saw an overrun first aid station. Did you know about that?"

"I know the doctor who was overrun."

"That morning," Victor says, "Lionel Trilling was standing on the steps, looking at all the wreckage. A wonderful critic, a person like that. He seemed in shock. He was stooped and gray and crushed, as though *he* had been beaten."

The terrain of the battle is important. You have to know the slopes and the clearings, the shelters and the defilade areas. You want to know the stones of a place and where a man can hide.

Columbia, the battlefield, was cleverly designed.

Because land is scarce and expensive in Manhattan, the architects, among them Stanford White, tried for a spacious illusion with interconnecting plazas. Tended hedges serve as walls. The lowest land, the broad, grassy area around Butler Library, is called South Field. Past privets, the field extends eastward to a promenade in front of Hamilton Hall, the Van Am Quad. This system rises slightly toward a main pathway. College Walk, which bisects the campus east-west, is a broad avenue paved with octagonal blocks. Low Plaza rises in broad flights and marbled flats. The plaza is bordered by grassy areas and two plain fountains that shoot single streams of water. Above all stands Low Library, with its high Romanesque dome. Low occupies the highest ground, a leveled tract that sweeps from Dodge Hall on the west around the entire north campus, including, going clockwise, Lewisohn, Mathematics, Havemeyer, Uris, Schermerhorn, Avery, Fayerweather, Philosophy and Kent Hall. Beyond, to the north, the land descends again. The Low area is the vital center of the campus. This is where one finds four out of the five buildings that were occupied.

By the morning of Monday, April 29, Truman and Kirk felt they had gone as far as they could. They had sent Kenneth Clark, a black psychologist, to make a separate peace with the blacks. They had asked Theodore Kheel, a pre-eminent labor mediator, to propose a settlement. Clark failed and Kheel's opening proposals were spurned. Kheel expected to mediate further Tuesday, but Kirk and Truman had run out of patience. The time for mediation was done.

At noon Monday, Howard Leary, the commissioner of police, lunched with editors in the executive dining room of *The New York*

Times. Times luncheons have become command performances in New York City, particularly since *The Herald Tribune* perished. They are sophisticated exercises in public relations. *Times* executives get news tips from their guests—usually off the record—and a briefing on current situations. In turn, the guest, police commissioner or President, makes friends with the men who publish the most potent newspaper in Christendom. Howard Leary rode the *Times* elevators, and ate the *Times* shrimp cocktail and bantered with the *Times* brass. But, on the testimony of several people who were there, he did not announce the coming Columbia bust. "If it came up at all," says A. M. Rosenthal, now the managing editor of the *Times*, "and I'm not sure that it did, it was in a very general way." After lunch, Leary was driven downtown to his office at 100 Centre Street and back to work.

Sometime Monday afternoon, Columbia executives sent word to Centre Street. They wanted the occupied buildings cleared. One official Columbia report says that Grayson Kirk called Leary at 6 P.M., which is accurate but possibly misleading. Kirk did indeed telephone Leary then, but others, and possibly Kirk himself, had spoken to police officials earlier. New York policemen work eight-hour shifts, one of which ends at 4 P.M. Hundreds of policemen, in a dozen stationhouses, who had been scheduled to go home at four were ordered to remain. By midafternoon, the police officials were marshaling the manpower that they would deploy at Columbia toward dawn.

After talking to Kirk, Commissioner Leary assigned the Columbia operation to his direct subordinate, Chief Inspector Sanford Garelik. Although Sandy Garelik is a hard-nosed man, not civil libertarian but cop, some members of the force call him an intruder. The police department is an Irish Catholic preserve, and Garelik is a Jew. He was appointed during the unorthodox mayoralty of Fiorello LaGuardia and installed as chief inspector under unorthodox John Lindsay. Garelik is not as far right as the old Irish Guard, and that, plus his religion, makes him suspect to many New York police.

The plan, as Garelik and his assistants devised it, was functional. About a thousand policemen would be dispatched to the five Manhattan precinct houses closest to Columbia. They would be briefed in basements by their superiors and by Columbia spokesmen. Then they would be driven to staging areas near the campus. Hamilton was to be cleared first. That would defuse the racial bomb. Low would go next. Take the command post. Then Fayerweather, Avery, Mathematics. An arm or two might have to be twisted, but Garelik did not anticipate much violence. A thousand police, including members of the elite Tactical Patrol Force, could comfortably handle the four or five hundred students Kirk and Truman said were in the buildings.

Truman specified that not one, but two warnings were to be issued through a bullhorn before any buildings were cleared. First a university representative would speak, then a policeman. After that the police were to allow any rebel who wanted to quit free exit from the building without arrest. When the police actually entered, they would not carry clubs or blackjacks. In the event of violence, police surgeons would care for the injured on *both* sides. No police wagons were to roll on the campus. The vans would be left on Amsterdam Avenue and on Broadway. Finally, the bust would begin at 4 A.M., when most of the students were docile with sleep, and the campus was least likely to be overrun by spectators. "They promised all these things," Truman says sadly, "but they went back on their word."

By Monday, more than 250 journalists were wandering the campus, and the radicals, wiser here than Kirk or Truman, knew that an orderly bust was unlikely. Some wanted to make the bust as fierce as possible. "That way," one radical said, "the whole world will see the pigheadedness and brutality of the power structure." A number of extreme radicals held private meetings and discussed the best ways to goad police.

In one apartment, a girl remembers, there was a cold discussion on "rattling the pigs." "What we are dealing with," said the leader, a Columbia College undergraduate, "is a certain kind of Irish Catholic prudity, with a lot of sadism thrown in. We've seen these men before. They beat up a black kid and take graft, but they get off their rocks with a priest once a week. So they have this crazy sense that they're guardians of morals. They're the kind of guys who have a hard time with sex, a hard time getting hard is what I mean. So here's what we want to do. We want to shake them."

"How?" asked the girl, uneasily. About ten people were assembled in a building on West 113th Street.

"Well, you can always pick up your skirt. They won't know whether to jerk off or go blind. But if that's too rough, take 'em apart with words. Tell 'em their mother sucks black cocks, or takes black cocks in the ass."

The girl blinked. "The important thing," said the group leader, "is you got to use these words. I know that can be tough. We aren't all completely liberated. But if we use words like *sucks* about their mother, these fuckin' cops will blow like a balloon. And when they blow, they'll be there naked and the whole country will see the naked face, the naked ass, of fascism."

The coming bust troubled Rabbi Bruce Goldman. The rabbi focused his concern on medical help for injured students. He did not anticipate injury to himself. Late Monday, Goldman left his office in Earl Hall to chat with the Catholic chaplain, Father James E. Rea. The most sensible way to obtain adequate medical help on campus, the two clerics agreed, was to telephone H. Houston Merritt, dean of the College of Physicians and Surgeons and university vice-president for medical affairs. The conversation took place through intermediaries; Rea's secretary explained the concern to a secretary of H. Houston Merritt. "Hold on, please," Merritt's secretary said. When she spoke again it was to report a blunt reaction. "Dr. Merritt," she announced, "says that he wouldn't touch the campus tonight with a ten-foot pole."

Rabbi Goldman went home to 440 Riverside Drive at about 8 P.M. Toward 2 A.M. Tuesday his telephone rang. The caller said that the police were about to clear the campus. The rabbi dressed in haste, putting on a dark suit and a blue tie. Meanwhile on campus workmen were closing water pipes that feed sprinkler systems and fire hoses. The police action began by neutralizing a counterweapon.

At 2:15 Rabbi Goldman identified himself at the main gate and was admitted to the campus. He walked directly to the east side of Low. He wanted to reach the students in Fayerweather. Access down paths through the hedges was blocked by wooden barricades marked "Police Dept." A line of policemen stood in front of the horses.

"I'm a rabbi," Goldman began. "I want to get through."

"*Nobody* gets through," a uniformed patrolman said.

"I'm a Columbia clergyman," Goldman said. He is a compact, intense man who wears a neat beard.

"Look, Mac," said a policeman. "We don't care who you are or what you do. You don't get through."

"I am a chaplain." Rabbi Goldman pushed forward. Two policemen knocked him backward. Goldman staggered, but did not fall.

"Now just a minute here. This man is an official of Columbia University." James P. Shenton, a history professor at the college, had been standing nearby. He wanted to vouch for the rabbi. "He has a right to pass these barricades," Professor Shenton said.

"He got no rights," said a policeman, "except the right to ask us. He asked and we said no."

The rabbi abruptly lost his temper. "I have a right to function here," he said. "You can't deny me that right." He tried to push through again. One policeman punched him in the ribs. Another spun him. The first policeman drove a fist into him again. Rabbi Goldman found his footing and took a pad from his pocket. He wanted to record the numbers of the policemen. Another policeman stepped in front of Goldman. "Nobody writes down anything," he said. Goldman was shoved again, and finally knocked down. Someone kicked him in the back and made him gasp.

At 2 A.M. it was fifty-three degrees and somewhat misty. Abe Rosenthal of the *Times* was riding up to Columbia alongside Police Commissioner Howard Leary. Rosenthal had attended the musical *Hair*, which he enjoyed. Then he walked into the *Times* office "to read the tickers" in the newsroom. Everyone was talking about the coming bust. The police had tipped the *Times* and men attached to the Metropolitan desk were preparing a dummy story. *"Police tonight cleared students from all five occupied buildings of the campus."* Details would be filled in later. The *Times* wanted to get as much into type in advance as possible. Edition schedules shifted. The *Times* would make the Columbia story in almost all the next morning's late city edition.

At Columbia, Seth Shulman had wandered out of Fayerweather and joined a group standing in front of Avery. Josie Duke was waiting in Low, frightened but tearless. Truman and Kirk sat in a ground-floor office in Low. Dick Greeman had left the campus at 7 P.M., convinced the bust would not come that night. Andrea and Richard had returned to Fayerweather. Two hundred and fifty Harlem blacks filled Amsterdam Avenue from 110th Street and moved slowly, cautiously toward the campus. Mark Rudd left his office at Ferris Booth and walked about with a retinue and a walkie-talkie. Mounted police, their helmets reflecting street lamps, rode up and down on Broadway. To the north on Amsterdam Avenue near 120th Street, hundreds of other policemen were assembling.

"Hey," Cicero Wilson called out of a third-floor window in Hamilton, as the blacks of Harlem proceeded up Amsterdam Avenue. "Look, man. The brothers are on the move."

Suddenly, it seemed to the people on campus, police descended from everywhere. One truck, filled with wooden barriers, drove into the campus from Amsterdam Avenue. A column of policemen, perhaps forty in all, marched behind. A second column followed, and a third. One detachment moved toward Low, but the action now centered on Hamilton Hall.

Before the bland gaze of Alexander Hamilton's statue, forty police under Inspector Waithe pressed toward the timid cordon, ten young faculty men who were guarding the building with their bodies. With the inspector was a Columbia official. He held a bullhorn and read:

> On behalf of the trustees of Columbia University, the owner of this building, Hamilton Hall, I have been authorized to order you not to remain and you are hereby ordered to remove yourselves forthwith.
>
> All necessary precautions have been taken to assure your safety as you leave the building. The New York City Police Department is here to assure that.

Lights were being turned on inside Hamilton. Through the windows you could see blacks standing in the lobby.

A black police officer took the bullhorn. He repeated parts of the first statement, then added:

"We have been empowered by the trustees to remove anyone now occupying the building and to charge him with criminal trespass. If you leave now, you will not be arrested."

On a third-floor balcony, a black student cupped his hands and bellowed: "Speak a little louder, Uncle Tom."

The black policeman directed himself toward the faculty-student cordon. "If you impede us, you also will be subject to arrest." No one moved, but neither did the cordon lock arms. The police were strangely calm. Behind them the crowd filling the Van Am Quadrangle strained to see. Light played through trees, falling on the spectators in speckled patterns.

The police moved toward the faculty-student cordon in a wedge. "Excuse me," a black captain said over and over. "Excuse me please." He edged steadily ahead until he reached the front doors.

"Hey," a white policeman called, "anyone got a key? We forgot ours."

The lead officers began rattling the doors. "Someone call a cop," cried a policeman at the back of the column. "There's guys trying to break into this place."

But police were already inside Hamilton. The men, the spectators saw, approaching from the front were a diversion. Following subterranean tunnels that run for several blocks and join a half dozen buildings, the key police force, blue-helmeted and resolute, had crashed Hamilton Hall from underneath. The tunnels led them to the basement, and they moved briskly upstairs. Soon more than a hundred police were in the lobby. William Booth, the city human rights commissioner, accompanied them to observe arrests.

"All right," a black police officer told the crowd outside of Hamilton, "everyone inside has agreed not to resist arrest. They want to be arrested peacefully. There's nothing to see. Let's move along."

For all the vocal militance of Cicero Wilson, the blacks did not physically resist. In turn, the carefully watched police were gentle. Only the first group of blacks was handcuffed. After that, at the suggestion of William Booth, the cuffs were put away. The blacks, who had prepared saucers of vaseline to attenuate mace and who had formed an exit plan to protect their women, now left Hamilton Hall through the underground tunnels, quietly and without emotion. Eighty-six students were arrested. No one was injured.

On Amsterdam a few city employees walked among the blacks who had come from Harlem. "There was no trouble. No trouble. Everyone was treated with respect."

Word spread through the crowd. It shuffled to a stop. Men talked intensely. Then, as slowly as it had come, the crowd dispersed down Amsterdam Avenue.

The terror of a Harlem uprising was thus gently laid to rest.

Dr. Thomas Harper never saw the club that slit his scalp. He remembers pain, and stitches and a question that he was trying to answer, just before the blow.

Harper was the physician inside the executive offices on the second floor at Low. When the police entered, an officer, seeing Harper's years and medical jacket and sensing authority, said, "Can you talk some sense into these kids and get them to walk out?"

"If I could," Harper said, "I wouldn't. And I can't. I'm only the medical aide. These young people make decisions on their own."

Someone spun Harper. Someone else struck him from behind. Then —the scene lives in Josie Duke's mind—a third policeman began to blackjack Harper. The doctor fell gradually, a look of surprise on his face. He had never been blackjacked before. He sank to his knees. The police continued beating him. Blood stained his scalp. He made a guttural noise. Then he was down. Other policemen dragged him out of Grayson Kirk's office by his feet.

The police were working with their overall plan. First Hamilton, then Low, then the others. But David Truman had said there were no more than four or five hundred people in all the buildings; the police were alarmed to find more than one thousand. The crowd on campus,

perhaps fifteen hundred, worried them too. But their plans were well
drawn and their men were armed. No one yet knows whether the
blackjack assault on Tom Harper was plan or improvisation. It was the
first brutal incident of the night.

Each police contingent, one hundred to two hundred men, was
assigned to a building and placed under an inspector. Waithe, the
Negro assistant chief inspector for the entire city, supervised the
gentle bust at Hamilton. An inspector named Kowski was assigned at
Low Library. Inspector Kelly was in charge at Avery. Inspector Kra-
sewski drew Fayerweather. The individual police possessed various
expertise at handling riots. Several hundred came from the Tactical
Patrol Force, the elite six-footers who, the department advertises,
"undergo advanced training in the psychology of crowd control."
They also undergo training, on secluded fields in the borough of Rich-
mond, on how to charge, how to beat retreating men on the backs of
the legs and how to thrust the tip of a nightstick into genitals.

Other detachments were nonspecialized patrolmen. These men
were least certain of what they were to do. They were also irritable.
Many had worked a full eight-to-four trick at their regular precinct.
Then, suddenly alerted, they had to call home and say they could not
be there for dinner. After that they waited, in the cellars of precinct
houses, wasting hours at cards or in talk, but somewhat nervous, as
troops are nervous, not knowing what it is they have to face.

Also there were plainclothesmen. These men are not detectives.
New York detectives carry gold badges; plainclothesmen hold shields
of silver. Detectives look down on them. Much plainclothes work is
demeaning: petty vice, prostitution, bookmaking. Plainclothesmen
tend to be rough, cynical and venal. Finally, there was at least one
detachment of jackbooted motorcycle police. An oddly assorted
police legion stormed Columbia. According to Jacques Nevard,
then a deputy commissioner, "We sent the best force we could mus-
ter."

While the detachment entered Hamilton at 2:10 A.M., other columns
were marched into College Walk. One strode toward Low. At about
ten-minute intervals, additional columns closed on Avery and Fayerweather.

Like Hamilton, Low stands over a tunnel. The police, marching to
Low from Amsterdam Avenue, were not assigned to clear the building. Rather they were to restrain crowds and to clear corridors leading
to the paddy wagons that followed behind them. Despite Truman's
opposition, the police drove vans onto the campus. The sooner the

protesters could be stuffed into wagons, they felt, the better. The police were genuinely afraid of a massed uprising of rebels and spectators.

The Low faculty cordon was resolute. About forty police climbed the steps toward Low, marching directly toward the southeast entrance, where a few nights earlier Dick Greeman had been clubbed. Another column silently approached Low from the north. This detachment formed a police line twenty yards above the building, sealing one direction of escape. A third column proceeded through underground tunnels. The Low commune, now ninety-three strong, had less than half an hour of life.

The police marching toward the security entrance were led by plainclothesmen. The men had been ordered to display their badges, but many refused. Some, wearing lumber jackets, pinned shields to the insides of lapels. Two or three wore shields upside-down.

Students bolstered the faculty cordon. Many locked arms. It was two-thirty in the morning. The students chanted, "No violence. Cops must go. No violence."

The police stopped twenty feet from the swelling cordon. The groups faced each other in the dim light. A uniformed sergeant stepped forward. "You are obstructing the police. I warn you that if you do not move, you will be subject to arrest."

Someone in the crowd started to sing "Sans Souci," Columbia's anthem. He stopped when he forgot the words. The police moved closer, and the crowd burst into "The Star-Spangled Banner." Then the plainclothesmen, armed with sticks and handcuffs, closed with the cordon.

The plainclothesmen first attacked the flanks, peeling off men and shoving them hard enough to make them stagger. Dan Pellogram, president of the Student Council, stood at a fringe. A plainclothesman seized him, snapping Pellogram's neck. Then he kneed Pellogram in the groin, left him doubled over and moved on. The first yelps carried through darkness. "Crowd control by terror is legitimate," one police executive said later.

Uniformed police attacked the center of the cordon. The faculty members had locked arms. Against the sure and unified police charge, the faculty fell, almost en masse. One instant there was a line of well-dressed men, and the next the men were on the ground, face down. The uniformed police ran over them. They stepped on some. Nightsticks were out; the police beat several fallen men. It was light enough to see men writhe. Someone suddenly ran into the melee screaming, "Peace. For God's sake, peace." A plainclothesman slammed a forearm full into his face. The man fell and lay on the stones of Low Plaza, silent.

The plainclothesmen fanned more widely. They wanted all the area in front of Low cleared. A man was taking notes near a corner of Low. Two plainclothesmen ran into him, shoulders low, and drove him through the privet. They followed through the quivering hedge. Two students came up and helped the man to his feet. "I'm a campus reporter," the man said. The police beat the reporter and the two who tried to help him, whipping their clubs in short, punishing strokes.

A girl in jeans and a jacket watched from another fringe. She had no shoes on. A plainclothesman approached and she started to run toward Philosophy Hall. The plainclothesman cracked a fist into the side of her head. She did not moan or cry. She simply crumpled. The tactic of terror is devastating. Within ten minutes the entrance to Low Library had been cleared. The police marched in.

Inside Low, they joined the contingent that had entered Low through tunnels. They hurried up the marble stairs and opened the doors to Suite 202, old oak decorated with a small sign saying "Office of the President." Shoving aside desks and chairs with great speed, they dismantled the students' barricades.

Within Kirk's office, members of the commune sat on the floor in a circle. They were facing inward and singing "We Shall Overcome." A few had locked arms, which can be interpreted as resisting arrest. Many did not. They sang quietly. They could hear the police outside. Then Paul Carter, vice-provost, read the form statement: "On behalf of the trustees . . . I have been authorized to order you not to remain in Low Library."

A police officer read another statement: "Adequate measures have been taken to insure your safety." The only response was the refrain of the song. The police broke in. All the students stood up. Then the police attacked Dr. Thomas Harper.

The police fear of concerted action against them is understandable. They were foreign to Columbia ground, by all the traditions, and they sensed it. They didn't belong. People from their station, the Irish lower middle-class, who went to college, attended St. John's of Brooklyn, or St. Francis. A few good students made the Jesuit severity of Fordham. Poor students finished high school and studied at semi-professional institutes to prepare for police and fire examinations.

The policemen had dreamed their own images of the Columbia barony. One told me long afterward how let down he was: "I thought the place and the people up there would be real special. Instead, it was nothing but a lot of pinkos." But a great number of police came to Columbia, which they believed had discriminated against their class for generations, prepared to be let down, prepared to dislike what they saw, subconsciously or consciously prepared to hate.

* * * * * *

The policeman is sitting in a bar on Broadway, fourteen blocks from the Columbia campus, remembering some of the things he saw and did. "Go slow, very slow," the cop says. "Don't try and push me." Then, "Hell, I shouldn't even be talkin' to you at all."

The police, the best of them, are not proud of what they did during The Battle for Morningside Heights. Jacques Nevard, the former deputy commissioner for public relations, submits, "We were asked to step into the worst kind of scene—dispute among Columbia and its students and its neighbors. Any cop will tell you there's nothing worse than breaking up a family quarrel." A Captain Glaser in Nevard's office adds, "I wouldn't repeat to you some of the things they called our men." But in the end one leaves police headquarters certain that important cops are unhappy. They feel that there is nothing much to choose between radicals and academicians. They are only sorry they had to make the choice.

The policeman at the bar is an off-duty plainclothesman, identifiable as police by an assertive manner and by a small, significant bulge on his right hip. "You want a Scotch?" I ask.

"No. I drink beer."

The policeman is a stocky, black-haired Irishman, a bachelor of thirty-two, and he is worried that I might print his name.

"You can say I'm Irish," he says. "They ain't gonna identify me from that, but if you say who I am, you know, it starts some heat."

"Sure."

"It's better for you if you don't use my name. If you promise you won't use it, I can tell you more about what really went on."

"Well, sure. I promise."

The beer comes. The cop sips. He smacks his lips and sips again. "Good," he says. "What did they tell you downtown?"

"Not a helluva lot."

"They don't know what's going on downtown," the cop says.

It is a reasonable gripe of a workingman against his superiors. And this cop is a workingman. He works hard for a base of $8,700. He supplements it, I suppose, in little ways, as policemen do, but he is not wealthy. "Did you go to college?" he asks me.

"Until I started writing."

"I got in a term at St. John's. Then I had to quit and join the force. My father was dead. Believe me, I wished I coulda finished. If I had college, I coulda gone to law school. That woulda been something for my mother. It would have made her proud to have me be an assistant D.A." The cop is sipping as he talks. He chain-smokes cigarettes without a filter. "What I saw at the college was something terrible," he says.

"What college?"

"Columbia College. Kids acting like bums, and showing no respect for the law. These same kids who shoulda been down on their knees thanking the Lord that He had let them go to college. I woulda been on my knees myself."

More beers come. The cop grows expansive. "I get kinda sore at something, you know? Everything I got in life I worked for. It gets me sore when I see these kids, who been handed everything, pissing it away, talking like bums, dressing like pigs."

"Did they *call* you pig?"

He has black eyes; they glare like lamplights. "Where'd you hear that? It's some joke, ain't it, a rich kid calling a police officer pig. These smart-ass college kids think they're so big they can get away with anything they want. I don't have to take that, particularly from smart-ass college kids."

His jaw is set and he glares with remembered anger. "But you agree to take certain abuse," I say, "when you sign up to be a cop."

"All right," he says. "But I got limits. My mother doesn't have to take abuse." He continues very quietly and evenly.

"I'm up at Columbia. I'm trying to get people moving. They're maybe not moving. I'm a little scared myself. Not much, but a little. And I gotta shove. I shove. There's some girl sitting down. I tell her, *MOVE*. She sits where she is and she looks at me and says, wait a minute. I wrote it down." The cop reaches into his wallet and takes out a folded piece of white paper.

"I wrote it down, in case I ever got to testify on any of the stuff that went on." He stares at the worn paper and reads: "Your sister sucks off your mother." He reads it in a monotone. Then he carefully replaces the paper in the wallet.

"So I hit her," he says. "I hit her good. I made her cry."

* * * * * *

The policeman who beat Thomas Harper eliminated an important witness. It could be easy in the event of later trouble to dismiss the testimony of young radicals as irresponsible. A bald-headed physician, however, could prove formidable. The police dragged Harper out of 202 and into a hall. There he was handcuffed.

"My bag," Harper said. "I have to get my bag, so I can treat injuries." Blood was running down the back of his head.

"You don't need it, Doc," a plainclothesman said. "We'll take care of anyone who gets hurt." Harper tried to rise and the plainclothesman pushed him back.

In the corridors, police formed gauntlets. One file of police wearing leather jackets stood in the office of Kirk's secretary. Another gauntlet formed in the ground-floor rotunda, where Dean Hovde would welcome the autumn frosh.

Inside Kirk's office, patrolmen waded into the circle of singing radicals. One seized Tony Papert, spun him to his feet, and shoved him toward the exit. Papert was handcuffed to a boy he knew only as Paul. The two ran the gauntlet. A few police chopped at them with blackjacks, but police fury was still developing. Papert and Paul were pushed into the rotunda, unhurt.

Josie Duke was arrested soon afterward. A policeman grabbed her and she tried to spin away. The policeman seized her arms and squeezed them. Josie tried to kick him. Then the policeman spun her and she was shoved into the corridor and handcuffed. She was not beaten in the gauntlet, but later, as she was being pushed into a patrol wagon, a policeman put an arm on Josie's shoulder and said, "How did you like it in there?"

"What?" Josie said.

"Did you get pregnant?"

With vans parked on College Walk outside Low Plaza, the police pushed the communards outside. The plaza could be kept permanently clear. People kept darting in and out, but the police had made their point. No spectators walked close to the police lines.

The gauntlet outside was rougher than the one within. Students were shoved down flights of stone steps, and dragged by their feet and knocked head first. A kind of cry arose, composed of a dozen individual shouts of pain. There was no apparent logic to the police action. They seemed to select victims on whim. One bearded boy, stumbling down the steps, was suddenly set upon by a plainclothesman with a blackjack. The man beat the boy. "Don't," the boy said. "Please, don't."

A girl cried, "Stop that." The plainclothesman continued the beating. "Stop hitting David," the girl screamed.

The man beat David to semiconsciousness. Under the beard, David's face began to swell. Then David was rolled out of the way. He was not prominent in the commune, and he had said nothing to provoke the police. Friends had difficulty recognizing him for several days.

"But why?" a girl was crying, as the Low commune died. "Why," as she climbed, trembling, into a van, "do you bastards have to be so bloody?"

Later a police officer told a Columbia official, "When kids go limp or refuse to be budged or touched, all you can do is push and drag them. To carry each one individually takes three times the force. It takes four policemen, one for each leg and arm. And it's slower. If we'd had the manpower, we still would have been there half the night. We had to do it the way we did."

The Columbia official did not ask why it was necessary to array TPFs into a gauntlet, and the police have never tried to explain, nor do they concede officially, that the gauntlet was there.

What was happening in Low, one veteran policeman insists, unofficially, was a rebellion against Garelik-Lindsay. "Pretty much on the level of captain on down. A lot of the men wanted to make Garelik look bad." Men with significant rank organized the gauntlet. Men with rank watched the beating of Harper. None moved to stop it.

Avery, housing the architecture students, was the first building that the police had to attack frontally. No tunnels led within. The main police column approached College Walk, then turned north past Low Plaza. Scores and then hundreds of observers trailed the police.

Avery stands thirty yards west of Low. At 3 A.M. the grounds before Avery lay in darkness. The brightest light issued from illuminated fountains, dry now, at Uris Hall. The police took darkness as their shield.

Hedges border a plaza before the doors to Avery. Silently, plainclothesmen moved in, rows of bulky men tramping along the hedgerows. About one hundred uniformed police massed before the doors. Behind, wedging them, a crowd grew. Some put the number at nine hundred.

The young people jeered and chanted. "Cops must go. Cops go

home." In front of the police, men stood in a silent cordon. Professors of architecture were there, Percival Goodman, Alexander Kouzmanoff, Raymond Lifchez, and students, including Seth Shulman. From the second floor of Avery rock music blared. The police were uncomfortable, even frightened. A university spokesman and a police officer read the eviction demand hastily. While the policeman was talking, someone in the cordon broke and cut into the hedges. Plainclothesmen beat him with saps. A sap is a small truncheon sheathed in leather. It does not break the skin the way a blackjack does, but it inflicts equal pain.

The men in the cordon locked arms and sang "We Shall Overcome." "Get 'em, get the commies," someone shouted. The men continued to sing.

Deep in our hearts
Thy will be done
We shall overcome

A police charge stifled the hymn. The uniformed police advanced, throwing people aside toward the hedges and the plainclothesmen with saps. One man was lifted and thrown completely over a hedge. A woman, standing in front of the building, was spun, her arms twisted behind her back. She screamed and screamed. Some uniformed police lashed out with walkie-talkie aerials. The police did not trample this cordon so much as punish it. A professor staggered out of the mass, bleeding from the head. He fell across a concrete pavement, moaning. Professor Lifchez was beaten until he could not stand or walk. Seth Shulman decided that the best defense was to lie on the ground, curled into a ball, with hands clasped over his head. The police were unidentifiable in the darkness. They had no one to account to. And they were scared. The elements mixed to a ferocity.

Police burst into the foyer of Avery. A small group sat there. The police grabbed the students and shoved them into the darkness outside where others were still beating professors.

A police vanguard drove up five flights. The sixth floor was dark and empty. The police cast their flashlights down corridors and went to the fifth floor. There they found a group singing. Others ran down farther. Near the second floor, on the marble staircase, Robert Thomas, Jr., a district reporter for *The New York Times*, was watching.

Police were pouring into Avery. "Hey, what are ya doing?" someone shouted at Thomas.

"I'm with the *Times*."

"No press," a policeman shouted. "No goddamn press."

Police began to swing at Thomas. The reporter found his press card, a little colored cardboard badge signed by Howard Leary, and, spinning and tumbling down the stairs, he held it as high as he could. It was no armor. A policeman swung a handcuff into Thomas's scalp. Twelve stitches later closed the wound.

A gauntlet formed. The police on the fourth and fifth floors handcuffed students to one another in pairs and started them down the stairs. Farther down, other police kicked them. Some stumbled on the stairs. The police kept prodding.

One protester, semiconscious and bleeding from the head, was dragged down the outside steps of Avery, feet first, by a policeman.

"Can't you see?" a young woman screamed. "That's a human being you're doing that to."

The policeman never looked up. "He could walk if he wanted to," he said.

Another girl, in jeans, kicked out as a policeman dragged her outside. Two plainclothesmen pulled her to a tree in the courtyard and they rhythmically beat her head against the trunk. "Fuck you," she yelled. "Oh, fuck you, you bastards. Oh."

Two men moved to her rescue. Plainclothesmen grabbed them and pulled them down. One of the men screamed as saps landed. The sound of saps continued. Avery was cleared in twenty minutes. By 3:20 A.M., the Architecture Commune had been destroyed.

Fayerweather, with its tumult of graduate students, was next. The building stands directly east of Avery, separated by a small plaza. Rabbi Bruce Goldman had weathered the first police attack near Low. Now he joined the cordon standing before the south steps at Fayerweather. Goldman linked arms with Alexander Erlich, a professor of economics, and Sidney Morgenbesser, the professor of philosophy. Three students, victims at Avery, ran wildly in front of them. One was bleeding from head wounds. Blood covered his face, his neck, his chest.

"How did this happen?" Rabbi Goldman asked.

"The police kept beating me."

At that moment Goldman saw fresh police contingents marching on Fayerweather from both north and south. The units, about 150 uniformed men and at least 20 plainclothesmen, walked slowly. An officer had decided a slow pace would maintain calm.

Leonard DeFiore, assistant director of admissions at the School of

Engineering and Applied Science, read the warrant on behalf of the trustees. A police captain took the bullhorn and called: "We have orders to clear the area. Please move away and do not obstruct the police in their work."

Immediately—before anyone who wanted to leave could have escaped—someone barked an order: "Take posts." The police arrayed themselves in a wedge and charged the cordon. Rabbi Goldman took successive blackjack blows to the left side of his head. Someone picked him up and threw him forward. The rabbi landed on his midsection. Someone struck him from behind. In pain, he thought, *there should only be faculty behind me; plainclothesmen must have infiltrated our cordon.*

Rabbi Goldman stumbled to his feet. A punch crashed into the left side of his head. He fell again. He was stunned. He could hear screaming. To his right, a girl was lying on her back, hysterical.

The rabbi tried to rise again. He wanted to comfort the girl. A policeman kicked the back of Goldman's head. In the half-dark, a student who recognized the rabbi fell over him, using his own body as a shield.

The rabbi was dazed. Three other students ran to him. They lifted him and dragged him to a gate at Amsterdam and 117th Street. There, as tenderly as they could, they placed the rabbi on the roof of a parked car. Later they carried him to a first-aid station that had been thrown up on South Field. Wendy Donn, a registered nurse, washed his wounds.

Past the cordon, police dismantled the barricades at Fayerweather. They proceeded up a wide marble staircase to the top story, and began to work down. Two groups of students on the fourth floor were singing "We Shall Overcome." The police moved in roughly. It was here that the policeman took a sharp bite to the belly. One girl bit a policeman's fingers, drawing blood. Again the police organized a gauntlet.

On the third floor of Fayerweather a large lounge had been barricaded. The police pounded down wooden doors, breaking the lock. Then they faced a barrier composed largely of red leather chairs. No singing greeted them here. "Pigs," people were shouting. "Fucking fascist pigs." The police threw aside chairs and pounded at the radicals. They shoved them from the lounge toward staircases that run down a wall facing Amsterdam Avenue. No one outside could see what the police were doing. Fayerweather—Marx's Park—was "cleared" by 3:50 A.M. By an official police account, seventeen people were injured. Since the same account insists that only five people were injured at Avery, the police statistics appear to err on the side of underestimating police violence.

Mathematics was the last to fall. Across campus from Avery, this commune, mixing a hard-line radical core with a good number of visiting adults, had devised a rigorous defense. Each step on the staircase was slicked with soap or vaseline. Activists on the second and third floors stood ready with chairs. As the police scrambled up, those who did not slip would be bombarded.

A contingent of 150 policemen reached Math at 3:45 A.M. A conservative claque followed the police, calling, "Go get 'em." Conservatives climbed the steps of Earl Hall, southeast of Math, for a better view of police massing. Between the buildings, Brooke G. Schoepf, a medical anthropologist, and Robert Furtz, a fourth-year student at Columbia medical school, spread white blankets on the lawn. A young physician named Desmond Callan and a medical orderly named Kelly Snodgrass joined them. A police officer approached and said, not harshly, "You better not stand here. You'll get run over." The four moved the aid station to what they hoped would be a safe position. Even before the police moved, they had a patient. One boy, standing in the faculty-student cordon outside the building, watched the police assemble and began to cry. He was treated for "an acute anxiety reaction"—hysterics.

Fifty plainclothesmen milled near the aid station. They wore no badges. Instead they had buttons of green. The buttons told other police that they were colleagues but protected anonymity. "Hey," a plainclothesman shouted to Miss Schoepf, who was wearing a white jacket. "They're gonna need you soon."

A reporter from the FM radio station WBAI arrived, bleeding from a scalp wound. Callan examined him and cleaned the injury. The reporter, carrying a portable tape recorder, continued to describe the scene.

"You'd better lie down on a blanket, and take it easy," Callan said, "until the bleeding stops."

A police officer, seeing the tape recorder, told the reporter, "Okay. Move."

"This man is injured," Dr. Callan said. "He should not be moved."

"If this man stays," said the policeman, "I'll clear the whole lot of you out of here."

The reporter staggered away.

Spotlights played on the area. You could see the action at Math clearly. A group of newspaper reporters stood behind the police. From the steps of Earl Hall, the conservatives shouted, "Get 'em." The administration warrant and the police warning were read through bullhorns. From the fourth floor of Math someone leaned out and shouted, "Fuck you, cops." A group called in unison, "Up against the wall, motherfuckers." The police did not respond.

The front door was barricaded and chained shut. Policemen pried the door with crowbars and used a small saw to cut the chains. When the doors opened, the police confronted a towering stack of furniture. The Math radicals foraging in many offices had created the greatest of all barricades. Still the police worked quickly. The forward men disentangled pieces of the barricade, mostly chairs, and passed them back. Other police set them on the sidewalk. If you could forget what you had seen at Avery or Fayerweather or Low, you might have thought you were observing a model police action.

But the police were still nervous about being wedged. A ranking officer approached a line of TPFs and pointed toward the conservative students standing on the steps of Earl Hall. "All right," he said. "Clear 'em out."

The TPFs bolted up the steps of Earl toward the young men who had been urging the police, "Go get 'em."

You could hear individual shouts. "No, no. Not us. We're with you."

"Hey, what are you doing? We're on your side."

The charging TPFs closed with the conservatives. One neatly dressed boy was thrown against a hedge, his crew-neck sweater torn. He lay trembling. Other TPFs approached. "I'm with *you*," the boy screamed. Then he lunged to his feet and ran.

Inside Math, the police made their way up the soapy stairs very slowly, some on all fours. They were helmeted. From above, students threw chairs. The police backed away.

An officer shouted through a bullhorn, "Anyone throwing chairs will be charged with assaulting an officer. *Assaulting an officer.* You can go to jail for ten years." The barrage stopped. The police resumed their climb. On the second floor, students, among them the chair throwers, waited. From higher still, you could hear *"Up against the wall—"*

The police seized the protesters, some of whom fought back, and shoved them down the slippery stairs. Radicals skidded and bounced to the ground floor. There they were handcuffed and hurled outside. The police there had heard about the chair throwing. They used blackjacks and clubs against the handcuffed students. Sometimes as many as four pummeled one. "You're not supposed to beat them," one girl shouted. "You're not supposed to do that." A uniformed policeman turned and yelled at her: "We'll show these black-white motherfuckers to tangle with us."

The beatings continued. They were not worse than the beatings elsewhere, only more visible. John Kifner, a *Times* reporter, watched, then hurried to Dodge to telephone the metropolitan desk. "I want to do a story about the police outside Math," he said. He began to describe the violence.

There was a brief discussion on the desk. Then Kifner was told, "We don't think it's worth a separate. We'll give you rewrite and they'll take enough for an insert in the general lead."

By 4 A.M. Math was cleared. The police had done the job they were hired to perform. But they were not finished. Police rage was far from spent.

June Finer had set up her aid station on South Field. Victor and Celia were standing there. So were conservative students, frightened now. The reigning mood of the South Field crowd was to protest. No one knows how many people filled the field; estimates run from fifteen hundred to two thousand, and walking among them you could hear shouts of outrage.

"Hey, what are you doing on my campus?"

"Cops must go."

"Cops eat shit."

"Up against the wall."

After a while one chant became most common. The Columbia crowd bellowed at the police: "Sieg Heil. Sieg Heil. Sieg Heil."

A few minutes after four, the police began their charge. They overran June Finer's aid station and they knocked over a man in a white jacket who shouted, "No. I'm a doctor."

The police advanced, whipping the nightsticks their inspectors promised would be left in the station houses. They picked individuals at random, boys and girls, men and women, and beat them. You heard the sounds and after a time you could distinguish between nightstick and blackjack against flesh. The crowd shrank toward the library, 375,000 volumes strong, named for Nicholas Murray Butler. The building was locked tight. The books inside were safe.

The police, arrayed in a loose picket line, drove the crowd toward a gate on West 114th Street, locked earlier to prevent the escape of protesters. Panicked people managed somehow to climb these gates, which are ten feet tall. Then, for no apparent reason, they rushed toward Broadway. One policeman, standing on the corner of Broadway and 114th, started as he saw a crowd of ragged, panicked Columbia people rushing toward him. "Hey," he shouted in alarm, "just what the hell is going on in there?" No one could tell him because no one had yet realized that the police had now become the rioters.

In all, 712 persons were arrested, about three-quarters of them Columbia students. By dawn, 89 faculty men and students had been treated at nearby hospitals. Their wounds ranged from a fractured jaw to gashed scalps and broken ribs. Scores, and possibly hundreds of others, sought treatment from private physicians or at other hospitals. There is no statistical way to appraise the injuries. "To grasp it all," suggests John Hastings, the Columbia assistant vice-president, "you have to think in terms of battle. Only in war do you see anything like what went on."

The maintenance men were at work early, cleaning the strewn lawns and replacing tulips.

13 THE MEANING OF MEANING

EARLY dawn fused with morning after, and everyone shared horror. Eleanor Raskin and Josie Duke and Tony Papert were among hundreds locked into cells at the Tombs. Their cellmates were drunks, whores, junkies. "I'll admit it was a little greasy," Josie says.

Professor Sidney Morgenbesser, Bob Thomas of the *Times* and Rabbi A. Bruce Goldman lay in emergency rooms of St. Luke's Hospital, awaiting treatment. One physician recognized Goldman as a rabbi and shook his head. "Didn't you people learn anything from Auschwitz?" he said. "Do you still have to be pushy?"

Seth Shulman, dry-mouthed with sleeplessness, visited his girlfriend, who made coffee. He remembered that a *Times* photographer had been shooting pictures while he stood in front of Avery and that his father always read the *Times*. He telephoned Boxford, Massachusetts, then, to say that he was neither seriously hurt nor under arrest.

Richard Greeman was at the wheel of his Volkswagen. He was using it to drive injured students to hospitals, where they would be treated more promptly than at St. Luke's. Once the Volkswagen was caught on Broadway in a charge of mounted police. Greeman heard the clatter as the horses swept close by, towering over his little car.

Grayson Kirk made his way back to his office before 5 A.M. The room was a rubble of blankets, half-eaten sandwiches, knapsacks. Kirk had been silent about the police violence. Now he leaned against the pale green wall, placed one hand to his face and said, "My God, how can human beings do a thing like this?"

But quickly, remarkably quickly, horror and despair passed. The radicals soon were released on bail. None of the injuries was fatal. Kirk's office was cleaned. Shortly he was saying that "at Columbia we have protected the integrity of all institutions."

A day later the Ad-Hoc group considered calling a general strike. But Alan Westin, the chairman, yielded to his senior colleagues and adjourned the meeting before a vote could be taken. Even the activist faculty was incapable of action. The tenure men, the Joint Faculties, established an executive committee to "study and recommend changes." The administration canceled classes until May 6.

On May 21, students reoccupied Hamilton Hall. This time the police, called at once, cleared the campus less violently. "We'd learned," a deputy commissioner says. But this time, too, police pulled guns. "It is remarkable," Dean Hovde concedes, "that no one was shot." The commencement following Columbia's 214th academic year was held on Tuesday, June 4, in the vast and not quite finished Cathedral of St. John the Divine. While Richard Hofstadter was making a moderate plea in behalf of the university—"distinguished these many decades because it has been doing *some* things right"—three hundred members of the graduating class rose under their mortarboards and walked out. In front of Low Library, an anti-commencement had been organized. Dwight Macdonald spoke, and Harold Taylor and Professor Alexander Erlich, who said he was not afraid to address the people before him as comrades. Erich Fromm, the psychoanalyst, cited Nietzsche's remark that "there are times when anyone who does not lose his mind has no mind to lose." Rabbi Goldman offered the invocation. "Let us close our eyes for a moment," he said, "that we may see again the vision that we follow. Inspired by this hour of challenge, let us return to the canvas and paint, each of us, the portrait of a life filled with beauty, with justice and with truth."

Then summer came with a sweep of heat and the adventurous spring receded more swiftly than anyone had thought possible.

Now Kirk is gone, Truman is gone and even Rabbi Goldman has been dismissed. The alumni who support his office decided that he was too emotional and rather too radical. After a respectable interval, nine months I think it was, they gave him notice. But he remains near the campus.

Faces change rapidly at a university, where four years is a career. In the autumn of 1969, another new class entered Columbia. From that day forward most students at Columbia College would know about the riot only second-hand. They had been schoolboys in the spring of 1968.

Mark Rudd was no longer at Columbia. He had elected to become a professional lecturer, for fees as high as $750. Josie Duke was gone from Barnard. As she put it, she had become "an organizer of campus women for radical action." Later in an Episcopal church she became Mrs. John Marshall Geste Brown, Jr., "which doesn't mean that I will leave the movement." The original six radical demands now seemed remote. In point of fact, almost any protesting student who wanted to be readmitted *was* readmitted. Most criminal charges were dropped. The gymnasium may never be built. Construction has stopped, supposedly permanently, and the site gapes, a scar on a green slope of Morningside Park. Even the autocracy of the Columbia president is being checked. The trustees have approved a faculty senate.

These changes are significant; more change than anyone anticipated on the April day when Harry Coleman was imprisoned. But ultimately they are peripheral. Ultimately, Columbia the multiversity remains almost precisely what it was. The endowment stays in real estate, and two hundred apartments are being kept vacant, during an extreme Manhattan housing shortage, to facilitate future expansion. Government research continues to be the primary work at Columbia. Some of the radicals are asking themselves and others, "What the hell did we win anyway?"

Columbia itself is a poor place to look for the true outcome of the Battle for Morningside Heights. It is as absurd as looking for the significance of Gettysburg among the weathering cannon in the field. The effects spread in time and place.

"In a democratic society," Lord Bagehot wrote a hundred years ago, "it is the responsibility of people in positions of power not to reveal the impotence thereof." Before Columbia '68, various universities had been challenged from time to time. But the challenges, except at Berkeley, 1964, were tentative, and Berkeley itself was beginning to appear as an isolated happening. In the weeks before Columbia '68, there were comparatively modest student protest movements. Afterward, the deluge. The men in positions of power at Columbia had revealed their impotence. Students everywhere, most of whom had never read Lord Bagehot, saw the revelation and understood. College presidents and deans no longer frightened anyone. Mark Rudd lifted the visors of the old guard and found that the helmets were empty.

If Columbia had only demonstrated impotence, it would have been important. But Columbia illustrated more. That is why other Battles for Morningside Heights dominate other springs. The Columbia radicals, loud, crude, sloppy in scholarship, stumbled—there is no better verb—into an attack on the two great flaws in the American system. The first is racism. The second is what Eisenhower mislabeled the military-industrial complex. It is really the military-industrial-*intellectual* complex. Other flaws gape, in beleaguered America, but not so ominously. Racism threatens to split the country. The military-industrial-intellectual complex threatens to destroy the world.

At Columbia, these flaws came into brilliant focus. Here was a university whose racism not only kept out black students, but whose agents literally bullied blacks out of the neighborhood. Columbia trustees taking over park land from blacks, whose park it was in point of fact, offered a crumb with suffocating virtue. "A chance," as one Negro puts it, "to piss in Columbia's own urinals."

Editorialists have clouded the issue. Typically, *The New York Times* attacked the radicals as "a rule-or-ruin minority." On May 1, 1968, with the university's indecencies blatantly exposed, a *Times* editorial writer composed the following under the title "The Columbia Community": "The wisdom and dedication of the faculty are essential to the task of [review and reform] which when accomplished will enable the university to turn once again to its mission of teaching, research and public service." The faculty's dedication to anything beyond self-interest is surely questionable. Teaching, as we have seen, is a minor aspect of the Columbia "mission." Much of Columbia's research is dangerous. And its sense of public service, notably as far as the black public goes, is anachronistic and misguided.

This sort of editorial has helped marshal the middle class against the student rebels. It has had no effect on the rebels themselves. The brightest of them see it for what it is. It is not calculated dishonesty. It is simple cliché thinking—nonthink, which is worse.

In *The Protestant Establishment*, E. Digby Baltzell, of the University of Pennsylvania, distinguishes between caste and aristocracy. A truly aristocratic community is open to anyone, from whatever beginning. A Jew or a black or a Pole climbs to the top of an aristocratic society if he is qualified. In the aristocracy Baltzell advocates one might find Bayard Rustin (black socialist), Gregor Piatigorsky (Russian-Jewish cellist), at the same eating club as Adlai Stevenson III, Nelson Rockefeller and Max M. Fisher (Jewish philanthropist-industrialist). The qualifications for membership are intellect, spirit and, I suppose, the price of a meal. What we have developed in America,

Baltzell argues, is not aristocracy, but caste. In a caste system, the individual is chained to his past. Avenues are closed and doors are barred because a man is black, or Jewish. No eloquence by Rustin, no performance of the Dvořák concerto by Piatigorsky, can win either man certain club memberships; and no acumen by Mr. Fisher seems likely to win him a seat on the board of General Motors.

Columbia is a perpetuator of caste. Under Nicholas Murray Butler, it perfected an anti-Semitism that was no less vicious because it attempted to be bland. The Columbia of Butler did not discriminate against Jews. "However," as one spokesman put it, "we feel we want a national balance to our student body, so we employ geographic quotas." Columbia College in the city of New York limited the number of "New Yorkers" it would accept. In this instance, New Yorker was euphemism for Jew. Columbia would not be moved under urging, pleading or modest protest.

Court action begun by the late Rabbi Stephen Wise and legislation forced a change in policy. The Wise suit asked that Columbia's tax exemption be revoked, because Columbia violated constitutional guarantees on religious freedom. As Rabbi Wise knew, his suit had no chance in the climate of that time. But it attracted publicity and, within a few years, a New York State law was passed. The law prohibited educational institutions from discriminating.

Columbia College opened to Jews. As many as half of a recent entering class has been Jewish. Since World War II, Columbia has taken Jews onto its tenure faculty, seemingly freely, but there remains the sticky matter of the wasp deans.

Elitism, grudgingly yielding to law, public sentiment and the fact that Hitler gave anti-Semitism a bad name, was a seminal cause of Columbia's clash with blacks. The genteel anti-Semitic Columbia 1945 was the forerunner of anti-black elitist Columbia '68.In the anniversary spring, 1969, a black man with a beard stood on the Cornell campus—buildings had been occupied—and shouted: "We want black people in here from Harlem and Bedford-Stuyvesant. We want an open enrollment. We are told blacks are not qualified, that ghetto schools are inferior, that blacks need prerequisites.

"Listen," the black man thundered on the plain above Cayuga, "if Lyndon Johnson, a C student from an unaccredited Baptist College, is qualified to be President of the United States, you tell me why a child from a ghetto school is not qualified to go to Cornell." The man was there because of what happened at Columbia. His speech was a natural development of the gymnasium issue. And in spring, 1970, '71 and '72, one can be sure, there will be further natural developments, as the blacks resume storming the American educational system.

In a sense, the blacks are recent immigrants. For almost a hundred years, their emissaries were allowed into the white society. Paul Robeson could sing (until he sang politically) and George Washington Carver could invent and, after much pain, Jackie Robinson was allowed to play baseball with seventeen white men. But the black mass was walled out in "a kind of colonial system within the United States," as Gene McCarthy put it. Now blacks, crashing the society, would join America through the educational system as immigrants have always joined. Earl Warren's Supreme Court understood with supreme wisdom that the place to begin incorporating blacks into society is the elementary school.

The black condition, like the black reaction, is extreme. They have been extremely victimized. In the wake of the radical uprising, Columbia stood almost naked, revealed as a prime victimizer. And not only Columbia, but American higher education generally. The university community, almost twenty years after Brown versus Topeka, had not opened to blacks. As someone suggests, "They were still getting used to all those Jews." We look for leadership from universities, and find that Columbia College at the time of the radical onslaught had only sixty-six black students. One result was Rap Brown on campus. Another result was focus, a massive black understanding that the great university, even as the southern grade school, was the enemy.

Might as well sit in here, as at George Wallace's public schools. They screwin' us in different ways, but they both screwin' us.

Two realities dominate academic intercourse with the American war machine. The first is the university as a corporation lusting for profit. The second is the professor as whore. University professors do not concede that they sell out when they undertake research for defense or intelligence projects whose end results they do not control. They are doing necessary work, consulting, contributing to the national security. They talk, much as Eugene Galanter did, in self-justifying jargon. It always seems to be a matter of special circumstance. But one current story is applicable. A man approaches a willowy patrician blonde whose looks have overwhelmed him. "If," he says, "simply to have your body, I give you $50,000, buy you a chalet in Switzerland and beg to make love to you under the Alpine moon, would you let me?"

The blonde at once says, "Of course."

"Well," says the gentleman, "how about right now in your bedroom?"

"What do you think I am?"

"I've established that," says the gentleman. "Now we are haggling over price."

In *Das Kapital*, Marx writes, "All means for the development of production transform themselves into means of domination over, and exploitation of, the producers; they mutilate the laborer into a fragment of man, degrade him to the level of an appendage of a machine." *Not only the machinist in the auto industry, but also and equally the professor in the knowledge industry.*

The academic man studies Marx more carefully than the radical youth. He wonders at Marx's insight, storms at Marx's blindness. In the end he may compose a monograph. But the academician is caught in a professional delusion. He sees himself as commentator incarnate. It is the illusion of professors that they stand outside the stream of history and current affairs, that inexorable laws do not apply to them. But the truth is that Columbia faculty salaries are subsidized by the American war machine and that a considerable number of Columbia professors are direct contract workers for Defense, State and their subsidiaries.

How many? Some say 40; some say 150. There is nothing free or open about faculty work for government. There is no free exchange of fact or idea here. All that one research team could develop was this: faculty involvement in the war machine is wide. The participation is secret. Getting one professor to comment on other professors who are doing war work is about as difficult as getting one surgeon to say publicly that another surgeon is a butcher.

We have not come very far in our investigation of the professor as war profiteer, but what Columbia taught, and surely this is a great deal, is that the investigation must be made.

The stars were right for the Columbia rebellion. Perhaps not in fifty years will another time come when events, personalities and geography so coincide. With Martin Luther King newly dead and graduate deferments abruptly stopped and the American President an object of scorn; with Eugene McCarthy and later Robert Kennedy saying, each in his way, the system may be wrong; with Grayson Kirk bumbling; with the Ivy League college on the lip of a ghetto usurping black land, and with campus radicalism coming again to life; with the Vietnam War stretching toward a bloody eternity, the time was right for Rudd and Papert and the rest.

For all Marcuse's words, the radical movement lives by examples. Marcuse speaks of an irrational society that permits Auschwitz by silence and that creates Hiroshima, and the student response is empathetic but detached. Vietnam was something else. It was real as the television news, where blood is red and injured colonels sob. Vietnam was proof of the irrational society; it was just the kind of proof radical leaders needed.

The leftists, Josie Duke and the others, consider their movement a moment in history possessed of purity and inevitability. "It had to be," Josie says. "It had to happen," seconds a young man. I think it did not have to be and without Vietnam would never have begun. It is one thing to be a middle-class idealist, disturbed in an unfair society in which your lot is pretty good. It is another to be an idealist who, upon failing two or three courses, will be dispatched to insensate Asian war.

The college movement is related to Vietnam, and Vietnam is related to the American system. If Vietnam ended, the white middle class might very well stop its march to the polarities and move back toward the center. But will the American system permit Vietnam to end? Will the generals and the militaristic politicians and the industrialists and their lobbyists and the professors? Or are we in America wedded to a succession of small wars that stimulate the economy and are controllable, except insofar as which of our children are killed? The answer to these questions transcends my research and goes beyond the purview of this book.

It is a brisk November day on the Columbia campus. The weather is invigorating and tomorrow the public is going to elect Richard Nixon President of the United States. We are replacing, one student says, "a venal Texan with a warlike Quaker." Outside of Hamilton Hall, on the Van Am Quad, the white middle-class radicals have organized a picket line. "Don't vote tomorrow," is what the picket signs say.

They pass singly and in twos, a boy who will be an accountant and another who will sell Chevrolets and one who will teach and a girl who at nineteen is going to fat and a thick-necked boy and a thin vague girl and a boy with Harpo Marx's hair and now a girl to turn men's heads. She is trim and five foot five and wearing a green knitted dress that clings. Her dark hair is drawn back. Her dress is covered with a design: the inverted Y, as a peace symbol. As she walks in the picket pattern, one notices her buttocks, against the patterned wool.

This November day the New York public schools are closed. The teachers have struck and the city government, like Columbia in crisis, has been uncertain. Two Negro boys, twelve or fourteen, have wandered onto the Columbia campus and are standing close to the picket line and watching. Then one strides to the girl in green and pats her right buttock, brown hand briefly on green cloth.

She starts, and turns. The boy is Negro. The white girl is helpless before the blacks. "Crow-jimism" young radicals call this phenomenon. She resumes walking her racetrack pattern, her mouth set firm.

The boy giggles. He turns to his friend and says something softly. The other Negro shakes his head. Next time the girl comes around, the boy darts out and grabs her with two hands. In succeeding passes the escalation continues. Finally after four or five turns, the friend joins and the girl in green, who is sheathed in peace symbols, is having her bottom probed by pubescent blacks.

"Now cut that out," she says at length.

The boys retreat, but they have won. Had they been white, they would have been rebuked at the first foray. The white radical is helpless before aggressive blacks. How can one rebuke the symbol of oppression, the primary victim of what one is pledged to fight?

Not very well, as the girl demonstrated. This is a lesson black leaders know by heart.

Columbia, unlikely Concord of the student movement, was quiet in the spring of 1969. The white radicals tried to occupy Fayerweather and Mathematics, but found no general support. A single court order put them to rout. A sensible, but surely uninspired man, Andrew Cordier, made a few moves toward liberalization of university structure and the white radicals lost their base of support.

But the blacks? The blacks are different and they know it. They held Hamilton for a few hours and then, responding to black leadership, abandoned it. At Columbia, spring, 1969, was not their time. But on two dozen other campuses, the blacks disrupted, occupied, shouted, demanded. Their drive to join society cannot be easily blunted.

Already black power and student power may be fusing. While the white radical is always tempted to return to the middle class, in a sense to go home again, the young black has no home to which to go. As the two movements come together, leadership of the radical students will darken.

I wonder about the twelve-year-old boys I saw election day. When they get to college, if they get to college, what will be their concept of power and right?

I think they will remember the lesson they learned the day before the country turned to Richard Nixon. As I write these lines, I remember Edwin Markham's "The Man With the Hoe":

> How will the future reckon with this man?
> How answer his brute question in that hour
> When whirlwinds of rebellion shake all shores?

In assured and swinging academic circles, the poem has fallen out of favor.

EPILOGUE

LITTLE MORE than a year after what had appeared to be its
victory, the Students for a Democratic Society babbled into ci
As a democratic, radical organization, the SDS died in Chicago
June 1969, at the querulous age of nine.

After the Columbia uprising, SDS chapters burgeoned and i
membership increased to almost 100,000. SDS had become the
leftist student group in American history, but as power came
dents, so did power's traditional handmaiden on the left, factio
One wing, the Revolutionary Youth Movement, called R.Y.M
youth as a class in the vanguard of the fight against the ab
capitalist America. To them youth and the blacks were a
heroic breed. The other large faction, the so-called Worker-
Alliance, described blacks and in a sense students as a subgrou
a generally oppressed American proletariat. One has to have li
the left for a time to comprehend the fury of such dogmatic st
The first of the appendixes that follows outlines the bewilder
tions within SDS, as I found them while preparing an art
Esquire magazine during the summer of 1969.

After the Columbia uprising, Mark Rudd traveled to the 19
convention in Michigan, expecting, I am told, to be rece
triumph. Instead, he was spurned. He was "a movie-star type,
tion of the press, a personality cultist and hopelessly shallow." I
Klonsky, a hulking Californian, and Bernardine Dohrn, an att

225

sharp-featured graduate of the University of Chicago Law School, won the principal offices in the national SDS.

During the academic year that followed, the Worker-Student Alliance quietly built a power base within local campus machinery. When the SDS convened at a dismal complex of halls on the south side of Chicago in 1969, the W.-S.A. held a narrow plurality among 1,500 delegates.

The '69 convention, rather like the convention of a major party, began with test votes. Klonsky, wearing old pants and a camp T-shirt, proposed that the press at large be admitted provided that each reporter paid a $25 fee and signed an affidavit that "he won't testify against us." However, the *Times* was to be barred. A *Times* national correspondent named Anthony Ripley had already testified before the House Internal Security Committee. Ripley was under subpoena and what he said, in effect, was that his published accounts of the 1968 convention were correct. Still Klonsky said, "No *Times*."

The Worker-Student Alliance wanted no "capitalist press at all." According to its spokesman, "The capitalist press will distort what happens because they always distort. Bar them all." The W.-S.A. resolution carried by about 3 to 2. From this moment on, June 18, not more than an hour into the convention, the R.Y.M. faction, which controlled the chair and national offices, knew it was outnumbered. Subsequent days offered comedy, hysteria and finally a drill that traces to Munich, 1923.

Both major groups wanted an issue to win swing delegates and, on the night of June 18, both reached the same stratagem: they would support women's liberation. The result was self-canceling. Jeff Gordon of W.-S.A. protested that R.Y.M. security guards, assigned to search delegates, were "feeling women's breasts." A R.Y.M. band from New York came out against a California radical pamphlet with a bare-breasted woman on the cover.

R.Y.M. next sought black support. On June 19th and 20th, spokesmen for the Black Panther Party attacked W.-S.A. But two Panther leaders, presented with a captive white audience, lost discipline and began to talk like burlesque comics. They advocated "pussy power." In angry frustration, Bernardine Dohrn finally led a R.Y.M. walkout. Her group gathered in a room near the main hall and began to evolve a doomsday device.

The W.-S.A., now meeting under a new chairman, broke itself into workshops. Groups moved their chairs, gathered, facing one another,

and discussed racism, imperialism and how it was essential for young radicals not only to teach workers, but to learn from the workers as well. The point about blacks, people said over and over, was that they were a part of the oppressed proletarian class.

It was almost eleven o'clock when Jared Israel of W.-S.A., a black-haired New Yorker who had moved to Boston, concluded a private meeting with Mike Klonsky. He returned to the main floor and asked for attention. "Look," he shouted, "I have information that the R.Y.M. people are finally coming back here. When they do, please don't hiss or chant. All we need is a fight. Then the Chicago pigs will bust us all."

Israel was preaching docility because, as far as I can learn, Klonsky and Dohrn had urged it on him. Docility was what the R.Y.M. people wanted. It was critical to their careful plan.

A file of R.Y.M. women, Valkyries, left the closed room. A dozen marched through the passageway into the main hall and formed a line about the podium. The girls stood shoulder to shoulder saying nothing. The podium itself was unoccupied.

A column of R.Y.M. security guards came next. These men ringed the radical Valkyries. Two columns now protected the lectern.

A double line of men followed. Ten Black Panthers were in the lead. The file marched to a point in front of the hall, split into two columns and strung themselves out until the W.-S.A. was completely encircled. Someone stood up.

"Sit down," a R.Y.M. man yelled.

"I didn't try to get up," a W.-S.A. member explained later, "and neither would you. It was scary."

The W.-S.A. had been taken in. Their disarrayed people, sprawled about in workshops, were surrounded. Now the R.Y.M. elite marched unchallenged to the podium. Big Mike Klonsky, who reportedly carries a gravity knife, leaned toward the microphone. "We have agreed there will be no fights. I'm sure there will be none."

The W.-S.A. was too startled to respond.

Bernardine stepped forward. "In the last twenty-four hours," she cried, her voice grinding, "we in the next room have been discussing principles. We support the national liberation struggles of the Vietnamese, the American blacks and all other colonials. We support all who take the gun against U.S. imperialism. We support the governments of China, Albania, North Vietnam and North Korea. We support women's liberation!"

Backed by the security men, the shrill revolutionary held the room. "All members of the Progressive Labor Party, W.-S.A. and all who do not support these principles are objectively racist and counter-revolutionary. They are no longer members of SDS."

Too late, W.-S.A. began to chant. Pointing fingers at the podium and thrusting in rhythm, the W.-S.A. people cried: *Shame! Shame! Shame!* But Bernardine's group, having declared itself the winner, was walking out. With muscle and with trickery, the minority had read the majority out of SDS.

Late that night R.Y.M. people secured the files, the mailing lists and the names of contributors from the old SDS national office on West Madison Street. The next day the W.-S.A. elected John Pennington as chief officer. The desperate R.Y.M. now was forced to consider Mark Rudd.

Rudd conceded that he was a creation of the capitalist press. "But," he argued, "I *am* the one guy that everybody knows. We need an identifiable leader now." Although many regarded this as cynicism, Rudd was elected national secretary of one faction of the splintered SDS. I telephoned afterward, and asked, "Which is the real SDS?"

"You're talking to him," Rudd said.

Participatory democracy, like the SDS itself, lay in ruins.

At Columbia that August the mood was cheerful. Andrew Cordier was promoted to the presidency. He would no longer be merely acting, chief executive. Cordier celebrated by appearing on a national television program, where he spoke of "new dialogues and new communication." In September, the new University Senate adopted a resolution "putting Columbia on the record for immediate withdrawal" of American soldiers from Vietnam as "the most reasonable plan for peace." It was another season now, twelve years after Sputnik and several months after the United States had rocketed two mortals to the moon. Although the Senate members were sincere, "immediate withdrawal" had become popular and safe.

Certain specifics of structure and viewpoint at Columbia and indeed at all campuses were changing. The basic issues were what they had been, and no thoughtful man could believe, even for an instant, that The Battle for Morningside Heights was done.

A Guide to SDS Factions

	Revolutionary Youth Movement I (R.Y.M. I) also called "The Weatherman"	Progressive Labor Party-Worker-Student Alliance (W.-S.A.)	Revolutionary Youth Movement II (R.Y.M. II)	Labor Committee	Independent Socialist Clubs
PROMINENT MEMBERS	Mark Rudd, Bernardine Dohrn, Jeff Jones, John Jacobs.	Milt Rosen, Progressive Labor Party Chairman; John Pennington, Jeff Gordon, Jared Israel.	Mike Klonsky, Bob Avakian, Carl Davidson.	Steve Fraser, Tony Papert.	Mike Parker, Ron Tabor.
ORIGINS	Born out of unified student movements at Columbia and Midwest campuses in 1968-9.	Split from Communist Party in 1961 as protest against Khrushchev revisionism.	Formed during 1969 when Maoists of California's Bay Area Revolutionary Union (B.A.R.U.) joined with a small number of Chicagoans.	Formed in 1968 during a threatened strike against New York City Transit Authority when students joined with West Village and tenant groups.	Descended from old-line anti-Communist Leftist groups.
SLOGAN	Power to the People.	Power to the Workers.	Ho Ho Ho Chi Minh/N.L.F. is going to win.	Let's go, Mets.	None.

229

VIETNAM

U.S. should get out now. Vietnamese have been fighting a thirty-year war and should not be criticized.	U.S. should get out now. Ho Chi Minh sold out by talking at Paris and by taking arms from Soviet revisionists.	Same as R.Y.M. I.	U.S. should get out now, but it is no socialist revolution. Socialism is a world movement and Ho fought as a nationalist. He should have been encouraged toward world socialism.	U.S. should get out now, but North Vietnamese and Vietcong leaders are Stalinists, incapable of establishing a workers' democracy.

RACE

Blacks are an internal colony and must be liberated by gaining right of secession. Their fight will be a spearhead of socialist revolution. Whites must follow black leadership.	Blacks are a super-exploited section of the working class, and should join with the Progressive Labor Party. Working class can solve race problem by establishing dictatorship of all proletariat, including blacks.	There are two possible courses for the black revolution in the U.S.: socialist or an alliance of black workers with petty bourgeoisie for self-determination. Blacks must make their own choice.	A black-white alliance in common struggles for common material demands is the cornerstone of the future socialist society.	Whites should support black demands but expand them to class demands.

COMMUNISM

We are revolutionary Communists. So are the people of Cuba, and North Vietnam, but not the people of the U.S.S.R. They are revisionists.	We are Communist. China and Albania are true Communist countries. Soviet Union is capitalist.	We are Maoists. We support China, Albania, oppose East Germany and Czechoslovakia. We sympathize with Rumania, North Vietnam and North Korea. The Soviet Union is very evil.	We are socialists. To be truly socialist, "red" countries will need revolutions in the West, setting up massive exchanges of capital goods.	We are socialists. All "red" countries are not Communist, but Stalinist.

SEX

Women can be part of the international liberation army, fellow fighters in the struggle. Puritanism allied to Mao's.	Guys can live with girls but they must respect them. Puritanism allied to Stalin's.	Respect women, but it's acceptable to fight for women's rights and day-care centers. Puritanism allied to Nixon's.	No stated position, but anti-Puritan.	The same as the Labor Committee.

EDUCATION

More admissions for blacks, as a tactic to shut down schools.	Workers should not demand admission to colleges. Colleges teach bourgeois values and twist free minds.	More admissions for blacks.	Better education for everyone to increase productivity, eliminate poverty.	Universal free higher education.

231

TAXES

No stated position.	Taxes are going up because capitalists exploit other people.	End the Vietnam war tax.	Tax income is being wastefully invested by the U.S. government and business.	The same as R.Y.M. II.

REVOLUTION

There may be a minority revolution by blacks. Youth, an oppressed class, can join, along with white-collar workers who are also proletarians. Revolutionaries should not waste time combatting specific social ills but instead should fight police, teachers, social workers—i.e., all pigs.	Workers can be made to learn to recognize government as their enemy because it suppresses their strikes. Communists (i.e., the P.L.) should accompany workers in trade-union struggles and point this out.	P.L. is partly right but fails to put enough stress on blacks in the struggle. Weatherman faction is adventurist.	Socialists must get themselves together, see where they are tending and form a worker-student-black coalition to bring about, with as little violence as possible, the world socialist state.	P.L. is generally right, but undemocratic. A democratic revolution is possible in America.

232

APPENDIX II
The University as War Contractor

No figures illustrate the dangerous and self-serving military-academic complex more clearly than the hundreds of millions of dollars that the Defense Department invests in university contracts each year. Columbia is not the only university war contractor, nor is it the greatest. Columbia is simply a major war contractor, one of many possible planners of World War III.

The following are figures on the twenty-five largest university war contractors for fiscal 1967, according to James Ridgeway's *The Closed Corporation: American Universities in Crisis*. Figures obviously vary from year to year.

CONTRACTOR	VALUE OF DEFENSE CONTRACTS
1. Massachusetts Institute of Technology	$92,423,000
2. Johns Hopkins University	71,041,000
3. Stanford (including Stanford Research Institute)	45,592,000
4. Cornell (including Cornell Aeronautical Laboratory)	23,814,000
5. California (all divisions)	17,353,000
6. **Columbia University**	**16,416,000**
[IDA]	15,823,000
7. University of Michigan	13,714,000
8. Illinois Institute of Technology Research Institute	13,517,000
9. University of Illinois	10,961,000
10. Pennsylvania State University	9,808,000
11. University of Washington	5,618,000
12. University of Pennsylvania	4,833,000
13. Princeton University	4,831,000
14. Ohio State (includes research foundation)	4,795,000
15. University of Texas	4,618,000
16. George Washington University	4,534,000

17. Harvard University   4,247,000
18. California Institute of Technology   4,189,000
19. University of Dayton   3,860,000
20. Duke University   3,380,000
21. University of Denver   3,271,000
22. University of Miami   2,879,000
23. Carnegie Institute of Technology   2,836,000
24. New Mexico State University   2,811,000
25. Syracuse University   2,716,000

APPENDIX III
The Slump in Columbia Scholarship

Columbia's academic standing declined under the stewardship of Grayson Kirk. The following is from a report of the American Council on Education.

COLUMBIA DEPARTMENT	NATIONAL RANK IN 1957	RANK IN 1966
Economics	4	14
English	5	10
History	2	9
Mathematics	7	12
Philosophy	4	11
Physics	3	12
Political Science	4	9
Sociology	3	18

A COLUMBIA CHRONOLOGY

Because the Columbia uprising neither began nor ended as a local incident, the chronology includes many recent events, not directly of Columbia but directly related to it, from student riots in Spain to the murder of Martin Luther King.

1754	King's College chartered in New York "to promote liberal education" and to foster unity in polyglot colony. Begins with eight students, one professor.
1760	King's acquires own land near Hudson River on lower Manhattan Island.
1767	School of Medicine founded.
1776–85	All classes suspended during Revolutionary War.
1787	King's reopens, renamed Columbia.
1810	New York State legislature establishes Columbia structure in "act relative to Columbia College."
1811	Protesters disrupt Columbia commencement, force faculty to flee, beat off police. Several fined for "riot."
1857	Columbia College moves to site, near 49th Street, now Rockefeller Center.
1858	Law School founded.
1864	School of Mines, now Engineering, founded. Frederick A. P. Barnard assumes Columbia presidency.
1869	Barnard study indicates dismal future for liberal arts colleges. He proposes Columbia concentrate on graduate and specialty schools.
1886	Teachers College founded.
1889	Barnard College founded.
1890	Graduate Faculty in Philosophy founded. Seth Low succeeds Barnard.

237

1892   Graduate Faculty in Pure Science founded. Trustees acquire 18 acres on Morningside Heights.

1896   Columbia declares itself university. College now refers to undergraduate school of arts. Low dedicates Morningside campus. Trustees retain 49th Street land.

1902–45   Presidency of Nicholas Murray Butler. Columbia adds schools of Business, Dentistry, Library Service, Social Work, Journalism.

1917   Butler dismisses two faculty members who oppose U.S. war policies. Professor Charles A. Beard resigns in protest.

1920   Butler runs for Republican Presidential nomination; draws 69½ votes in convention that opts for Harding.

1931   Butler shares Nobel Prize for peace.

1934   Harold C. Urey wins Nobel Prize for chemistry. Columbia Faculty now among four or five finest in U.S. Butler perfects techniques to limit number of Jewish students admitted.

1946   School of International Affairs founded, tightening Columbia affiliation to U.S. Department of State.

1948   Religious quotas in educational institutions outlawed by N.Y. legislature.

            Dwight D. Eisenhower appointed president.

1950   Eisenhower takes leave to direct NATO.

1952   Elected President of U.S., Eisenhower resigns Columbia position.

1953   Grayson Kirk named fourteenth president of Columbia.

1953   Eisenhower ennui blankets U.S. campuses; students describe themselves as "the quiet generation."

1957   U.S.S.R. launches Sputnik. Ennui shattered. Space-race begins. Pentagon budget and university enrollment start unprecedented increase.

January, 1959   Castro's guerillas enter Havana, overthrowing Batista, a favorite of U.S. State Department.

October, 1959   Wisconsin graduate students publish first issue of *Studies on the Left*. U.S. New-Left movement starts.

January, 1960	Columbia announces that it will lease park land for new gymnasium.
February, 1960	Black students open lunch-counter sit-ins in Greensboro, N.C., draw wide support from northern white students.
June, 1960	SDS founded in New York.
November, 1961	Three thousand City College students boycott classes to protest administration ban against Communist speakers. Student activism growing.
April, 1961	Cubans armed by CIA land at Plaza Giron in Bay of Pigs; are routed.
May, 1961	Freedom Rides begin.
June, 1962	SDS adopts Port Huron Statement.
October, 1962	Cuban missile crisis seemingly brings world close to nuclear war.
May, 1963	Martin Luther King leads bus boycott in Montgomery, Alabama.
November, 1963	Paris police attack students demonstrating against conditions at French universities.
July, 1964	Harlem explodes into first major riot since World War II. Black unemployment rising. Thousands of northern students go South to help "Freedom Schools" in Mississippi.
August, 1964	Johnson administration charges North Vietnam with unprovoked attack on U.S. destroyers in Gulf of Tonkin.
September, 1964	Free Speech Movement appears at Berkeley. More than 800 students arrested.
January, 1965	Madrid students demonstrate; want to form independent student associations.
February, 1965	Johnson administration begins regular bombing of North Vietnam.
March, 1965	King leads Selma-Montgomery march. More than 25,000 students appear for Washington demonstration called by SDS to protest Vietnam policy. SDS rapid growth begins.
April, 1965	Johnson administration dispatches Marines to Dominican Republic.
May, 1965	Student demonstrators disrupt annual N.R.O.T.C. ceremony at Columbia.

July, 1965	President Johnson increases military strength in Vietnam from 75,000 to 125,000 men. (By the end of 1965, more than 200,000 Americans were on the ground in Vietnam; by the end of 1967, the number was almost half a million.)
August, 1965	Thirty killed during riots in Watts, California.
October, 1965	Across country, 100,000 march against Vietnam War.
January, 1966	New York Parks Commissioner criticizes Columbia gym plans.
February, 1966	Columbia CORE protests gym.
March, 1966	Militant J.C.R. student movement forms in France.
February, 1967	Twenty Columbia students prevent CIA recruiter from interviewing prospects.
March, 1967	Under threat of student strike, Columbia administrators agree to withhold class rankings from draft boards.
July, 1967	Columbia Trustees authorize filter agreement with Robert Strickman. Neighborhood rally at gym site protests planned construction.
December, 1967	Rap Brown warns that Harlem will burn down gym.
January, 1968	After Senate investigation, Columbia Trustees return filter rights to Strickman. Vietcong's Tet offensive overruns seven cities, upsetting Washington line that U.S. is winning war.
February 28, 1968	Columbia students join local residents in militant protest against gym.
March 12, 1968	Running without machine help and speaking out against Vietnam policy, Sen. Eugene McCarthy almost upsets Johnson in New Hampshire primary.
March 16, 1968	Robert Kennedy rushes into presidential race, announces candidacy.
March 22, 1968	French students, protesting arrests of J.C.R. members, seize building at Nanterre campus of University of Paris.
March 27, 1968	One hundred Columbia students enter Low Library demanding Columbia disaffiliate from IDA.
March 31, 1968	Johnson announces he will not run again.

April 2, 1968	McCarthy wins Wisconsin primary.
April 4, 1968	King assassinated in Memphis; wide rioting by blacks.
April 9, 1968	Mark Rudd interrupts Columbia memorial for King, accuses Columbia of racism.
April 18, 1968	Students riot in seven Spanish cities; Falangist Minister of Education, Lora Tamayo, resigns.
April 22, 1968	Six leaders of IDA protest at Columbia placed on probation.
April 23, 1968	Battle for Morningside Heights begins. SDS and SAS rally at sundial. Dean Coleman imprisoned. Demonstrators adopt six demands.
April 24, 1968	A.M.: Frightened and rejected by blacks, white students leave Hamilton Hall. Some occupy executive offices in Low Library. Police rescue Columbia Rembrandt. P.M.: Blacks release Coleman. Low Commune swells. Architecture students occupy Avery Hall.
April 25, 1968	Students occupy Fayerweather Hall. Ad-Hoc Faculty Committee forms to mediate dispute. Harlemites rally on Broadway in support of black students, march across campus. Gym construction stopped.
April 26, 1968	Students occupy Mathematics Hall, their fifth building. Fear of Harlem and protests by Ad-Hoc Faculty dissuade Kirk from calling police. Rap Brown, Stokely Carmichael hold press conference on campus.
April 27, 1968	Students crowd into occupied buildings. Ad-Hoc Faculty cordons Low.
April 28, 1968	Conservative students form outer cordon at Low. Radicals throw provisions to demonstrators.
April 29, 1968	Ad-Hoc Faculty appeals to trustees and to Mayor to intervene.
April 30, 1968	In early morning, city police clear more than one thousand from five buildings. Students, faculty chased and beaten. Ad-Hoc Committee dissolves.
May 2–14, 1968	More than 1,000 French students seize Nanterre campus; demonstrations spread, threatening De

	Gaulle government. Columbia reopens, but few classes are held.
May 21, 1968	Hamilton reoccupied. Police arrest 138, then clear campus, several drawing guns.
June 4, 1968	Hundreds walk out of Columbia commencement.
July, 1968	Liberation School flourishes near Columbia. Students talk of new uprisings in fall. Private detectives patrol campus.
August, 1968	Trustees accept Kirk "resignation"; Andrew Cordier appointed acting president.
September, 1968	SDS attempt to disrupt registration fails. Classes open normally.
April, 1969	Riots sweep U.S. campuses, but attempts at new Columbia sit-ins fail. Cordier obtains court orders to clear buildings, then has protesters arrested.
June, 1969	SDS collapses in factional fight at Chicago.
August, 1969	Cordier becomes fifteenth president of Columbia. University appears victor in Battle for Morningside Heights; still, Cordier concedes, new confrontations possible.

FULL NAMES OF GROUPS

CIA	Central Intelligence Agency. Prime U.S. espionage apparatus.
CORE	Congress of Racial Equality. Increasingly militant and increasingly nonwhite protest group.
J.C.R.	Revolutionary Communist Youth. A leading radical student movement in France.
IDA	Institute for Defense Analyses. Private corporation, heavily funded by Pentagon, and deeply involved in war research, contracts with university personnel.
N.R.O.T.C.	Naval Reserve Officers Training Corps.
SAS	Students Afro-American Society. Organization of black activists on Columbia campus.
SDS	Students for a Democratic Society. Largest student radical group in U.S. history until 1969 split.
SNCC	Student Nonviolent Coordinating Committee. National group active in organizing students as workers for equal rights of Southern blacks.

INDEX